Giants
of
Steam

THE FULL STORY OF THE
NORTH BRITISH LOCOMOTIVE CO. LTD

Rx class 4-6-0 No. 201 climbs the grade near Karoonda on 12th October 1965 with a fully loaded goods train. This locomotive was built by North British in 1913 for the 5ft 3in gauge South Australia Government Railways. *John Southwell*

The imposing front end of the Victorian Railways R class Hudson 4-6-4. These impressive engines were built by NBL in 1950, to order L7, and were amongst the company's finest products.

Mitchell Library Collection

Giants
of
Steam

THE FULL STORY OF THE
NORTH BRITISH LOCOMOTIVE CO. LTD

Rodger P. Bradley

OPC
Oxford Publishing Co.

Soon after its entry into service, one of the new L1 class 2-6-4 tank engines, No. 67760, is captured on shed at Grantham, in the early British Railways livery. No. 67760 was built at Hyde Park, under order L991, and sported works number 26598. In company with the K1 and B1 tender locomotives, these Thompson designs were part of a standard range being introduced by the former LNER, a great many of them built by NBL.

Rail Archive Stephenson

A catalogue record for this book is available from the British Library.

ISBN 0-86093-505-1

Library of congress catalog card number 94-73828

Oxford Publishing Co. is an imprint of
Haynes Publishing
Sparkford, near Yeovil, Somerset, BA22 7JJ

Printed and bound in Great Britain by
BPC Hazell Books Ltd
A member of
The British Printing Company Ltd

Contents

Not that far from home, almost new K1 class 2-6-0 No. 62008 just outside Edinburgh Waverley station in July 1949. This photograph was actually taken in the Princes Street Gardens, and clearly shows the NBL diamond plate on the locomotive's smokebox. During 1949, British Railways introduced its first standard liveries, and the K1s were treated to lined black, but with the lion and wheel insignia on the tender sides. No. 62008 was built by North British at Hyde Park, to order L992 in 1949 and carried works number 26613.

(W. J. V. Anderson, Rail Archive Stephenson)

Foreword

As a member of the Reid family, it gives me great pleasure in introducing you to this book on the history of the North British Locomotive Co. Ltd, of Glasgow, Scotland.

As you will read, my family was involved with N. B. Loco for some considerable time, spanning two World Wars and the Great Depression years, encompassing their consequential manufacturing upheavals.

Assembling a book of this Company's history is no mean achievement, involving months of painstaking research, interviews and the collation of material. Whilst necessary to illustrate the broad aspect of activities carried on, some chapters cover technical aspects of of the N. B. Loco, showing the development of steam locomotive advancement through the years, until its demise through the introduction of diesel and electric traction.

Being part of our national heritage, it is important that all these activities be recorded for posterity, before they are lost for ever.

In the practical field, sterling efforts are also being made to save and preserve where possible, examples of the company's products, so that future generations will be able to have a practical insight into the ingenuity and workmanship of the period.

Sir Hugh Reid, Bart.,
Honorary President,
North British Locomotive Preservation Group

The 19D in this illustration shows the NBL diamond plate on the side of the smokebox, and although perhaps not so famous as other classes, led Sir Nigel Gresley to remark that these were "one of the best designs the world has ever seen".

Courtesy: South African Transport Services

Introduction and Acknowledgements

In 1903, Neilson, Reid & Co., Dübs & Co., and Sharp, Stewart & Co. were amalgamated to form the North British Locomotive Co., bringing together a long history of expertise, success and excellence in building steam locomotives for railways at home and abroad. Curiously, it did not come into being to build locomotives because of a need for these machines, but was formed to counter the commercial competition of foreign locomotive manufacturers, in particular the Baldwin Co., of the USA. All of the predecessor companies had been in the business of building steam engines for many years, and were already responsible for some very famous locomotives, including the first 4-6-0 to run in Britain, and the famous Caledonian Railway No. 123. Around the world, the expanding British Empire was building railways in South America, Australia, China, India, and of course Africa. Many European railways too were operating steam engines built by the three companies that merged to form NBL, from France, through Norway, Austria, Spain, Germany, and even Russia. The pedigree of these famous companies was beyond question when it came to consider the question of countering the North American builders in particular, and their efforts to break into the markets of the British Empire.

Sharp, Stewart & Co. had moved to Glasgow from Manchester before the turn of the century, whilst the famous Neilson, Reid & Co., had largely been in the hands of the Reid family for many years, and Dübs & Co. was established south of the River Clyde in the 1860s. The diamond shaped builders plate was originally the impression on the bricks used in the construction of the Dübs works in Polmadie, although for some years after the merger, the three works still applied their previous style of plate. Through all of the changes within the industry, the steam locomotives that carried the famous North British diamond plate will always be remembered for their quality and reliability, and their work on railways all over the world. The combination of three of the UK's largest steam locomotive builders in 1903 resulted in the largest railway locomotive builder in Europe, and reinforced the reputation of Glasgow as the centre for engineering excellence.

It is undoubtedly true that NBL was at its most successful, and profitable, in the years between 1903 and 1920, and as a result of this, was able to weather the trauma of the economic slump of the 1920s and 1930s. It came very close to closure during that time, and one of its three plants, the Atlas Works, ceased to manufacture locomotives, was closed, and even offered for sale. Again during the inter war years, North British delivered some famous locomotives for home and abroad, including the LMSR's 'Royal Scot' class, the Southern's 'King Arthur' series, and many of South African Railways' locomotives. India too, continued to dominate in NBL's order books, whether for the 5ft 6in gauge, metre gauge, or even diminutive 2ft gauge locomotives for the Darjeeling & Himalaya lines. The company was saved by the onset of World War II, and continued to build large numbers of steam locomotives, but despite a mini boom in orders shortly after the war, the writing was clearly on the wall for steam traction. During the war, the famous 'Austerity' locomotives were built in huge numbers, whilst immediately afterwards, orders culminated with the famous LNER B1 Class 4-6-0. During the late 1940s and early 1950s, some of the largest locomotives were built for South Africa, Spain and India, through a difficult period when the company was trying to come to terms with the move away from steam, by almost all of the world's railway companies. NBL had built many hundreds of industrial locomotives too, and it was in this area that it saw an opportunity to move into diesel traction, including sales of its more popular "Miner" series of underground locomotive.

The transition from building steam to building diesel and electric locomotives was never successfully achieved by any British locomotive builder, and ironically perhaps, the Baldwin organisation, which had been the catalyst for the formation of NBL, succumbed to the same fate. North British never achieved a successful transition, despite strenuous efforts in the 1950s, but this was too little, too late. Even when some of the larger colonial railways were busy electrifying main lines, in the 1920s and 1930s, and providing major orders for locomotives and equipment, the North British Locomotive Co. could not see a future for non-steam railway locomotives. Sadly, this lack of foresight, even before the Second World War, proved ultimately to be the undoing of this giant of steam, but its memory lives on in the large number of preserved engines, all over the world.

The famous North British diamond plate still represents the best of British steam traction, and the enthusiasm for the preservation of the locomotives, and other remains of the products that came from the Glasgow works, ensures that the legend will continue.

In progressing the research for this book I was surprised to find how little has been recorded in print about this famous company, and the major part it has played in the development of railways almost everywhere. In trying to draw together some of the pieces of its story, I am indebted to many people and organisations around the world. In particular I must thank Willie Dewar, Chairman of the Springburn Museum Trust, and former NBL employee, whose enthusiasm for the locomotives and work of the people of Springburn knows no bounds. To all of the staff at the Mitchell Library in Glasgow, without whose enthusiasm and dedication the photographs and records of this famous company would not be available, and to Ian Gordon in particular for his help and encouragement. Others who have provided help and information, and to whom I offer my sincere thanks include: Graeme Carter, Vern Ross and the New Zealand Railway & Locomotive Society, Queensland Railways, Westrail and State Railways of New South Wales. I would especially like to thank Kim Bird of the State Transport Authority South Australia, for his most generous help, and the use of information from 'Steam Locomotives and Railcars of SAR', by Bird, Fluck and Sampson. Of the many other organisations I would like to thank Malawi Railways, Norwegian State Railways, Canadian National, Transnet Museum South Africa, National Railways of Zimbabwe, Central Railway of India, Victoria Railways, Bytown Railway Society, and Canadian Pacific Archives. Here at home, Ken Livermore and the

North British Locomotive Society, and Bill Howie and Hunslet Barclay. Thanks too, are owed to Roger Shenton, Phil Cousins, and Birmingham Railway Museum for a number of photographs of NBL built engines at home and abroad. For permission to use some of the line drawings of British locomotives, I am indebted to the *Railway Gazette International*, for a selection of weight diagrams. Last, but by no means least, to my wife Pat, who as always with inestimable patience, has given much support and encouragement.

1

Pioneering Locomotive Builders

In 1903, the first new locomotive to be constructed by the North British Locomotive Co. appeared, bearing the works number 15723. This was an interesting choice of number, and was arrived at by adding together the latest works numbers of the three constituent companies at the time of the amalgamation. In this way, it could be suggested that the new company had the experience and expertise of the building of more than 15,000 steam locomotives. This would clearly be a useful publicity technique, although the separate companies, Messrs Dübs & Co., Neilson, Reid & Co., and Sharp, Stewart & Co., had achieved nothing like that number of locomotives built. At the time of this great amalgamation, the works of the three celebrated builders were combined and created the largest single manufacturer of steam locomotives in Europe. The next 60 years of the history of North British provided considerable variety, and commercial highs and lows, for this specialised steam locomotive builder, culminating in its eventual demise in 1962.

If the directors of the amalgamated companies had had their way, at the outset, the new organisation would have been known as the 'British Locomotive Co.'. However, it was not to be, since a small company had already been registered with that title. Curiously, no records have been uncovered that indicate that the company ever built locomotives! The North British Loco. Co. had indeed an extensive heritage to draw on, and the engineering and innovative skills, recognised all over the world, from Glasgow and the established industrial base of the Western Scottish lowlands.

The oldest of the three companies, Sharp, Stewart & Co., had set up its works, not in and around Glasgow, or the Clyde, but in Manchester. Even more curiously perhaps, the company's engineering base was in making machine tools, and equipment for the textile industry. The two native Glasgow companies, Dübs & Co., and Neilson, Reid & Co., had a common ancestry, to a degree, since Henry Dübs, who had been a managing partner in the latter company, established his own operations south of the Clyde in 1863. Neilson, Reid & Co. was the largest of the three companies, and had been established in 1837, just four years after Sharp, Stewart had been formed in Manchester. Intriguingly perhaps, Neilson's were able to provide the established factory for Sharp, Stewart to move into, in the shape of the Clyde Locomotive Works, which was in fact owned by Walter Neilson. Sharp, Stewart, as the company had become, moved to Glasgow in order to reduce manufacturing costs, since labour costs were lower, for the same skills, and the premises rates were lower in Glasgow than Manchester.

The principal economic activities of the region centred on heavy industry, textiles and railways, and the fact that James Watt, improver of the steam engine, undertook this development at Glasgow University, adds to the excellence of the engineering reputation of the area. Glasgow and the Clyde have had a long industrial history, based on the coalfields, and the availability of the mineral wealth of the area

The 2-4-0 wheel arrangement for passenger locomotives was very popular in the mid to later 1800s, and each of NBL's predecessors built them in numbers, for various railways at home and abroad. They were much used on Scottish railways, and this example was built by Dübs & Co., to their order 11E in 1865.

Bryan Jackson

In the year before the great amalgamation, Sharp delivered these 4-4-0 locomotives to the Cape Government Railways in South Africa, built under their order E1199 at the Atlas Works. Africa was to prove one of the most fruitful sources of work for not only the predecessor companies, but later, the North British Locomotive Co.

Bryan Jackson

just like the industrial heartland of England. The development of foreign trade, as crucial to the locomotive manufacturing business, as any other industry, was aided by Glasgow's position, and the establishment of trade routes with the rest of the world was made easier. Steam and transport were synonymous in the Victorian era, and the reputation of the Clyde based engineering and shipbuilding industry was at its highest. These developments were not accomplished in isolation, and the companies that formed the backbone of the Scottish engineering and manufacturing industry formed close associations with one another.

In 1831, some six years before Neilson's fledgling locomotive building company came into being, the Glasgow & Garnkirk Railway was opened – the first in Scotland – and predecessor of a number of short railway lines. These new lines, forming the nucleus of the railway network, precluded further development of a canal system, and saw the increasing use of steam locomotion as the prime mover for the new transport system. However, even before these major developments, various tramways had been in existence, and the adoption of steam power for mineral and coal lines followed the same pattern as elsewhere, such as the route from Kilmarnock to Troon. The new transport system was in turn both fostered by, and assisted the growth of the industrial revolution in this area, but which resulted in the concentration of heavy industry, engineering, and other primary industries, in the West, Central Lowlands.

Although James Watt had established the suitability of the steam engine as a prime mover around 60 years earlier, it was not until after the vital work done by George and Robert Stephenson, and the success of *Rocket* in the Rainhill Trials of 1829, that steam railway locomotives began to revolutionise land transport. The manufacture of the new locomotives was not only taken up and adopted by colliery engineers, but by cotton mill engineers, and marine engineers. The latter were instrumental in developing its use in the shipbuilding industries of the Clyde, whilst the cotton industry, and its engineers in the Manchester area saw to it, that it was put to work in the modern textile factories. They were however not slow to realise that its application went far beyond stationary steam engines, driving weaving and spinning machinery, and applied the new technology to traction, and rail transportation in particular.

The Manchester Connection
The story of North British Locomotive Co. really begins with the building by Sharp, Roberts & Co., of the locomo-

tive *Experiment,* for the Liverpool & Manchester Railway, followed rapidly by engines numbered 2, 3, and 4, for the Dublin & Kingstown Railway. Richard Roberts, who was a partner in the firm of Sharp, Roberts & Co., with John Sharp, was the driving force behind the company's move into the locomotive building business. Roberts himself, and the company, were renowned for the design and manufacture of equipment for the textile industry, and as a designer, one of his claims to fame, was the first metal planing machine and a screwcutting lathe. Roberts' contribution to the success of the company he joined, after he came to Manchester in 1816, was very important, especially in the development of textile machinery. He it was who had invented the self-acting spinning mule in 1825, although it was a contributory factor in the burning down of the company's works by Luddites.

However, company history actually goes back a number of generations of the Sharp family, who had been known in Manchester as joiners and builders. From this family, Thomas Sharp diverted activity into the business of manufacturing products made in iron, and set up his base in Market Stead Lane. By 1811, Sharp, Greenleaves had been established in New York Street, and possessed a warehouse in Oxford Street wharf. The next decade saw a growth in the family business, with the company name changed to Sharp, Brothers, and John Sharp becoming a partner in 1823. John, and his alliance with Richard Roberts, set the trend for the next, successful developments. Richard Roberts had, in fact, been made a partner in 1822, of the company, Sharp, Roberts & Co., Engineers, at their Globe Works, in Faulkener Street. Whilst Roberts' ingenuity, and craft had earned the company an enviable reputation, even the fire of 1825 actually had some benefit. After this unfortunate incident, Sharp, Roberts & Co. expanded its activities, and acquired a site in Great Bridgewater Street, to provide the first of the company's Atlas Works.

The 1830s were a period of invention and activity, and the application of steam power to transport, especially perhaps on land, was growing rapidly. In 1833, the inventive Roberts again produced something of a dramatic development, with a steam powered 'road engine' which was driven for about a mile and a half along Oxford Road, through the centre of Manchester. This particular experiment was a disaster, coming to grief by way of a boiler explosion in the streets of Manchester, later in 1834. Needless to say it was not repeated. However, in that same year, the export of three engines of the 'Hibernia' class for the opening of the Dublin & Kingstown Railway, was followed by orders for many more steam locomotives. The 'Hibernia' class engines themselves were a development of Roberts' earlier experimental road locomotive, with vertical cylinders driving the connecting rods for the 5ft diameter wheels through a cumbersome bellcrank arrangement.

The home market produced significant orders for what became known as the 'Sharp Singles', in the twenty years from 1837 to 1857, enhancing the company's reputation. By later standards these were lightweight engines indeed, and using the same 5ft diameter wheels fitted to the Irish engines, resulted in a locomotive weighing no more than 12.5 tons! The first UK orders for the mainland came from the Grand Junction Railway, with 12.5in dia. by 18in stroke cylinders, carried between the frames, under the smokebox.

The design was in fact based on Stephenson's 'Patentee' type, and the Grand Junction orders marked, in fact, Sharp, Stewart's return to railway locomotive building. John Roberts, undoubted mechanical genius that he was, had not, it seems, grasped the relative simplicity of the steam engine, and his over complication in the design of the Irish engines was not repeated.

In 1838, the 2-2-2 *Atlas,* was typical of the company's designs, incorporating sandwich frame plates, each welded in one piece. This provided a significant mechanical improvement over previous types of sandwich frame construction, where axle guards were simply bolted on, the company were probably the earliest to use this method of construction. Another reported 'first' for the company, was the inclusion of weights in the wheels, to balance the rotating masses, and reduce the damaging effect on the track of the locomotive. Early versions of the Sharp 2-2-2 included wooden lagged boilers, and a steam dome mounted just behind the chimney, a feature that became synonymous with Sharp Brothers construction techniques for many years.

In 1843 the company moved premises, establishing its famous Atlas Works. Following the death in the previous year, of Thomas Sharp, and the departure from the partnership of Richard Roberts, brothers John Sharp and Thomas B. Sharp, together with a new partner, John Robinson, continued the business as Sharp Bros. From that time on, in addition to locomotive building, the company manufactured large numbers of machine tools. On the locomotive front, the 'Sharp Singles', with their 2-2-2 wheel arrangement, continued to be sold in large numbers, and by 1857, some 600 engines had been built. The later builds had 5ft 6in or 6ft diameter driving wheels, and 15in to 16in bore, by 20in stroke cylinders. The later series of 2-2-2s had predominantly 5ft 6in diameter driving wheels, and the heating surfaces varied from 750 sq. ft. to 970 sq. ft., and 80 to 100lb boiler pressure. These locomotives were exported in some numbers, to European destinations including Denmark, France, Italy and Germany. With imitation said to be the sincerest form of flattery, some early French locomotive builders, reportedly, copied the design.

A similar design, but with 6ft 6in wheels was built for the London, Brighton & South Coast Railway in 1849. The class of 15 engines were instrumental in enabling the railway company to improve its services, and did some good work. These 2-2-2 wheel arrangements were very popular for passenger engines at this time, both at home and abroad, the type establishing Sharp's reputation. The company constructed other 2-2-2 types in the early days, with outside cylinders, mainly for German railways, although a tank engine version was built for the London & Birmingham. For the London & North Western Railway, Sharp's built the most powerful 0-6-0 for freight duties, along with the first 20 of McConnell's renowned 'Bloomers' for passenger service. These engines were very successful, and from the mid 1850s, worked the LNWR's heaviest expresses for around 25 years, developments of which could be found in subsequent designs that were built by the railway company themselves.

Sharp Bros underwent another change in 1852, when John Sharp retired. There then arrived one Charles Patrick Stewart, whose contribution to the continued success of the company was significant. Thomas Sharp, brother of John, retired a short time later, with Mr. Stephen Robinson taking his place, and in 1863, the organisation became a limited liability company, under the name of Sharp, Stewart & Co.

Export orders for the company continued in good measure throughout the 1850s and 1860s, to France, Germany, Spain, Holland and Egypt. In Spain, engines built by Sharp, Stewart during the 1850s, were reportedly still at work in the 1920s, some 70 years later. In Holland, almost the entire locomotive stock for the Rhenish Railways were built in Manchester, whilst in addition to Egypt, other exotic locations for export orders included Demerara and India. France continued to be a lucrative market for the company, and the fashion for engines of the Crampton design saw Sharp,

Order E466 from Neilson in 1876, was a typical British goods locomotive, in this case for the London, Chatham & Dover Railway, depicting No. 156.

Bryan Jackson

Stewart exporting engines to that country's Northern Railway in 1860. These unusually designed engines, with their large single driving wheel at the rear of the locomotive, were not especially long lived, although the Sharp, Stewart engines worked express trains out of Paris for the towns of northern France, in turn with their French built counterparts.

In the same year that the Crampton design was built for France, the injector, invented by M. Giffard was first brought to Britain. Sharp, Stewart were instrumental in its success for locomotive applications, although there are two versions of how the device came to be manufactured in this country. The first attributes Charles Stewart with seeing the device at work on a steamboat in France, and that he at once secured patent rights for making it in the UK. The second, and more colourful account, sounds more plausible. It has been reported, in a book, entitled *The Theory and Practice of The Injector*, by an American author named Kneass, that two sample injectors were obtained by the French representatives of two British locomotive building companies. In Sharp, Stewart's case, the engineer tasked with assembling the device in this country, without apparently, any instructions being supplied or available, connected up the appropriate delivery, steam and overflow pipes correctly, and got the device to function.

After raising steam on a locomotive to test the device, it did indeed prove to be getting feed water into the boiler, and upon seeing this, the head of the company at once secured the sole rights for its manufacture in the UK. It is reported too that getting the device accepted as a normal part of the steam engine's equipment was difficult, and initial trials seem to have been accompanied by subterfuge. After its arrival in this country, under the auspices of James Gresham, who was in charge of Sharp, Stewart's injector department, and later of Gresham & Craven, applied various improvements to the original Giffard design.

For the company as a whole, the 1860s continued to see the expansion of export trade, and in particular, extensive contracts from South America, following an order from the Sao Paulo Railway. This period also saw the earliest introduction of eight-coupled locomotives, with an 0-8-0 tank engine for Mauritius in 1867, and a couple of years before this, an eight-coupled locomotive for India. Some years later, during the 1880s, Sharp, Stewart built the first eight-coupled heavy freight locomotive for a British railway company, although this typical Sharp, Stewart design had been exported in large numbers overseas. The proud owners of this first example of an 0-8-0 tender locomotive in the UK, were the Barry Railway Co. In terms of quantity, the output from the Manchester company, considering the newness of the technology, was good, averaging in the 26 years to 1870, when the 2,000th engine was built, no fewer than 75 locomotives a year. The pioneering spirit of the company saw them build the first tender locomotive for Japan, which was set to work on the 3ft 6in gauge Imperial Railways in 1871.

At this time, Sharp, Stewart produced a double framed 0-6-0 goods engine, where the locomotive's inside frames were carried through from front to back buffer beam instead of, as previously, being fixed to the front edge of the firebox. The obvious strength that this gave to the structure first appeared in a locomotive called *Manchester,* which saw the light of day in 1862. In fact, the engine, with its 'revolutionary' inside frames, was sold to Egyptian Railways, where it survived for over 30 years, before being broken up in October 1895.

Locomotives for the home railways continued to be a substantial part of the order book, with the later 1800s seeing orders from the Midland Railway, to Matthew Kirtley's designs, and the famous 'Mail' engines for the London, Chatham & Dover Railway. Locomotives with a 2-4-0 wheel arrangement were popular at this time, and although not a pioneer, Sharp, Stewart built a number of inside framed types, one of which was exhibited in Paris in 1878. In fact, this engine was purchased by the Paris & Orleans Railway, running express trains for many years. The P & O placed an order with Sharp, Stewart for a further 40 locomotives in 1882-3, but to the railway company's own designs, and with a 2-4-2 wheel arrangement. Exports to Europe continued during the 1880s, with orders from Austria and the Western Railway of France, amongst others, and which included engines built on Webb's system of compounding. The 4-4-2 wheel arrangement became popular on the Continental railways, with a leading bogie, and trailing wheel with radial axleboxes. The company actually introduced this design, although the first 30 went to the London, Tilbury & Southend Railway, it was more popular for export than home markets.

The 1880s produced the second relocation of Sharp, Stewart, from the Atlas Works in Manchester, where the lease on the premises had expired, to Glasgow. In 1884, the Clyde Locomotive Works was established at Springburn in Glasgow, and in 1888, Sharp, Stewart took a controlling interest in the Glasgow premises, which were renamed the Atlas Works. The last recorded locomotive to come off the Manchester Works' production line was works No. 3423, built for the Bridgewater Trustees. In Glasgow, a healthy

The oldest of the three companies that went on to form the North British Locomotive Co., was Sharp, Stewart & Co. This company came to Springburn from Manchester in the late 19th century. It continued to build on its reputation for excellence, which included these fine 4-4-0s, built at the Atlas Works for the Midland Railway Co. This is No. 2436.

Mitchell Library Collection

start was made at the new works, with an order for six 4-4-0 passenger locomotives for the metre gauge lines of the Argentine Government Railways. The Clyde Locomotive Co. was the result of Walter Montgomerie Neilson's apparent desire to return to the locomotive building business, after spending a number of years out of engineering altogether. The new works were set up across the main North British Railway line out of Glasgow, in the Springburn area, and as the Clyde Locomotive Co., only eight orders were taken, between 1886 and 1888, three of which were for South America, whilst the very first locomotives were a batch of six 4-4-0s ordered by David Jones for main line service on the Highland Railway. In fact, from Clyde's order E6, the locomotives that were built, were outshopped as Sharp, Stewart locomotives. In effect, Walter Neilson's new company was a failure, and the first order from the Highland Railway was the only major order built by the new company, before the works was bought by Sharp, Stewart. Neilson found it very difficult to win orders, and eventually he sold the works to Sharp, Stewart. Interestingly, the very first locomotive built by Neilson's new company, named *Bruce* by the Highland Railway, was displayed at an exhibition in Glasgow in 1886, before entering service.

The success of Sharp, Stewart in securing orders from railways around the world continued after the move, although most of the work came in large measure from overseas railway companies. Orders for compound engines continued to arrive, with 27 2-8-0s on the Worsdell and Von Borries system for Argentina in 1899. The Netherlands too saw large numbers of locomotives coming out of the new Atlas Works in Glasgow, and smaller numbers of locomotives for the home markets, in particular the Midland Railway.

At the time of the formation of North British Locomotive Co. in 1903, there was still a member of the Sharp family associated with the business – J. H. Sharp, grandson of a founder of Sharp Brothers. The final tally of steam types built by Sharp, Stewart during its independent existence totalled no less than 5,014 engines from the Manchester and Glasgow works.

The Neilson Heritage

Whilst Manchester was the birthplace of the oldest of the NBL triumvirate, in Glasgow, in 1836, Mitchell & Neilson set up the first of the major Scottish locomotive building companies. In fact, the younger partner in that company was one Walter Montgomery Neilson, son of the famous James Neilson, who had invented the 'hot blast' process in 1828, which revolutionised the manufacture of iron. The famous Neilson family also had a hand in the rapid growth of shipbuilding on the Clyde, with Walter's uncle, John Neilson, being responsible for the building in 1831 of the good ship *Fairy Queen* – the first iron ship constructed on Clydeside. Walter Neilson though was almost something of a child prodigy, since, by 1836, when Mitchell & Neilson were recorded as being in business in McAlpine Street, he was only 17 years of age.

In 1837, the first evidence relating to any locomotive building activities of the company are recorded, but with works in Hyde Park Street. The premises in McAlpine Street were reportedly used as offices, whilst the works in Hyde Park Street were being fitted out. However, there was very little locomotive building carried out until about 1843, prior to which the company was known as Kerr, Mitchell & Neilson, and then Kerr, Neilson & Co. By 1845, the firm was known as Neilson & Mitchell, although Mr Stewart Kerr left the company shortly after its establishment in Hyde Park Street. James Mitchell would seem to have been something of a mysterious character, since no real evidence

exists about his activities in engineering prior to teaming up with Walter Neilson, other than the fact that he had been connected with the Camlachie Foundry.

Although the company has historically always been said to have been set up in 1837, in the five years up to the building of the No.1 locomotive for the Glasgow & Garnkirk Railway, most of the output from Hyde Park Street were stationary engines. The most famous of these was the magnificent example built to supply power for hauling trains up the Cowlairs Incline from Queen Street station in Glasgow, on the Glasgow & Edinburgh Railway. The steam engine, built by Kerr, Neilson in 1842 was a typical piece of Victorian mechanical engineering, combining functionality with the ornate embellishments so typical of the era. A tribute to the quality of the engineering skills of the emerging Neilson tradition, is the fact that this stationary engine remained in service until six years after the amalgamation in 1903.

No story of the development of North British Locomotive Co. could be considered complete without reference to this steam engine – albeit a stationary one – which served the North British Railway's trains well for 67 years! The engine was built as a result of opposition to a high level terminus for the railway, from the powerful Edinburgh & Glasgow Canal Co., which forced the railway company into the construction of the Cowlairs Incline, descending the 1¼ miles to Queen Street station from Cowlairs. The engine supplied by Kerr, Neilson was an 80hp beam engine, with two cylinders, each of which had a diameter of 3ft, and a stroke of 6ft, and no less than eight boilers were provided to maintain the supply of steam. Although the arrangement was costly for the railway company, and tank engines were tried unsuccessfully in 1844, the rope-worked incline, with its 2½ miles long ropes lasted until the 20th century!

Under the name of Neilson, Mitchell, the company continued to build both railway locomotives, stationary and marine steam engines at the Hyde Park Street Works, until 1855. At about that date the company, whose name was changed to Neilson & Co., ceased the stationary and marine side of the business, and concentrated on locomotive building. A number of different home railways were buying locomotives from Neilson, Mitchell, most of which were in Scotland, and with a significant number being built for industry, which was developing rapidly at this time. During the 1840s and into the 1850s, the company boasted one or two, soon to become famous names, including Benjamin Connor, who was Works Manager, Henry Dübs, Patrick Stirling and James Reid. Henry Dübs joined the ranks in 1858 as Manager of the Hyde Park Street Works, but later set up on his own following a dispute with Neilson & Co., forming the third member of this group, Dübs & Co. Connor, Reid and Stirling were of course notable locomotive engineers in their own right, Stirling and Reid coming from Caird & Co., although the two gentlemen then went to Sharp, Stewart & Co. for a time, before finally coming to rest with Neilson.

Not long after Henry Dübs was appointed Works Manager, in succession to Benjamin Connor, it was decided that the Hyde Park Street Works were becoming too small to support further growth. In fact, the works in Finnieston was advertised for sale in 1859, with the advertisement indicating that the Hyde Park Street foundry had been founded in 1837. It was given to Dübs to plan and oversee the move to the new works in Springburn, the main reason for which was to give better access to the rail network. Work started on the new premises in 1861, which were named the Hyde Park Works, as a token of respect for the works in Finnieston, which had served the company well up to that time. The new plant was not only located near the main rail routes, but only a stone's throw from the

The third member of the triumvirate that went on to form 'The Combine', Neilson, Reid & Co., had been in the steam locomotive business since the 1840s. This particular example of the work of the men from Hyde Park, was delivered to Western Australia in 1895, and built to Neilson's order E740.

Bryan Jackson

Caledonian Railway's works at St Rollox and the North British Railway's Cowlairs Works.

Dübs planned the layout of the new works, and master-minded the move of machinery and equipment from Hyde Park Street in Finnieston, to Springburn. The works was moved on horse drawn wagons, up the steep gradients of High Street, Castle Street, and Springburn Road, to their new location, with, according to tradition, 'adequate refreshments' being provided for those involved.

Before the move to Springburn, the Hyde Park Street Works had already been expanded, with a new foundry, and boiler shop, to cope with the increasing volume of orders. Through the 1850s and into the 1860s, orders were received from the various railways in India, especially, and this continued throughout the company's independent existence. Amongst the more exotic locomotives built by Neilson & Co. was the ice locomotive for Russia, in 1861. This locomotive hauled three passenger coaches, themselves fitted with sleigh irons, between St Petersburg and Cronstadt, carrying the mails over a specially cleared track, which was fully signalled. On occasions, the locomotive also worked over country sleigh roads, other than the main track. In design it included 5ft driving wheels, which were provided with projecting steel spikes to increase the grip on the snow tracks. The boiler supplied steam to 10in by 22in cylinders, with the connecting rods driving an intermediate shaft, which was, in turn, connected to the driving wheels with coupling rods.

In place of a leading pair of carrying wheels, or bogie, a sled assembly was fitted, with leaf spring suspension, and a worm gear steering mechanism which allowed the sleigh assembly to turn on a front mounted pivot. The engine was steered from the front – not a nice place from which to drive – given the likely conditions! – and water was carried in a saddle tank, with the whole assembly weighing in at 12 tons.

The locomotive output of Neilson & Co. followed the trend shown on a number of railways, with a particular liking for the 2-4-0 wheel arrangement. Benjamin Connor, when working for the Caledonian Railway designed a 2-4-0 for the railway, which was built by Neilsons and others between 1858 and 1864. The Eastern Counties Railway were also provided by Neilson & Co. with a 2-4-0 type in 1859, which exhibited typical Neilson features, such as the flush firebox casing, with the steam dome placed on top. The four-coupled design was adopted by several leading

Scottish railways in the 1860s, with an 0-4-2 wheel arrangement and outside cylinders, for mineral traffics, and many were built by Neilson & Co.

The mineral wealth – in particular, the coalfields – were rapidly being exploited in the 1850s, and in 1857, Neilson & Co. built a number of four-wheeled saddle tank engines for ironworks and colliery service. These were a unique design, with a single 10in diameter by 16in stroke cylinder, carried below the footplate, at the rear, with a complex arrangement of valve gear, driving the 3ft 2in coupled wheels.

The early 1860s brought the early use of large single driver passenger engines, with the first of the 8ft singles for the Caledonian Railway, to Benjamin Connor's design appearing in 1859. Connor had recently left Neilson & Co., though perhaps something of his influence remained, since the company built three of this 8ft 2-2-2 passenger engine for Egypt, one of which was exhibited in London in 1862. Neilson's association with the Caledonian, continued with building more locomotives to Connor's design, along with the railway company's own works at St Rollox. In 1868, Neilson & Co. built for that railway a 2-4-0 with, at the time, the largest coupled wheel diameter (7ft 2in), of any locomotive in Britain.

In 1863, company changes were again in evidence when Henry Dübs resigned as managing partner, to set up in the locomotive building business on his own account. The effect on Neilson's was to leave the company with neither a manager, or a chief draughtsman. In order to fill the gap left by the departure of Dübs', who had so recently planned and managed the move to the new works in Springburn, Walter Neilson appointed James Reid as managing partner. Reid had risen to become chief draughtsman at Caird & Co. in 1851, also in Hyde Park Street, and finally Works Manager, before leaving for employment with Sharp, Stewart in Manchester. The loss of his chief draughtsman must have been even greater, since draughtsmen with locomotive experience were thin on the ground. Neilson's solution was to recruit one Edward Snowball, who paid a chance visit to Hyde Park in 1863, and stayed for 38 years. Snowball was at the time, Locomotive Superintendent of the Scinde Railway in India, and had previously been chief draughtsman at Robert Stephenson's Newcastle works. He had a reputation for being a perfectionist, and his eye for detail was a major part of the 'Neilson character' displayed by steam engines all over the world.

Neilson's continued interest in the general, as well as locomotive, engineering industry is emphasised by a plea for help, which came from none other than Ferdinand de Lesseps, then building the Suez Canal. De Lesseps' problems with the construction of the canal centred on the equipment in use, and which was not proving adequate for the job in hand. Walter Neilson's advice and involvement was a key factor in the final success of this project. He continued to play an active part in the progress of Neilson & Co. until 1876, when he left the business. Some aspects of the circumstances that led to Walter Neilson leaving the company he established are obscure, but although there are reports of Neilson relinquishing control of the company to James Reid, he clearly did not retire. Following James Reid's appointment, he was made a partner in the firm, but his partnership was coming to its end, and a dispute with Neilson, after the extension of that agreement, gave Reid the option to buy Neilson out. The disagreement between the two men clearly left Neilson feeling bitter, and reportedly financially out of pocket to a considerable degree, whilst Reid was able to obtain sole control of the company by 1876.

Neilson and Reid clearly got on with each other, at least in the early days, but from 1876 onwards, the company at Hyde Park was directed solely by James Reid, and engines turned out from Hyde Park have been described as Reid engines. James Reid was the sole partner in Neilson & Co. until 1893, when his four sons; Hugh, Andrew, John and Walter joined the company. As an engineer, James Reid's reputation was considerable, but his outstanding influence on the Hyde Park company was not recognised until after his death, in 1894. The company's name was changed to Neilson, Reid & Co. in 1898. Walter Neilson's activities in the later 1870s and early 1880s seemed designed to cut himself off from locomotive engineering, and he spent much of that period out of the country. The exact reason for his return to the industry are not known, but return he did, and set up the Clyde Locomotive Co. in Springburn, as noted earlier, which became the site of Sharp, Stewart's new works in 1886.

James Reid, in addition to his direction of Neilson & Co., was active in the social life of Glasgow, becoming a member of Glasgow Town Council, President of the Institute of Engineers and Shipbuilders in 1882-4, and Lord Dean of Guild in 1893. The railway companies and locomotive builders had frequently been at odds over who produced the best locomotive designs, with the specialist locomotive builders, naturally, supporting the view that the railway companies should not build their own engines. In 1882, James Reid's Presidential Address to the Institute of Engineers and Shipbuilders in Scotland, included a forthright attack on the railway companies habit of building their own locomotives. This view, that the locomotive builders knew best how to design and build engines in a cost effective manner, was resurrected occasionally, and apparently at times when locomotive orders from the home railways were less frequent. Having said that, Neilson & Co. secured large numbers of orders from Scottish railways in particular, but rather less of railways in England. Export orders were always the lion's share of the Hyde Park construction shops, as indeed they were for Neilson's competitors.

The Reid family of notable products included 25 4-4-0 tender engines for the Grand Trunk Railway in Canada, then running on 5ft 6in gauge track. A curiosity of this design, which was essentially American, was that bar frames were not used, instead, a shallow plate frame was adopted, and firebox casings, in true Neilson style, were flush. A notable achievement by Neilson & Co. was the building in Britain of the first 2-6-0 Mogul locomotive, although this was in an order from South America in 1866-69, and shared with Kitsons of Leeds.

The early 1870s saw Neilson & Co. building 30 of the Midland Railway's famous 800 class 2-4-0s, to the designs of Matthew Kirtley. These locomotives were very successful in service, and were employed during 1875/6 on the Midland's heaviest Anglo-Scottish express workings. Neilson continued to build for the Midland, with 20 engines of the 890 class ordered in 1871. This class were put to work on the Midland's Pullman trains running out of St Pancras, following their introduction into the UK in 1874. The Midland were not the only customers for the 2-4-0 design, with the North Eastern Railway ordering ten of its 901 class from the Glasgow builders in the 1870s.

In the early 1870s, there was a school of thought concerning passenger tank engines, many of which were four-coupled, that side tanks reduced adhesive weight as they were gradually emptied when working. Neilson & Co. built, to North Eastern Railway design, an 0-4-4 'back tank', in which the water tanks were carried over a rear bogie. A similar design was built for the Caledonian Railway in 1873/74, with outside cylinders and water tanks at the rear. This was typical of American practice, where it was known as the 'Forney' type, although it never became popular in Britain. Neilson & Co. built many of the standard 0-4-4 passenger tanks, more typically fitted with side tanks, such as those completed for the Midland Railway. The latter railway company provided Neilson's with orders for the 'standard' 0-6-0 goods locomotives, with their massive double frames, and designed by Matthew Kirtley. An interesting technical development was the generally accepted view that boiler tubes be reduced in diameter from the then almost universal 2in, to something less, and on the Midland, the Neilson built Class 890 2-4-0s were equipped with 1.5in diameter tubes. The boiler's performance was reportedly significantly better than that of engines equipped with the 2in diameter tubes, with a tube length of between 11ft 3in

Perhaps the most famous steam locomotive to have been built by Neilson was the No. 123 of the Caledonian Railway. Famous for the part it played in the Anglo-Scottish races to the north in the 1890s, it is equally famous for the engineering skills that made it such a legend amongst railway locomotives. No. 123 can still be seen, sadly not in steam, but in the Museum of Transport in Glasgow.

Mitchell Library Collection

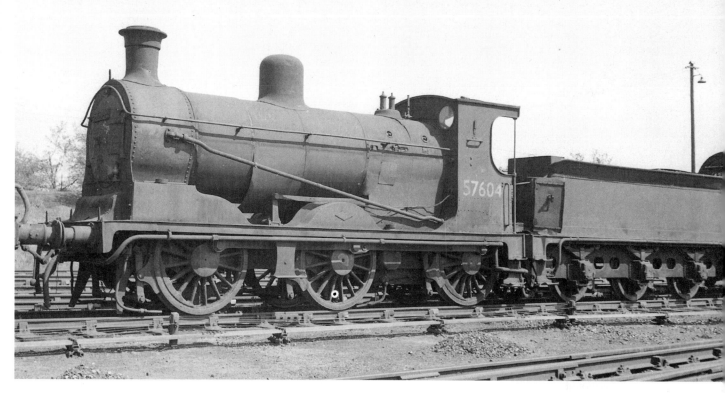

This ex-Caledonian Railway McIntosh 0-6-0, BR No. 57604, was built by Dübs & Co. in 1900, and this view, taken of the engine in British Railways days at Carstairs, on 3rd June 1963, is ample testimony of the quality of the builder's work. On the centre splasher, the so familiar diamond builder's plate, later adopted by NBL, carried Dübs works number 3882.

Roger Shenton

and 11ft 9in. Of course, different railways, and different engineers had their views, although there was a consensus that the tube diameter of 2in was too great. In this case, Neilson's collaboration with their customer resulted in a very successful locomotive design.

For passenger traffic, the 4-4-0 was becoming very popular during the later 1870s, and Neilson's built some less than successful engines for the Caledonian. These were outside cylindered machines, and were intended to replace the single driver locomotives then running the Carlisle

expresses. However, their boilers proved inadequate to provide sufficient steam to enable the engines to haul some of the heavier trains. They were subsequently reboilered by Dugald Drummond, and their performance improved appreciably.

Dübs & Co.
Henry Dübs was a strong character by all accounts, and his original employment by Neilson in the 1850s seems to have had two purposes. On the one hand, his then Works Manager, Reid, had little locomotive engineering skills, whereas Dübs had worked for Beyer Peacock in

Even older than No. 123, was this fine example of Caledonian Railway motive power, No. 48, in the design developed for the railway by Benjamin Connor, and built by Dübs & Co.

Mitchell Library Collection

Manchester, and Neilson believed that his connections would assist in bringing orders to Glasgow. However, the relationship between the two men must have been difficult, with both having forthright views on technical subjects. The move of Neilson & Co. from Finnieston to Springburn, and the laying out of the works did, as mentioned, come to provide the beginnings of serious differences between the two men.

By the early 1860s, these differences seemed to be going from bad to worse, and the straw which reportedly broke the camel's back came in the shape of a dispute over governors for stationary engines within the Hyde Park Works. Neilson cites a particular example of Dübs' stubbornness in refusing to produce a governor to Neilson's designs, indicating that Dübs believed he could design and build a better device. After disagreeing over the design, and the apparent point blank refusal to build Neilson's design, Dübs offered to resign the partnership and leave the company. The differences between the two men cast neither in a good light, with Neilson's prejudices revealed in his description of Dübs as a "pig headed German". In 1863, Henry Dübs left the company, and set up his own locomotive manufacturing company south of the Clyde, in the Little Govan (Polmadie) area, and which later came to be known as NBL's Queen's Park Works.

Neilson and Dübs had agreed that Dübs' new company would not be established within a radius of three miles of Neilson & Co.'s Hyde Park Works, since Neilson was aware that Dübs would soon find friends to assist him set up this rival company. Dübs clearly set about the task with a will, and in 1864, the construction of the new works began. Dübs was, naturally, closely involved with the planning and layout of the works, and the machine tools were all supplied by Whitworth & Co. in Manchester, at a total cost of £16,467. The ingenuity and vision of Dübs as a locomotive engineer was well known, and, interestingly, during the building of the new works, this ingenuity led him to use the clay excavated for the foundations, to produce the bricks that were used in the workshops' construction.

Barely a year after the construction work started, the first locomotive from the first order was delivered to the Caledonian Railway. This first locomotive was an 0-4-2 tender engine, with 5ft 1½in coupled wheels, and 16½in by 22in cylinders, to works order number 1E. Perhaps reflecting Beyer-Peacock's description of Dübs as having a slack attitude, and an easy temper, following completion of the first engine, a party was thrown by Dübs, in recognition of the event. Dübs' new works were christened the Glasgow Locomotive Works, and by the early 1870s, the company was so successful that it had become the second largest locomotive building works in Britain.

Dübs & Co. produced the first chairman of the later North British Locomotive Co., and its familiar diamond-shaped builder's plate, in addition to securing the skills of at least part of the drawing office of Neilson & Co. In fact, Henry Dübs persuaded Neilson's Chief Draughtsman, one Sampson George Goodall-Copestake, to join him, and the first NBL Chairman, William Lorimer, started work for Dübs & Co. in 1864. The familiar diamond-shaped works plate was derived from the pattern moulded into the bricks used to construct the works, and later adopted for use on North British built locomotives.

From an organisational perspective, Dübs & Co. were a pioneering company, when in 1866, they became the first engineering company to employ female tracers in the drawing office. The idea was reportedly suggested to Henry Dübs by a friend, who was also an artist, and ventured to suggest that ladies could be trained to produce duplicate copies of engineering drawings. At that time, the Victorian sense of propriety was something of a barrier, and the conviction in the minds of engineers and others that women simply could not do the work. Dübs' experiment, in which his company provided the necessary training was obviously successful, as tracing in engineering drawing offices all over the world became primarily almost a women only occupation! It is perhaps only recently that any reduction in the employment of women to trace engineering drawings has been seen, and subsequently through the use of computer aided design systems.

William Lorimer, who joined Dübs in 1864, became 'Principal Assistant' to Henry Dübs in 1867, and in 1875 a partner in the company. Following Henry Dübs' death in 1876, Lorimer was made Managing Partner, a position he occupied until the formation of NBL in 1903. At the time of Dübs' death, the various partners were; Mrs Dübs, Adam Paterson, Henry Dübs, Charles Dübs, William Lorimer, and Sampson George Goodall-Copestake.

The locomotives built by Dübs & Co. were both popular, well built and successful, and in addition, the company had achieved a considerable degree of innovation. Oddly perhaps, the aspect of the locomotive builders' innovative designs and manufacturing techniques supported James Reid's theory about the design and construction of railway locomotives. Apart from an extensive range and catalogue of orders from home and overseas railways, one of Dübs & Co.'s most long lasting inventions was the crane engine, which was first put to work in iron and steel works. During the period when the Fairlie locomotive was becoming successful, Dübs and Copestake designed and patented a special coupling, first applied to a pair of Dübs tank engines coupled back to back. The idea was to provide similar rigidity and traction to that of the Fairlie design, with a novel, and inexpensive form of articulation. Although the idea gained some publicity in the 1870s, its application was not taken up widely.

The home railways were a frequent source of orders for Dübs & Co., with the Caledonian, Highland, North British and Midland placing most orders with the company. Some of the Midland's most well known locomotives, including the 0-6-0s and 4-4-0s, to the designs of Samuel Johnson. Major examples from the Highland included the famous 'Ben', 'Jones', and 'Castle' class locomotives. The latter formed the basis of a design supplied some years later, under the North British Locomotive Co. banner, to France, whilst no less than 47 orders were taken for industrial locomotives at home.

Abroad, the greatest number of locomotives built at Dübs works were sent to India, Burma, Brazil and Argentina. Out in the far east, orders were taken from Australia and New Zealand, and a smaller number from China Japan, and the Philippines. Out of Africa, only the Cape Government and Natal Government Railways produced any volume of orders, with two orders from Egypt and one from the Sudan for the War Office. In Europe, orders were taken from Spain, Russia, Norway and Sweden, with Dübs designs introducing compound working to Norway, with a 4-4-0 type. In fact, in Norway, both standard gauge and 3ft 6in gauge engines were supplied. European orders in general though were few and far between, and the growth of locomotive manufacturing throughout Europe contributed to the demise of this market for the three Glasgow based companies. By the time North British came into being, orders from Europe had declined to almost nothing, with only occasional orders from the French War Office and the Paris-Orleans Railway.

One of the more interesting aspects of introducing new steam locomotives to foreign countries seems to be the effect that the then new technology had on the lifestyles. A

more curious reaction than most was apparent with the building of a couple of locomotives for China, representing the first Glasgow built engines for that country. In 1886, two 0-4-0 tank engines *Flying Victory* and *Speedy Peace* were despatched to China, where their arrival met with strong opposition from local landowners. In fact, it was claimed that these 'mechanical monsters' were desecrating sacred burial grounds of the ancestors, and coolies were bound and thrown in front of the advancing engines, and eventually, the train was forced to stop – but not before it had run over the hapless victims. The railway was finally forced to close after 20 men had been killed, and the engines were scrapped. A peculiar locomotive built by Dübs, was the steam traction engine *Abdul Aziz*, for the Ottoman Company, in 1866. Like the Neilson designed ice engine for Russia, this unusual locomotive was controlled from a steering platform at the leading end, complete with a marine type steering wheel.

Other products from Dübs' Glasgow Locomotive Works fared much better than the first Chinese engines, and the quality of the workmanship was of such a high standard that many engines could be found in service more than half a century later. A good example of the longevity of Dübs products may be cited by a couple of 2-4-2 tank engines despatched to Queensland in 1881, and completed over 40 years in plantation service, with one of them still at work in 1950, after being sold to the Tasmanian Hydro-Electric Commission. Another long lived locomotive was built for New Zealand in 1873, and named *Mabel*. This engine completed no less than 75 years service, and was rescued for preservation in Otago. In North America, quite clearly, competition from Baldwin, Lima and Alco was fierce, although Dübs managed to secure orders from the Canadian Pacific Railroad, for both 4-4-0 and 4-6-0 designs. The latter type continued to be supplied by the new North British Locomotive Co. from 1903, for a time, and was followed in later years by locomotives for the Newfoundland Railway.

By the late Victorian era, the pre-eminence of the Glasgow based locomotive builders was being challenged around the world, and although the skills and experience were not questioned, the locomotive market was being rapidly exploited by many other companies. The development of the locomotive building capacity of the Baldwin Locomotive Works in particular, had a profound effect on the three Glasgow companies, and it was clear that drastic action was needed to retain some economic viability. That major change was brought about in 1903, when the three companies were merged, and their combined skills and experience brought into being the largest specialist locomotive builder in Europe.

2

The Great Amalgamation

In 1903, Europe's then largest builder of steam locomotives came into existence, as the North British Locomotive Co., formed from the three major Glasgow based manufacturers. With the wealth of experience and expertise that the triumvirate of Sharp, Stewart, Neilson, and Dübs & Co. brought with them into this new organisation, future prospects looked decidedly good. At the time of its formation, the new company employed around 8,000, and the works at their peak, occupied 60 acres within the City of Glasgow. 'The Combine' as it became known was sandwiched between the Cowlairs Works of the North British Railway, and the St Rollox Works of the Caledonian Railway, and was at the heart of the Springburn district. The railway had, over many years come to represent the community of Springburn, and its engineering excellence was renowned all over the world, and was emphasised with this change. The third railway manufacturer in this new organisation had established works in the Little Govan, or Polmadie area, south of the Clyde, but Henry Dübs had been intimately involved with the setting up of a major part of the Springburn heritage. In fact, the setting out of Neilson's Hyde Park Works, and the move from the old works near the Stobcross Quay, was masterminded by Henry Dübs. The Glasgow Locomotive Works of Henry Dübs was set up in the Polmadie, or Little Govan area as a result of agreement with his former employer, Neilson.

The reasons behind the amalgamation of 1903 were economic, but with some disagreements between the companies – notably the departure of Henry Dübs in the 1860s, competition for orders was fierce. But, the driving force behind 'The Combine', was the rise of the engineering empire of Matthias Baldwin, and the volume of locomotives it was able to produce, at competitive prices. The orders for home railways were not so common as those for overseas, or industrial lines, since the pioneering era had passed, and railways were an accepted transport system. In addition of course, the home railways built many of their own locomotives, a feature of the railway business that was not so common overseas. There was still a great deal of railway growth and development elsewhere around the world, and like other UK companies, capitalising on the markets provided by the influence and control of the British Empire was a prudent direction.

The merger was really an attempt to protect the interests of locomotive manufacturers in Glasgow, according to reports in the contemporary press. But it was successful, and whilst there was little outward indication of change initially, the North British Locomotive Co. had work in progress for India, Japan, South Africa, Canada, and various railways in Britain. Back in the late 1800s, when Sharp, Stewart purchased the Clyde Locomotive Works, to escape the high rates of central Manchester, they also benefited from reduced labour costs. The wages of engineering employees were low everywhere, and conditions of employment often brought about conflict. At the time of the merger, industrial disputes were common, and the partners of the North British Loco. suffered from them just as other engineering works.

In principle, North British were bespoke locomotive builders, building to the individuals' requirements, but Baldwin's growth, and their prodigious output led to claims about the quality of the builders' output, as compared with those of British companies. The 'upstart' Baldwin company was challenging the Glasgow builders' supremacy even in the British Empire markets, and in 1902, Egyptian Railways ordered locomotives from the Brooks

D. A. Hendrie was one of South Africa's most celebrated locomotive engineers, and this order, L378, placed with NBL in 1909, was for 21 goods engines. The design was noted as 'Improved Hendrie', and similar to earlier orders (L56 & L61), placed in 1904. They were originally designated Class B, but subsequently reclassified Class 1.

Mitchell Library Collection

The industrial marketplace did not escape the men from North British, as order L52, for a solitary 0-4-0 tank engine, testifies. The order was placed according to records, on 31st December 1903, just in the first year of existence of 'The Combine' and intended for the Metropolitan Coal Co.'s Glasgow Works, and bearing the name *James Fergusson*, and was builder's No. 16350.

Mitchell Library Collection

Locomotive Co. (later Alco), and Dübs & Co., for comparative trials. Similar trials were held between a Baldwin built goods engine, and one from the Neilson stable, with results reported in the Egyptian press to the effect that the Neilson engines performed better.

In the five years before the formation of NBL, Baldwins' locomotive output had risen from just 901 engines, to no less than 1,533, and the company was continuing to expand, but not just in North America. This was clearly a matter of serious concern for the three Glasgow builders, and shortly after the turn of the century, when it was reported that Neilson, Reid & Co. were building 200 locomotives a year, with 2,500 men, Baldwin were turning out 300 a year, with

only 1,400 men. The reaction from British builders, and railway industry observers to this explosion in output was to attempt to rubbish the American products. Prior to the formation of NBL, the British locomotive builders' attitudes certainly carried an air of smugness, and whether at home, or abroad, the specialist engine builders felt they could turn out steam locomotives better than the railway companies themselves. In the years and months leading up to the founding of NBL, these attitudes, together with perhaps overpricing of their products, were responsible for the loss of orders to the North American, and indeed, German locomotive builders.

At the time the North British Locomotive Co. was formed, the steam rail motor was very much a popular method of working trains on branch lines, and one of the new company's first orders was for the Barry Railway in South Wales. Under order L68, NBL built two such examples, which carried running numbers 1 and 2, following their delivery in 1904. Both were built at the Atlas Works, formerly the workshops of Sharp, Stewart, and shown here is No. 2.

Bryan Jackson

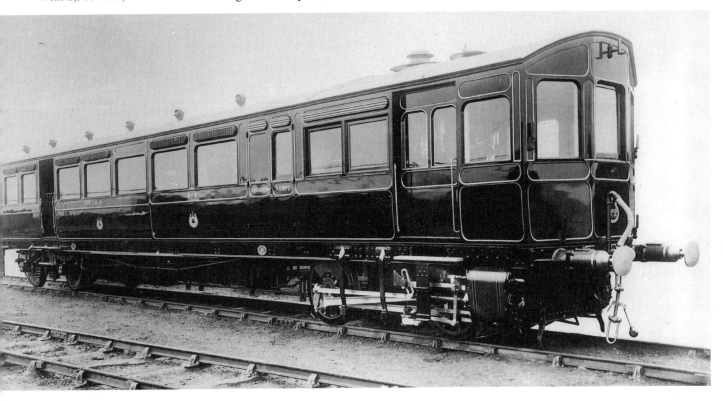

The 100 and more privately owned railways in Britain before 1923, ordered large numbers of steam engines from all of the North British antecedents. This fine example of a common enough tank engine design was from one of the smaller companies, the Furness Railway, No. 103. Five of these 0-6-2 tanks were built at the Atlas Works in 1903, to order L17.

Mitchell Library Collection

The press was not slow in seeking out instances of less than successful performance of American built products, whether at home, such as the Midland Railway's 2-6-0s from Baldwin, or out in the Far East. A report in *Engineering* stated that Japanese Railways were discarding American built engines, in favour of their British built counterparts. Having said that, the same journal noted soon afterwards that Baldwin had received a repeat order for 18 locomotives for Japan. The contemporary press were loyal to Britain's locomotive industry, but in striving to bolster the UK products, demonstrated some disregard for the foreign engineering companies, and railway operators. For Britain, pricing was perhaps the straw that broke the camel's back, and the loss of an order to Baldwin, by Neilsons, for locomotives for the Port of Calcutta. The row that followed, involved J. C. Baird, Member of Parliament for Glasgow Central, and included accusations that the British Government were handing out orders to the USA and Germany for Indian railways, indiscriminately. The end result of this difference of opinion between the British builders and the Government, was a pompous letter to *The Times*, with Neilson, Reid & Co., Dübs & Co., and Sharp, Stewart & Co. as joint signatories. The last couple of paragraphs of this letter are particularly interesting;

'The present difficulty has been caused by the simple fact that we are filled with orders sent to us from all parts of the world by companies who know our work and who in forecasting their needs prefer to wait for us, rather than go elsewhere, while obviously they do not regard our prices as prohibitive.

With regards to the future, if the Indian railways are prepared to accept the cheapest engine offered without regard to quality of material and workmanship then the capacity of the existing establishment is quite ample to satisfy demand. On the other hand if it is proved that the British engine though not the cheapest in the first cost is the most economical in working and maintenance and the Indian railways are prepared to restrict themselves to British manufacturers in future we are prepared to take such steps as may be necessary to meet any future demand.'

In retrospect the attitude of the locomotive builders seems very strange. They appeared to be adopting the position that the railway companies should wait for the builders to deliver when it suited them, rather than meet the railways' need for an appropriately priced engine, delivered when it was required. So far as Indian orders were concerned, railways in the heart of the British Empire were saying that the locomotives supplied by the likes of Baldwin, and the German builders, were no more expensive to maintain and operate than their more expensive British offerings.

A letter to *The Times* was one thing, and an effective response to the competition quite another, but the growth of Baldwin in the USA had, if it had done little else, brought the North British Locomotive Co. into being, and the locomotive industry in Britain back to commercial reality. Ironically, at the time the company was formed, the difficulties of finding a name even caused problems. The use of the fine sounding British Locomotive Co. had to be dropped, because of the existence of another engineering company of that name, and settling on North British Locomotive Co. was not without its problems. Confusion with the then North British Railway, with its works in Springburn, also headed by Reid, was obvious. A lawsuit brought against the company by consultants H. T. Van Laun was more surprising. These consultants claimed that they had set out to amalgamate the Glasgow locomotive builders and an English manufacturer, back in 1899. In the legal action that took place, the consultants claimed payment from the three Glasgow builders of £34,207, or 2.5% commission for setting up the North British Locomotive Co. H. T. Van Laun had indeed been asked by Dübs, Neilson, and Sharp, Stewart to plan the formation of the amalgamated company, but without a formal contract, the case for compensation was not upheld by the courts.

In 1902, the works of the three former companies were sold to the newly formed North British Locomotive Co. – 'The Combine' – for £1,020,000. The shareholders of the former companies also received £278,417, 13s6d for work in progress, which was apportioned as follows;

Neilson, Reid & Co.	£108,949 1s 4d
Sharp, Stewart	£75,985 10s
Dübs & Co.	£93,843 2s 2d

And, for stocks and materials, the following amounts were agreed;

Neilson, Reid & Co.	£31,886 17s 4d
Sharp, Stewart	£22,840 17s
Dübs & Co.	£15,106 8s 1d

From the above it is clear that Neilson, Reid & Co. had easily the most work in progress, followed closely by the works of the one time Neilson partner, Henry Dübs. Sharp, Stewart, with their illustrious reputation, were equally clearly not so busy as their neighbours in Springburn, though nonetheless were constructing large numbers of steam engines at that time.

There is an interesting comparison to be made at this point, with the fixed assets valuation of NBL, when the company was at the end of its life almost sixty years later. The value of land and buildings for instance, in 1960, was £1,120,000, only £100,000 more than had been paid for the three works back in 1902. To this 1960 price though, the value of plant and machinery, fixtures and fittings was added, bringing the total to £2,297,100, representing the worth of 'The Combine', 57 years after its formation. In the last ten years of its existence however, NBL was, sadly, making considerably less than half of the profits that it had in the first years of its life. Given the depreciation in value of the £, then this was clearly a disastrous situation.

The influence of the Reid family on the new company may be judged by the presence of no less than three directors on the Board, with Hugh Reid as Chief Managing Director. At the outset of 1903 the new company, its directors, and organisation was as follows:

Chairman	William Lorimer
Deputy Chairman & Chief Managing Director	Hugh Reid
Managing Director – Hyde Park	Andrew Thomson Reid
Managing Director – Queen's Park	William Lorimer Jr.
Managing Director – Atlas	John Hutchinson Sharp
Managing Director – London Office	John Frederick Robinson

Other Directors:
John Reid
Walter Montgomery Neilson
Alexander Wilson
Charles Ralph Dübs

An interesting comment appeared in the Company's 50th anniversary publication, stating that *"Celebrations in various forms took place, not only the formal events, but much more informally and certainly exuberantly amongst the men affected by the transition."* Clearly, on such reports, the event was welcomed – certainly this was true within engineering circles, if contradictory to the reportedly staid and sober attitude of the Neilson, Reid, or Sharp, Stewart organisation. Celebrations of this nature were more likely to come from the Dübs camp, where, it will be recalled, the late Henry Dübs was 'accused' of having a lax attitude to his employees, and indeed he had left Sharp Stewart's employ with this reputation. The Dübs family association with the new company was short lived, since Charles Ralph Dübs, Henry Dübs' son died in the same year that 'The Combine' came into being. For three years after the formation of NBL, the former Dübs works was still referred to as the 'Glasgow Locomotive Works', but on 29th December 1906, NBL announced that this site was to be known as the Queen's Park Works.

The North British Locomotive Co., began trading in 1903, and by the end of the year, 51 orders had been received for 335 steam locomotives. Of these first orders, only six were for home consumption, including two for Ireland, three for industry, and a single order from the Furness Railway, totalling only nine locomotives. The remaining 45 orders and 326 locomotives were for export, and primarily to British colonies. This stark contrast between home and overseas orders was, with only occasional exceptions, a feature of the work of the company throughout its history.

The early years of The Combine's existence were very much along the lines of business as usual for the three

Not all of the Robinson designed ROD 2-8-0s were actually put to military use during the First World War, and this NBL built example is seen in later years in LNER days. North British had also built 50 of these locomotives for the Great Central back in 1912, under order L496. The classic Robinson, Great Central Railway design is in original condition in this view, and sports LNER running number 6277.

P. Ransome-Wallis

Above: The 'Stobcross Crane' may be missing in this view, but the location for shipment is still Finnieston Quay on the River Clyde. Locomotives from all three predecessor companies left for all points of the compass from here. This view shows an NBL built 4-6-0, No. 230-338, *en-route* to France, for French State Railways – 30 of these were built in 1911, at Queen's Park, to order L442.

Mitchell Library Collection

Below: Another view of North British products at the delivery phase. In this case, one of 20 4-4-2s, being unloaded at Port Said in Egypt, in late 1925. The locomotive was actually designed by the American builders Baldwin, one of NBL's main competitors. The fact that these locomotives were delivered to the British colony in Egypt caused much aggravation in the British locomotive industry, and not a little adverse comment in the press.

Mitchell Library Collection

works, and another six years were to elapse before the company had a single headquarters building, in Flemington Street, Springburn. In the new building, the drawing offices and various administrative offices were located, centralising these important functions, near the Hyde Park and Atlas works. The orders received by the company during these first years were shared between the works of the former Sharp, Stewart, Dübs & Co., and Neilson, Reid & Co., with the separate internal organisations continuing as before. By 1909, no less than 400 orders had been received. Similarly, on the 10th September 1909, when the new offices in Flemington Street were opened, a party was held in the quadrangle bounded by the offices. Performing the opening ceremony was Lord Roseberry, and although the primary function of the building was administrative, the top floor was given over to drawing offices, a lengthy description of which appeared in the contemporary railway press. The new building enabled the company to bring together the technical and commercial staff under one roof, and indeed, provided an important advantage as North British Loco. Co. competed with other suppliers for orders. At the time of the amalgamation, the equipment and fittings of the works attracted a great deal of attention in the railway press. The layout of the new works, on each of the three sites, included some of the latest machine tools, a number of which were designed and built by the companies themselves. Building machine tools was not uncommon, since Sharp, Stewart's had earned a reputation in this field for both the Manchester and Glasgow works, and examples of their designs were described in the engineering press.

Neilson, Reid & Co. was the largest of the companies, and taking the Hyde Park Works as an example – the layout of which was planned and implemented by Henry Dübs – back in 1864 – covered 14 acres, with mostly single-storey buildings, ranging from pattern shops, foundries, boiler, fabrication, and erecting shops. The paint shop was so designed that locomotives entered the shop at one end, on one of the two tracks, and left, completely painted at the other – an early form of mass production! As in most engineering works, perhaps the boiler, and fabrication shops come in for the greatest attention, and of course, in locomotive works, the erecting shops. NBL, like other compa-

nies, cast many items of fittings and other components in its own foundries, and the works also had joiners and pattern-making shops. At the time of the great amalgamation, the company was only able to manufacture iron castings, all steel castings being bought in from other suppliers.

The machine tools needed to build locomotives, or undertake most heavy engineering construction were, and continue to be varied although the belt driven lathes and steam hammers of the early 1900s have been replaced by sophisticated, computer controlled equipment. However, even in 1903, NBL was well-equipped, and owned some modern tools, with the Hyde Park Works materials yard fitted with electric pillar cranes. These cranes were supplied by the Leeds Engineering Co., who also provided the hydraulic shearing machine.

Hyde Park Works had nine gas fired forges, with the gas produced on site, supplying energy to a variety of furnaces for general forging, rivet and bolt making. This, like the other two works was very much a self-contained manufacturing unit at that time. The names of Kendall & Gent, Cravens, Noble & Lund, Butler & Co. and Hulse & Co. are as familiar today to engineers, as they were in 1903, when those names were seen on drilling and slotting machines, cranes, lathes and boring machines in the workshops of North British. The boiler shop contained stationary riveting machines, with the ability to handle the largest of boilers ordered by the railways of the day. Two machines were installed in Hyde Park Works, one with a 12ft 6in gap, the other a 17ft gap, each with the ability to exert a pressure of 50 tons.

The installation of the latest equipment in each of the former companies' works was driven almost entirely by competition, to achieve the rapid design and construction of locomotives. At the time of the amalgamation it was

Amongst the more unusual types built by NBL were these 0-6-0 'Abt' rack and adhesion locomotives for Queensland Government Railways, of 1914. In fact, this order (L615), for a pair of engines, was not the first, and dated back to the days of Dübs & Co., who had built similar locomotives. The first such order for NBL was received in 1905, as L152, also for a pair of 0-6-0 rack locomotives.

Mitchell Library Collection

Order L747, was placed in 1920, for 15 of these 4-8-2 Class 12A goods locomotives for South African Railways. These were a very successful design, and NBL built its first order in 1919, for 20 of the 12As, and its last in 1929, for a final 13 locomotives, bringing the NBL built total to 48 out of a class total of 67. They were only relegated from main line working following electrification progress, and were still at work on shunting duties in De Aar, some sixty years after their first arrival.

Mitchell Library Collection

believed that this combination would provide a recipe for success in the world market. The most severe competition for steam locomotives was coming from the USA and Germany, as well as other British companies like Beyer Peacock, Robert Stephenson, Hawthorn, Leslie and the Vulcan Foundry. Soon after the amalgamation, extensions to the Hyde Park and Queen's Park Works (then known as the Glasgow Locomotive Works), were made, with the not inconsiderable profits of the company being invested in up to date machinery and tools. The former Sharp, Stewart Atlas Works in Springburn was already equipped with modern plant, when they purchased the Clyde Locomotive Works, which previously occupied that site. Walter Neilson's return to the locomotive building business, with his new works in Springburn was not a success, but the benefit of the modern plant was reaped by Sharp, Stewart when they migrated north. Sharp, Stewart had in fact gone into voluntary liquidation in Manchester, and sold off their tools, plant and other equipment, before moving to Glasgow.

At the time of the amalgamation, and until 1909, the three works were self-contained units, although some centralisation of administrative activities was carried out at the Hyde Park Works. Ironically perhaps, Neilson, Reid & Co. had constructed new offices 20 years earlier at the company's Hyde Park Works, which were described as being 'handsome offices', which compared 'favourably' with other companies. Having said that the internal administration of the new company continued for the first few years, almost as before, at the separate works, but Hyde Park was adopted as the Head Office of NBL, until 1907. On 26th August of that year, it was announced that the new headquarters were to be built, just up the road from Hyde Park, in Flemington Street.

Not all of the activities of NBL were centred on Springburn, and offices were established in other cities, whilst a great many orders came to the company through agencies, and engineering consultants around the world. The new company got into its stride in the first decade, and in 1912 the main offices were located as follows:

The Central Argentine Railway came to Springburn in 1909 for 22 of these Von Borries compound Pacific locomotives. Built to order L383, they were Class P9A and carried running numbers 161–180, and 370–371, and works numbers 19095–19116. There were only two cylinders (one 19ins diameter high pressure, and one 27.5ins diameter low pressure), with the overall locomotive design produced by the railway company. They were intended for passenger services. *Mitchell Library Collection*

London Agents & Office
    Messrs Browning & Bertram,
    17 Victoria Street,
    Westminster,
    LONDON
A*rgentina*
    Messrs Franklin & Herrera,
    BUENOS AIRES
A*ustralia (New South Wales)*
    Messrs Gilbert Lodge & Co.,
    SYDNEY
Australia (Western Australia)
    Mr John Denny,
    PERTH
China
    Messrs Jardine Matheson & Co.,
    HONG KONG, and SHANGHAI
Chile
    Don Domingo Merry Del Val,
    SANTIAGO

The West African countries did not see such extensive railway development as elsewhere on the continent, and consequently, fewer locomotive orders came to Glasgow. This example, No. 10, arrived as order L300 in 1908, and five of the Emir class 4-8-0s were built to NBL design S530, at Hyde Park Works.
Mitchell Library Collection

Ordered by New South Wales at the busiest production period in North British's history, were these 20 Class 1 2-8-0 freight locomotives. The design was produced by the railway company, and the locomotives were built at Hyde Park Works in 1912.
Mitchell Library Collection

Spain
    Messrs Sheldon Goenaga & Co.,
    BILBAO
Portugal
    Mr A. W. Paterson,
    LISBON

The establishment of the new company may be seen in retrospect as a trade protection measure, rather than an attempt to respond to a growing market. The three works, although receiving orders at an impressive rate from day one, were supplying locomotives of a typically British, robust, not to say heavy construction. The stimulus for the 'rationalisation' of the British locomotive industry, was driven by India, as a major customer in the former British Empire. It is ironic to reflect that there are locomotives still in service in the subcontinent as the millennium approaches. Not surprisingly perhaps, the first order in the drawing office register, was also the first of the Indian Standard engines, as a counter to the American threat to the British locomotive industry.

Over the next few decades, during the golden years of steam railway traction, North British Locomotive Co., not only became a household name, but generated significant profits. This financial success was to be put to essential use in the years of economic depression, and enabled the company to continue some trade, where others had failed. The diamond-shaped plate attached to engines built by North British was only fitted to engines from Queen's Park, until the 1930s, with Hyde Park and Atlas works continuing to use their own designs.

In addition to its commercial success in the first 25 years especially, technically some interesting, and essential developments were seen coming out of the NBL workshops. The application of superheating, brass tubes fitted in boilers, early appearance of steel fireboxes, piston valves, and support for compounding showed the company had a sound grasp of technical as well as business developments. Some of the world's most famous locomotive types came from Springburn, from the LMS's 'Royal Scot' class 4-6-0, to Gresley's A1/A3 Pacifics, Class JA for New Zealand, and the famous R class Hudsons for Australia. Preserved examples of the latter took part in Australia's bicentennial celebrations. In Africa, many countries took delivery of Glasgow built engines, and in later years, some of the

largest Beyer Garratt types ever built, were put to work on South African Railways.

Some of the technical developments were obviously less successful than others, and perhaps in view of such failed experiments, like the steam-electro-turbo locomotive, NBL stuck to traditional steam engine building perhaps longer than was commercially prudent. But, the technical design and construction skills of the steam era have stood the acid test of time. Later years demonstrated the value of diesel and electric traction to many railways around the world, but changing the strategy of North British came too little, and too late to save the mighty organisation that grew out of the skills of the men of Springburn.

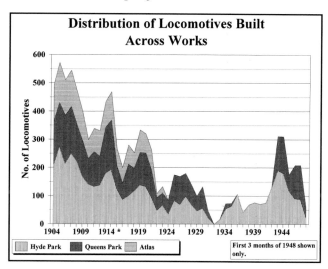

One of the earliest orders for NBL, came from Canada, with these two-cylinder compound 4-6-0s, built in 1903 to order L9. The photograph is actually taken from the company's sales and publicity cards, as shown by other photographs later in this book.

Courtesy Canadian Pacific Ltd

NORTH BRITISH LOCOMOTIVE COMPANY, LIMITED.
HYDE-PARK WORKS, GLASGOW.

Reference No. L 9.

GAUGE OF RAILWAY, 4-ft. 8½-in.

TYPE 4-6-0.—2 CYLINDER COMPOUND. **ENGINE.**

CYLINDERS { DIAMETER, H.P. 22-in. & L.P. 33-in.
{ STROKE .. .. 26-in.

WHEELS .. { COUPLED, DIAMETER. 5-ft. 3-in.
{ BOGIE, DIAMETER. .. 2-ft. 6-in.

WHEEL-BASE { RIGID .. .. 14-ft. 6-in.
{ TOTAL .. .. 25-ft. 2-in.
{ ENGINE & TENDER 52-ft. 8-9/16-in.

WORKING PRESSURE .. .. 210 lbs. per sq. in.

HEATING SURFACE { TUBES .. 2262½ sq. ft.
{ FIREBOX . 158½ ..
{ TOTAL .. 2421 ..

FIREGRATE AREA .. .. 32 ..

BOILER FEED, 2 INSPIRATORS No. 10 (HANCOCK).

TRACTIVE FORCE AT 60% } .. 25168 lbs.
OF BOILER PRESSURE }

WEIGHT { IN WORKING ORDER, 75 tons 5 cwts.
{ ON COUPLED WHEELS, 56 tons 19 cwts.

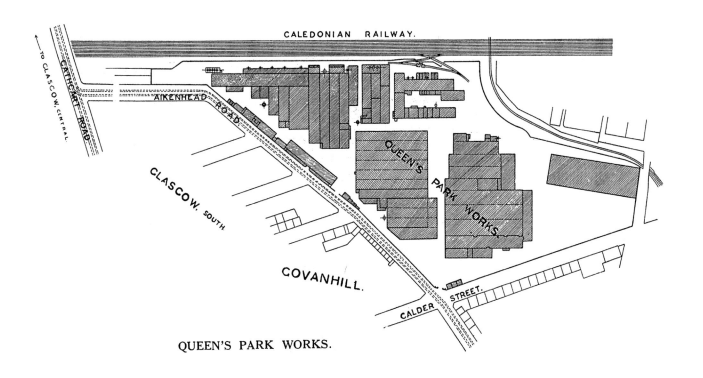

QUEEN'S PARK WORKS.

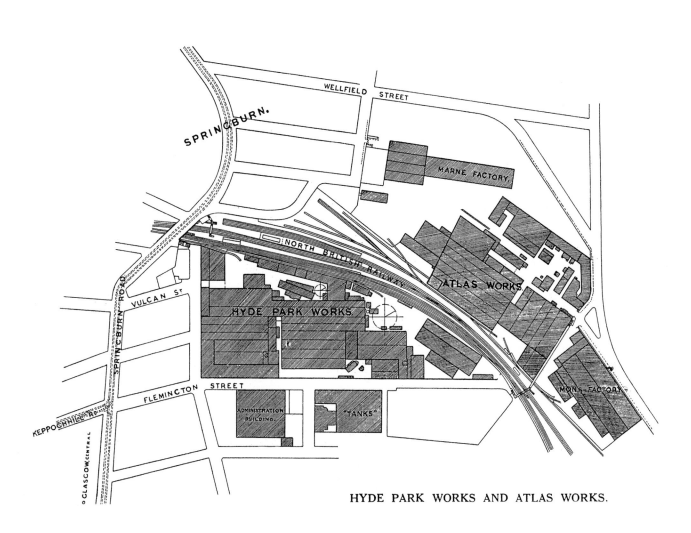

HYDE PARK WORKS AND ATLAS WORKS.

3

Home Orders 1903–1928

The three companies that formed NBL completed their final orders under their individual identities, and then continued the building of locomotives as before, but under the new company name. Neilson & Co. were in the middle of order number E898 for South Africa, Sharp, Stewart were building order E1200 for the Great Indian Peninsula Railway, whilst Dübs & Co. were completing order 4416E for Japan. Order L27 from the Great Southern of Ireland was originally placed early in 1903, but was delayed until 1904 for a pair of 4-4-0s, supplied without tenders. The progressive numbers were re-allocated to the 1904 order, and the original order L27 was cancelled.

The First Locomotives for the Home Market

In 1903, the first stirrings of non-steam traction were beginning to surface, and especially in the application of electricity. However, those early years for North British, perhaps with the exception of the Reid-Ramsay turbo-electric locomotive, steam power was most definitely the profitable route to follow. The first order received by North British for the home market came from the Furness Railway, on 26th June 1903, as order L17, although the War Office had placed an order two months earlier for a single 2-4-2 type. Out of the first forty orders received by the company, only one was for a main line railway company, two others were for industrial lines, and of course, the War Office engine already mentioned. The first 40 orders were placed between January 1903 and April 1904, only 16 months since the company was born.

Amongst some of the interesting early locomotives for the home market was a narrow gauge 0-4-0 for Woolwich

Arsenal, carrying works number 16032. The early years it has to be said, were very much dominated by NBL's continued success in exporting locomotives, although not a few engines were ordered by Scottish railways. In 1906, NBL's railway company neighbour, the North British Railway placed an order for a splendid 4-4-2 Atlantic type designed by W. P. Reid, the Locomotive Superintendent, a number of which were built by the company at Hyde Park Works, as well as by the railway company itself, and by Robert Stephenson in Newcastle. This design followed a fashion for the Atlantic type in passenger service on Britain's railways, although the Reid design had a larger diameter boiler (5ft) than most of its contemporaries.

The principal dimensions of these large passenger engines were: 20in by 28in cylinders, 6ft 9in coupled wheels, 3ft 6in bogie, and 4ft 3in trailing wheels, in a total wheelbase of 27ft 9½ins. The original, saturated boilers were pressed to work at 200 lb/sq. in., from a total heating surface of no less than 2256.2 sq. ft. These were large locomotives of their type, certainly by British standards, and weighed in at 121 tons, with a full complement of coal and water.

The North British Railway also ordered 0-6-0 goods engines, ten of which were under construction in 1906. A

In 1912, this 0-4-0 saddle tank was built in Glasgow for Bass, at Burton-on-Trent, to order L493 and in 1959 almost 50 years on, the diminutive No. 4 is still at work. Still at Burton-on-Trent, but for Bass, Ratcliff & Stratton, and carrying NBL works number 19848.

Roger Shenton

Above: The majestic lines of W. P. Reid's Atlantic design for the North British Railway, with its enormous, saturated boiler and clean lines, is ably demonstrated in this broadside view of *Aberdonian*. The first of 14 built by NBL under order L175, it was given running number 868 as shown here, with the remaining 13 numbered between 869 and 881 by the railway company.

Mitchell Library Collection

Above: The archetypal British 4-4-0, perhaps nowhere better expressed than in the Highland Railway's 'Ben' class ordered from NBL under orders L177 and L265. This view is of No.61 *Ben Na Caillich;* one of the four built at Queen's Park in the summer of 1908. All were built at the former Dübs & Co.'s works.

Mitchell Library Collection

Below: The LNWR, or self-styled 'Premier Line' could not apparently build everything at their Crewe Works. In 1915, no less than 20 of the famous 'Prince of Wales' class 4-6-0s were built by NBL, with the work divided evenly between the Hyde Park and Queen's Park works, under order L658 and L659. Another example of locomotives supplied without tenders. This is No. 2175 *Loadstone*.

Bryan Jackson

As the traffic on the Glasgow & South Western grew, NBL supplied 15 of these 0-6-0s, to the designs of James Manson, all of which were built at Queen's Park under order L521. NBL noted the running numbers as 71 to 85, but they were later renumbered, and this view of No. 300 shows clearly the powerful lines of the new design.

Mitchell Library Collection

year later, the Furness Railway came to North British again, for an 0-6-2 tank locomotive, as did the Maryport & Carlisle in 1908, for an 0-6-0 tender type, primarily used on coke trains, but occasionally seen on heavy excursion trains.

Further north, the Highland Railway came to NBL for 'modified' 'Ben' class 4-4-0s, to replace engines that the railway company had recently sold. These engines, four of which were built at Queen's Park Works, were essentially the same as the existing Highland Railway 'Ben' class, but with higher pitched, larger boilers, and safety valves on the firebox instead of the steam dome. In 1911, NBL completed 15 new 4-6-0 locomotives for the Glasgow & South Western Railway. The company had also ordered 15 0-6-0 goods engines, the first examples of which were constructed at Kilmarnock, by the railway, and the remainder in Glasgow. The railway company had moved its works to Kilmarnock in 1856 from Glasgow, and relocated near the Caledonia Works of Andrew Barclay, Sons & Co. Barclay were to play an important role in maintaining the products of NBL, following the Glasgow company's closure in April 1962.

A characteristic of British railway companies was a long standing commitment to building their own motive power, and this was certainly true of the period under review. Having said that, North British Loco. received orders from north and south of the border, including one for 20 of the London & North Western Railway's famous 'Prince Of Wales' class 4-6-0. These engines were also built by the

railway company at its Crewe Works, and by another Glasgow engineering giant, William Beardmore & Co. Although, looking at the orders coming in to NBL, during the pre First World War period, most home orders were from the Scottish railway companies. The North British Railway, in 1909, ordered more tank engines, as did the Highland Railway. The North British order included an 0-4-4T and on 0-6-2T - for working the Cowlairs Incline. The Highland Railway order was for an 0-6-4T, and was built at Queen's Park Works, with four of these engines used for banking on the Blair Atholl to Newtonmore section of the line through the Grampians.

The same year, 1909, saw NBL build two of the new, enlarged 'Ben' class 4-4-0s, as replacements for the Highland Railway's famous 'Skye Bogies' of 1874 vintage. The company had also recently sold four of the 60 class engines to P. W. McLellan, and Queen's Park Works delivered four of the new 'Ben' class as replacements.

In 1903 NBL supplied a new class of 0-6-2 tank engine to the London, Tilbury & Southend Railway, with 18in by 26in cylinders, 5ft 6in coupled wheels and weighing in at 64 tons 13 cwt. The railway company numbered them 69 to 74, and they were used primarily for goods workings, but in the summer they could often be found on excursion and boat train services. In the same year, NBL built another series of 12-wheeled tank engines, to designs which had earlier been supplied from the Atlas Works of Sharp, Stewart & Co. With 18in by 26in cylinders, 6ft 6in coupled wheels, and weighing 64 tons 14 cwt., they were used for

Ordered at the same time as the goods engines, were these new passenger 4-4-0s, six of which were built at Queen's Park, under order L522. The numbers carried in service, ran from 131, as depicted, to 136, although NBL's drawing office register lists the running numbers as 331 to 336.

Mitchell Library Collection

The Highland Railway placed three orders for these handsome 4-6-0 'Castle' class engines. This is No. 59, an example from order L668, placed in 1915, for the modified class.

Bryan Jackson

heavy passenger traffic. This order maintained a link between the Glasgow companies and the LT&SR, through Sharp Stewart and Dübs & Co., dating back to 1896. Although some earlier 4-4-2 type tank engines were supplied by Sharp, Stewart from their original base in Manchester.

The number of locomotives which NBL supplied to Scottish based public railways and industrial lines dominated the Glasgow builder's order books at home. Once again, in 1909, James Manson, the Locomotive Superintendent of the Glasgow & South Western Railway ordered a series of 0-6-0 goods engines from NBL. Manson and his team were also responsible for the design of a powerful new 4-6-0 passenger engine, then being built in the railway company's workshops at Kilmarnock. NBL's part in this development could, it may be said, have been that of taking the pressure off the railway company's works, and under order L402, supplying 15 of the 0-6-0 goods engines. The leading dimensions were:

Order No.	L402
Works Nos	19244 – 19258
Running Nos	47 – 61
Wheel arrangement	0-6-0
Wheel dia., coupled	5ft 1¼in
Heating surface	
tubes	1,286.00 sq ft
firebox	114.00 sq ft
total	1,400.00 sq ft
Grate area	18 sq ft

The original order for these engines was placed in March 1909, and they were constructed at the Atlas Works. Although, delivery was apparently somewhat leisurely since it was recorded that the 15 engines were delivered to the G&SWR between July and November 1910. This same railway company continued to be an important source of orders in the years leading up to the First World War, acquiring 4-4-0 passenger and 0-6-0 goods engines up to

1913. These particular orders were reported in the press as being similar in appearance to the engines recently built for the Highland Railway. This was an understandable comment considering that Peter Drummond had replaced James Manson as Locomotive Superintendednt on the G&SWR, and had come from the Highland Railway. NBL built both the 4-4-0 and 0-6-0 types, under orders L521 and L522, at Queen's Park works. The 15 0-6-0s were originally numbered 279 and 292 to 305 by the railway company, later becoming 71 to 85 in a renumbering scheme. The main dimensions of the goods engines were as follows:

Order No	L521
Works Nos	20113 – 20127
Running Nos	71 – 85
Wheel arrangement	0-6-0
Wheel dia., coupled	5ft 0in
Heating surface	
tubes	1,637.00 sq ft
firebox	147.00 sq ft
total	1,784.00 sq ft
Grate area	26.25 sq ft
Boiler pressure	180 lbs/sq. in.

These large boilered goods engines – the outside diameter of the shell was 5ft 3ins, and carried some 8ft 6in above rail level – were fitted with Stephenson type valve gear, and the increasingly popular piston valves. An interesting innovation in these engines, was the inclusion of Dugald Drummond's design of steam drier, which although not superheating proper, was alleged to improve the efficiency of the locomotive. These designs were a mixture of innovation and traditional techniques – the use of steam reverse on the one hand, with boiler feed pumps instead of injectors on the other.

Order number L522 was for six express passenger 4-4-0s

In November 1910, the North Eastern Railway ordered 20 of the famous Class Z Atlantics for express passenger duties. The locomotive shown in this view, No. 717, is one of the ten non-superheated engines, as order L436 placed at the same time as L437, which was for ten superheated engines. These latter were classified as Z1. All of the North Eastern Atlantics ordered from NBL were built in Hyde Park Works, and delivered in 1911.

Mitchell Library Collection

which showed a number of similarities with components and fittings on the goods engines. The passenger locomotives were originally numbered 131 to 136, although they were later renumbered 331 to 336, with leading dimensions as follows:

Order No	L522
Works Nos	20128 – 20133
Running Nos	131 – 136 (later 331-336)
Wheel arrangement	4-4-0
Wheel dia., coupled	6ft
Heating surface	
tubes	1,736.00 sq ft
firebox	148.00 sq ft
total	1,884.00 sq ft
Grate area	27.60 sq ft
Cylinders (2, inside)	19.5 in x 26 in
Wheelbase	
engine	24ft 9ins
overall	47ft 6ins
Weight (in w.o.)	
engine	61tons 17cwt
tender	45tons 5.25cwt
total	107tons 2.25cwt

Here again, steam reverse gear was fitted, but with feed pumps instead of injectors, and in this design, the piston valves were driven by Walschaerts valve gear. There was a common trend on the main Scottish railways at this time for large boilered engines, pitched well above rail level. This design added to their imposing appearance, and the G&SWR engines were painted in what was described as 'Highland green', but with standard G&SWR lining and lettering.

South of the border, one of the most important orders to arrive at NBL in 1912, came from the Great Central Railway, where the legendary James Robinson was the Locomotive Superintendent. The order was for 50 of the quite new 2-8-0 engines, which were later to find fame with the Railway Operating Department, in two world wars. Order L496 was not the first received by NBL from the Great Central, since in 1905, order L130 arrived for twelve of Robinson's new Atlantic type, which carried progressive numbers 16933-16944. The eight-coupled locomotives were built at Hyde Park Works, which in 1902, had also built three of Robinson's earlier 0-8-0 mineral engines, when the works had been under Neilson, Reid & Co. ownership. Two years before the 2-8-0 order was received, the arrival of superheating was seen to give an advantage in haulage power and efficiency over non-superheated engines, and J. G. Robinson initiated design work at Gorton on a new class of eight-coupled engine. The design was clearly going to be heavier than the 0-8-0, and was fitted with a boiler of the same design as those installed on the Atlantics, but was also equipped with the new Robinson design of superheater. The leading truck, larger cylinders and piston valves, along with the superheater, represented what might be referred to as a step change in technology. The first of these new 2-8-0 Consolidations emerged from the GCR's Gorton Works in Manchester in 1911. The Great Central's traffic was growing rapidly, and the railway's locomotive building capacity could not cope with the demand, and accordingly, they invited builders to tender for the provision of the new Class 8K locomotives.

At the end of 1911, with tendering negotiations in progress for the new engines, NBL was a prime contender, but the first order for 20 was placed in January 1912, with Kitsons of Leeds. Delivery of the Kitson locomotives was planned for the first to arrive in May, and the remainder by July, although unfortunately, the builder did not meet the agreed dates, and the first engine did not arrive until July. The Springburn management knowing that the Great Central would be needing more of these locomotives provided an incentive. They offered the railway payment by instalments for 50 new 2-8-0s. Euphemistically referred to as deferred payment, with each locomotive costing £4,500 each (£50 less than that agreed with Kitson & Co.), and payment made in ten half yearly instalments from January 1913. The railway company agreed to this arrangement, and the order was placed with NBL in February 1912. On the delivery front, NBL were confident – even allowing for the labour disputes (a coal strike occurred in that year) – that they could deliver quicker than Kitson's. In fact, the first of order L496 left Glasgow for Manchester in mid August as planned, and the remainder were indeed completed by the end of 1912. The main dimensions of the Great Central 2-8-0s built at Hyde Park were as follows:

Order No	L496
Works Nos	19854 – 19908
Running numbers	1203 – 1252
Class	8K
Wheel arrangement	2-8-0
Wheel dia.	
coupled	4ft 8in
leading	3ft 6in
Heating surface	
tubes	1,485.00 sq ft
s/heater	398.00 sq ft
firebox	154.00 sq ft
total	2,037.00 sq ft
Grate area	26.00 sq ft
Weight (in w.o.)	
engine	74 tons 7 cwt
tender	49 tons 18 cwt
total	124 tons 5 cwt

The Springburn built engines were two tons heavier overall than their counterparts from elsewhere, and the boiler was pressed to work at 180lb/sq in, compared to 170lb in the first railway built engines. The Robinson type superheater appeared on all the NBL built locomotives, whilst the earlier engines had been fitted with the Schmidt type. The major difference between the two was that the elements themselves were expanded into the superheater header in the Robinson type, whilst the Schmidt elements were fitted with bolted connections. The construction of the locomotives adopted plate frames that were thicker and heavier than existing locomotive designs, with massive steel fabrications for the valve gear motion brackets and drag boxes. This was an undoubtedly robust and reliable design, as its longevity was to prove, as did its choice for war service with the Railway Operating Division.

The ROD Engines for War Service
In total, 521 of these large 2-8-0s were built for the First World War, primarily for service in France, and of this number, no less than 369 were built by North British in Glasgow. The first order for the ROD 2-8-0s was placed on Valentines Day 1917, although this was not the first order for locomotives for war service. That particular place belonged to an 0-4-4-0 Fairlie type for 600mm gauge lines, and the order (L650) was placed by the French War Office in January 1915. In fact a number of orders placed with North British in the first year of the war, were from the French War Office, to a 2-8-0 design supplied for use on French State Railways.

Two generations of 2-8-0 for war service are captured in this view, both from the Springburn company. The leading engine is seen in its later guise, with changes applied by the new owners, the LNER. Although based on the Robinson, ex-GCR design, this design was selected by the Ministry of Munitions for service during the First World War. In LNER service, these were classed as O4/3, and this example carried works number 21808, built in 1917, to order L689. The ROD is seen here in April 1959, at Mexborough Shed. Behind is one of the War Department 'Austerity' locomotives taken in to BR stock.

Roger Shenton

Between February 1917 and October 1918 Springburn received eleven orders, five of which were constructed at Queen's Park, four at Hyde Park, and the remaining two orders were built at Atlas Works. The order, works and running numbers of the ROD engines are given below:

Order	Date Ordered	Works	Works Nos	Qty	Delivered	ROD Nos
L689	14/2/1917	Queen's Park	21768-21808	41	1917	1801 – 1841
L692	6/6/1917	Hyde Park	21819-21868	50	1917	1842 – 1891
L693	6/6/1917	Queen's Park	21869-21918	50	1918	1892 – 1941
L703	9/4/1918	Hyde Park	22000-22029	30	1918/19	1942 – 1971
L704	9/4/1918	Queen's Park	22030-22059	30	1918/19	1972 – 2001
L707	?/?/1918	Atlas	22080-22093	14	1919	1787 – 1800
L710	23/8/1918	Hyde Park	22104-22115	12	1919	2008 – 2013, 2015 – 2020
L711	23/8/1918	Queen's Park	22116-22127	12	1919	2021 – 2031, 2033
L712	24/10/1918	Hyde Park	22128-22177	50	1919	2034 – 2044, 2046 – 2048, 2051 – 2084, 2086 – 2087
L713	24/10/1918	Queen's Park	22178-22227	50	1919	2088 – 2137
L714	24/10/1918	Atlas	22228-22257	30	1919	2138 – 2167

Works	Orders	Engines built
Queen's Park	5	183
Hyde Park	4	142
Atlas	2	44

This highly successful design for the Great Central Railway was selected for service in France at the end of 1916, and its selection was attributed to the breakdown of the Nord Railway's locomotive operations. Interestingly perhaps, as production at NBL, and three other private builders was at its peak, the war ended, and not all of the ROD locomotives actually saw service in France. The final order received at Springburn arrived only two weeks before the armistice was signed, on November 11th 1918, and in fact, only just over half of all locomotives ordered were completed before the end of the war. The main dimensions of the ROD engines built in Glasgow were as follows:

Class	ROD
Wheel arrangement	2-8-0
Wheel dia.	
coupled	4ft 8in
leading	3ft 6in
Heating surface	
tubes	1,349.00 sq ft
s/heater	255.00 sq ft
firebox	154.00 sq ft
total	1,758.00 sq ft
Grate area	26.25 sq ft
Weight (in w.o.)	
engine	73 tons 17 cwt
tender	49 tons 7 cwt
total	123 tons 4 cwt

The first three orders were constructed with the above

particulars intact, and the only difference with these dimensions on later orders, was an increase in the total engine weight to 74 tons. Axle loads changed marginally between orders too, which was reduced by 6 cwt, from 17tons 7cwt, to 17 tons 1cwt. There were a number of detail differences between the earlier and later locomotives, and in comparison with the NBL built locomotives for the Great Central. Amongst these was the fitting of steam heating – since the engines were intended to haul passenger as well as freight trains, and twin air-brake cylinders from order L703 onwards. Of course, the slightly different 'standard' gauge on the Continent meant that the RODs were turned out with a different wheel profile to allow for the 5mm greater distance between the running rails. Another minor difference was the replacement of the Ramsbottom type safety valves with the Ross pop variety, and engines built under orders L710 to L714 had Robinson's 'Intensifore' lubricators, instead of the Wakefield pattern. In fact, NBL actually built 35 of Robinson's design of lubricator, until the Gorton Works of the Great Central began to supply them in quantity. Lastly, on the tender, although the orginal six-wheeled design was supplied, no water pick-up apparatus was provided, and the coal space was slightly bigger.

Of course, many of the NBL built 2-8-0s saw service in northern France, hauling troop, supply, and even civilian passenger trains, but many never arrived across the Channel. After the armisitice was signed, the locomotives on war service were brought back to the UK, at the same time as NBL was continuing to build in large numbers. The returning engines were stored in the south of England, mainly at Tattenham Corner, whilst the new engines from Glasgow were stored in dumps at Gretna and Immingham, with others going to work on the home railways. NBL's price per locomotive had increased during this work, from the original £6,030, to a basic price of £8,400 from the fourth order, to which was added the cost of labour and materials based on a value for each as at May 4th 1918.

The ROD engines had an interesting and varied career, and apart from their rental to the railway companies from 1919, many saw service on other railways around the world. Controversy surrounded the 'dumping' of engines at the end of the war, particularly in view of the railways' shortage of motive power, and prompted some Government action. In the UK, the railways were still under central control until 1921, and in December 1919 the Government stated that of the 300 heavy locomotives built for war service abroad, all but 30 or 40 were on hire to home railways. What the Government did not say at the time, was that the engines were still being built by NBL, after the signing of the armistice, and no arrangements for sale or disposal were announced. Between 1919 and 1921 the hired locomotives were operated by the GWR, LNWR, GCR, NER and Caledonian, amongst others, but in 1921, the Government required the return of these locomotives. The only exceptions were of course the engines purchased by the GWR and LNWR, whilst the returned hire engines were again stored in large dumps, at Gretna, Birkenhead, and between Chester and Rhyl. After being stored in the open for some two years, the locomotives had deteriorated, and the price that the Government wanted was never a possibility. In fact, when large scale sales of these 2-8-0s began in 1923, the price fell to less than 5% of the original cost to the Ministry of Munitions. Sales, which included large numbers of the NBL orders, included the 20 sold to the GWR, and 30 to the LNWR in 1919. These engines were delivered straight to the railway company from Glasgow. By 1925, the GWR had bought another 80, the LNER had obtained 173, and 18 were sold overseas. Further sales to the railways took place in the late 1920s, whilst some of the NBL built engines

stored at Gretna, were sent to Armstrong, Whitworth in Newcastle, prior to being dispatched to China.

More than 30 of the NBL built 2-8-0s were sent to China, some for industrial use on mining company lines, while eight were known to have been used on the Shanghai – Nanking Railway. Nine locomotives were sent out to New South Wales, also seeing service in the mining industry. By the time of the Second World War some of these engines had been cut up, but the majority were still in service, and a small number were back in war service again in the 1940s. It was on the LNER and GWR that the engines lasted longest, with major modifications, including reboiling on the LNER. On the GWR, and later as British Railways Western Region, a number of the Glasgow built engines were still at work on freight trains in the 1950s.

Back in 1912 a new type of locomotive was introduced to the railways of Great Britain, in the shape of the GWR's 2-6-0 'Aberdare' mineral engine, but in its GWR form, this was a unique type, with outside frames. J. F. McIntosh on the Caledonian Railway provided the first example of a typically British 2-6-0, with inside cylinders and inside frames. This design, or at least a similar one, was introduced by Peter Drummond on the G&SWR, with leading dimensions as follows:

Order No	L649
Works Nos	21172 – 21182
Running Nos	51 – 61
Wheel arrangement	2-6-0
Wheel dia.	
coupled	5ft
leading	3ft 6in
Heating surface	
tubes	1,133.00 sq ft
s/heater	211.00 sq ft
firebox	147.00 sq ft
total	1,702.00 sq ft
Grate area	26.25 sq ft
Weight (in w.o.)	
engine	62 tons 0 cwt
tender	45 tons 19 cwt
total	107 tons 19 cwt

Eleven locomotives were built by NBL to order L649, and were superheater fitted engines, but this time, in 1915, the boiler was fed by a pair of No.10 live steam injectors. The similarity in components and basic dimensions of all the NBL built engines for the G&SWR at this time is an obvious feature. A further five orders were received by NBL between 1915 and 1923, when the railways were grouped into the 'Big Four', and the G&SWR became part of the LMSR.

In the early years of the 20th century the 4-4-2 wheel arrangement for passenger tank engines was very popular with railways, examples of which were built by NBL for the North British Railway. In fact, the first of these, under order number L652, were built at Atlas Works, as an enlargement of an earlier North British Railway design, produced in 1912. In 1915, NBL began construction of these 15 locomotives, with two of their number in service by the end of that year. Under normal circumstances that would perhaps be an unremarkable feat, but considering the preoccupation of the works with construction and fabrication work for the war effort, some normal business was almost 'as usual'. At this time in the development of steam traction, superheating was gradually becoming more popular, with designs from a number of sources – those of Schmidt and Robinson perhaps the most well known. The new NBL built tank engines were fitted with the Robinson design, and in many areas, standardisation with earlier locomotive types for the railway company, was achieved. The main dimensions of the new superheater tanks was as follows:

Order No	L652
Works Nos	21203 – 21217
Running Nos	438 – 452
Wheel arrangement	4-4-2
Wheel dia.	
coupled	5ft 4in
leading	3ft 6in
Wheelbase	
engine	8ft 3in
overall	28ft 11.5in
Heating surface	
tubes	930.00 sq ft
s/heater	220.00 sq ft
firebox	95.00 sq ft
total	1,245.00 sq ft
Grate area	16.60 sq ft
Cylinders (2, inside)	19in x 26in
Weight (in w.o.)	
engine	73 tons 16 cwt
total	73 tons 16 cwt

There were in fact two orders for this class, built at the Atlas Works; L652 (for 15 engines), and a later order L740 (for six engines). For goods and mixed traffic work, tank engines with an 0-6-2 wheel arrangement were popular, and both the G&SWR, and North British railway companies ordered the design in 1915 and 1916. The North British order (L653), followed the 4-4-2 tank engines, and was the fifth in a series of orders for this type from the railway company. The order from the Glasgow & South Western (L656), was for six engines, and was the first of three orders, with the second order (L676) placed in the same year, 1916. Order L706 was the last of the G&SWR's orders placed with NBL, bringing the total number of engines built for that company to 28.

Home Orders 1903 – 1912

Railway	Year	Order No.	Works Nos.	Qty	Works	Type and Notes
Great Southern & Western of Ireland	1903	L3	16021-24	4	Hyde Park	0-6-2T to railway company's design
War Office	1903	L7	16032	1	Hyde Park	2-4-2T
Furness	1903	L17	16113-17	5	Atlas	0-6-2T
Mid. Grt Western of Ireland	1903	L19	16128-31	4	Hyde Park	0-6-0 to railway company's design
W. Baird & Co.	1903	L24	16182-83	2	Hyde Park	0-4-0T, similar to Neilson's E821
Wemyss Coal Co.	1903	L25	16184	1	Hyde Park	0-6-0T, similar to Sharp Stewart E947
Metro. Coal Co.	1903	L52	16350	1	Hyde Park	0-4-0T, similar to Neilson E863
Vickers Sons & Maxim	1904	L53	16351-52	2	Hyde Park	0-4-0T, same as L52
Great Northern of Ireland	1904	L59	16190-91	2	Hyde Park	4-4-0, without tenders, similar to Neilson E819
Great Northern of Ireland	1904	L60	16433-34	2	Hyde Park	0-6-0, without tenders, similar to Neilson E896
British Engnrs. Assoc.	1904	L64	16447	1	Queen's Park	0-6-0T
Wemyss Coal Co.	1904	L66	16463	1	Hyde Park	0-6-0T, same as L25
Barry	1904	L68	16466-67	2	Atlas	0-4-0T, steam rail motors
Strain & Robertson (For Chile)	1904	L73	16509	1	Hyde Park	0-4-0T, for Reducto Nitrate Co. Chile
Great Northern of Ireland	1904	L74	16510-11	2	Hyde Park	4-4-0, without tenders, same as L59
War Office	1904	L84	16601	1	Hyde Park	2-4-2T, same as L7
Great Northern of Ireland	1904	L87	16607-09	3	Atlas	0-4-0T steam rail motors
Barry	1904	L91	16628-33	6	Atlas	0-6-0T
W. Baird & Co.	1905	L106	16732	1	Hyde Park	0-4-0T, same as Neilson's E734
Midland & S.W.J.	1905	L114	16817	1	Atlas	4-4-0 new design
Strain & Robertson (For Chile)	1905	L125	16898	1	Hyde Park	0-4-0T, for Reducto Nitrate Co. Chile, same as L73
Great Central Railway	1905	L130	16933-44	12	Hyde Park	4-4-2, new Atlantics to Robinson's design
Great Northern of Ireland	1905	L141	17082-84	3	Hyde Park	0-6-0, without tenders, similar to L60
War Office	1905	L151	17223	1	Hyde Park	2-4-2T, similar to L84
Strain & Robertson (For Chile)	1905	L155	17262	1	Hyde Park	0-4-0T, for Reducto Nitrate Co. Chile, same as L125
Steel Co. of S. Wales	1905	L156	17263	1	Queen's Park	0-4-0T crane engine
Darwen Paper Mills	1905	L166	17321	1	Hyde Park	0-6-0T, similar to L25
North British	1905	L167	17322-31	10	Atlas	0-6-0T
Strain & Robertson (For Chile)	1906	L174	17368	1	Hyde Park	0-4-0T, for Reducto Nitrate Co. Chile, same as L155
North British	1906	L175	17369-82	14	Hyde Park	4-4-2
Highland	1906	L177	17398-400	3	Queen's Park	4-4-0 'Ben' class
W. Baird & Co.	1906	L188	17483	1	Hyde Park	0-4-0T, same as L24
Strain & Robertson (For Chile)	1906	L202	17667-68	2	Hyde Park	0-4-0T, for Reducto Nitrate Co. Chile, same as L155
Furness	1906	L215	17808-13	6	Atlas	0-6-2T, same as L17
Great Northern of Ireland	1906	L216	17814-16	3	Hyde Park	4-4-0, without tenders, similar to L74
Furness	1906	L220	17840-43	4	Atlas	0-6-0
Strain & Robertson (For Chile)	1906	L223	17852	1	Hyde Park	0-4-0T, for Reducto Nitrate Co. Chile, same as L202
G&SWR	1906	L226	17884-95	12	Hyde Park	0-6-0
Highland	1906	L227	17896-97	2	Queen's Park	0-6-0
W. Baird & Co.	1906	L229	17904	1	Hyde Park	0-4-0T
Strain & Robertson (For Chile)	1907	L243	18047	1	Hyde Park	0-4-0T, for Reducto Nitrate Co. Chile, same as L174

Highland	1907	L265	18269-72	4	Queens Park	4-4-0, similar to L177 'Ben' class.
Maryport & Carlisle	1907	L268	18285	1	Hyde Park	0-6-0
Great Northern of Ireland	1907	L269	18286-91	6	Hyde Park	0-6-0, without tenders, similar to L141
North Eastern	1907	L281	18355-74	20	Atlas	0-6-0 P3 class
W. Baird & Co.	1907	L286	18385-86	2	Hyde Park	0-4-0T, similar to L229
Strain & Robertson (For Chile)	1907	L289	18403	1	Hyde Park	0-4-0T, same as Neilson order E859
Steel Co. of S. Wales	1907	L290	18404	1	Hyde Park	0-4-0T to NBL design
London, Tilbury & SR	1908	L298	18504-07	4	Queen's Park	0-6-2T, similar to Dübs order 4468E
Strain & Robertson (For Chile)	1908	L327	18757-58	2	Hyde Park	0-4-0T, for Reducto Nitrate Co. Chile, same as L223
Strain & Robertson (For Chile)	1908	L328	18759	1	Hyde Park	0-4-0T, for Reducto Nitrate Co. Chile, same as L327
Midland & SWJ	1908	L333	18791-92	2	Atlas	4-4-0, same as L114
Highland	1908	L335	18803-04	2	Queen's Park	4-4-0 'Ben' class
Highland	1908	L336	18805-08	4	Queen's Park	0-6-4T
North British	1909	L344	18856-61	6	Hyde Park	4-4-0
North British	1909	L345	18862-67	6	Hyde Park	0-6-2T
North British	1909	L346	18868-79	12	Hyde Park	0-4-4T
North British	1909	L347	18880-89	10	Queen's Park	0-6-0
North British	1909	L357	18955-64	10	Atlas	0-6-0, same as L347
Highland	1909	L365	19011-12	2	Queen's Park	4-6-0 'Castle' class
Highland	1909	L366	19013-16	4	Queen's Park	0-6-4T
War Office	1909	L369	19019	1	Hyde Park	2-4-2T, same as L151 etc.
John Watson Ltd.	1909	L376	19048	1	Hyde Park	0-4-0T, similar to L290
D. Colville & Sons & Glasgow Corp.	1909	L377	19049-50	2	Hyde Park	0-4-0T, similar to L376
North British	1909	L382	19085-94	10	Hyde Park	0-6-0, same as L357
Midland & SWJ	1909	L388	19133	1	Atlas	4-4-0, same as L333
North British	1910	L394	19159-76	18	Hyde Park	0-6-2T, similar to L333
G&SWR	1910	L402	19244-58	15	Atlas	0-6-0
NBL – stock	1910	L406	19266	1	Hyde Park	4-4-0+0-4-4, steam turbo-electric locomotive
Midland & SWJ	1910	L412	19314	1	Atlas	4-4-0, same as L388
Strain & Robertson (For Chile)	1910	L413	19315-16	2	Hyde Park	0-4-0T, same as L289
Strain & Robertson (For Chile)	1910	L415	19320	1	Hyde Park	0-4-0T, for Reducto Nitrate Co. Chile, same as L155
Strain & Robertson (For Chile)	1910	L430	19371-72	2	Hyde Park	0-4-0T, for Reducto Nitrate Co. Chile, same as L328
North Eastern	1910	L436	19446-55	10	Hyde Park	4-4-2 Class Z Atlantic
North Eastern	1910	L437	19456-65	10	Hyde Park	4-4-2 Class Z1 Atlantic, superheated
G&SWR	1910	L440	19504-05	2	Atlas	4-6-0 381 Class
Strain & Robertson (For Chile)	1911	L473	19707	1	Hyde Park	0-4-0T, for Reducto Nitrate Co. Chile, same as L413
Strain & Robertson (For Chile)	1911	L474	19708	1	Hyde Park	0-4-0T, for Reducto Nitrate Co. Chile, same as L430
Midland & SWJ	1911	L479	19755-56	2	Atlas	4-4-0, same as order L412
North British	1912	L492	19828-47	20	Queen's Park	0-6-2T, same as L394
R. & G. Bass	1912	L493	19848	1	Hyde Park	0-4-0T
Great Central	1912	L496	19859-908	50	Hyde Park	2-8-0, later used as R.O.D. type
Furness	1912	L515	20071-72	2	Atlas	4-4-0
Furness	1912	L516	20073-76	4	Atlas	0-6-0
G&SWR	1912	L521	20113-27	15	Queen's Park	0-6-0, new G&SWR design
G&SWR	1912	L522	20128-33	6	Queen's Park	4-4-0, new G&SWR design
Highland	1912	L527	20160-63	4	Queen's Park	4-6-0, modified 'Castle' class
North British	1912	L528	20164-72	9	Queen's Park	0-6-2T, same as L492
Lanarkshire Steel Co.	1912	L532	20184	1	Hyde Park	0-4-0T, similar to L377
D. Colville & Sons	1912	L533	20185	1	Hyde Park	0-4-0T, similar to L377
Strain & Robertson (For Chile)	1912	L544	20282-85	4	Hyde Park	0-4-0T, same as L474
Coltness Iron Co.	1912	L545	20286	1	Hyde Park	0-6-0T, similar to Neilson's E839
Strain & Robertson (For Chile)	1912	L546	20287-88	2	Hyde Park	0-4-0T, same as L289

Railway	No. of orders	No. of engines	Avg. engines/order
North British	11	125	11.4
Highland	8	25	3.1
Great Central	2	62	31
G&SWR	5	50	10
North Eastern	3	40	13.3
Ireland	9	29	3.2
Industrial	36	48	1.33
Furness	5	21	4.2
Others	9	18	2
Midland & SWJ	5	7	1.4
Total:	93	425	4.57

The G&SWR 0-6-2 tank engines were very similar to the North British locomotives, but oddly perhaps, an increase in cylinder diameter from 18in to 18.25in was seen in the 'as built' condition. Out of a total weight of 65 tons, 50 tons was noted as being adhesive weight, or 77% of the total weight available for adhesion, making them eminently suitable for the work they were tasked with. In fact, like many 0-6-2s all over Great Britain, they were used frequently on moderately heavy goods trains, and mineral workings. For these latter, the G&SWR used them on routes in Ayrshire, on the severely graded lines south and east of Ayr itself. The leading dimensions of these particular tank engines were:

Order No	L706
Works Nos	22070 – 22079
Running Nos	1 – 10
Wheel arrangement	0-6-2
Wheel dia.	
coupled	5ft
trailing	4ft
Wheelbase	
engine	22ft 9ins
overall	22ft 9ins
Heating surface	
tubes	1,143.97 sq ft
firebox	118.12 sq ft
total	1,262.09 sq ft
Grate area	22.50 sq ft
Cylinders (2 inside)	18.25in x 26in
Boiler pressure	180 lb/sq. in.
Weight (in w.o.)	
engine	65 tons
total	65 tons

Whilst NBL continued to build locomotives during the war years of 1914 to 1918, and although these were mostly for export, quite a number of interesting types were built for the home market. The Highland Railway for example ordered six more engines in 1915, for two classes, with 4-4-0 and 4-6-0 wheel arrangements. The latter were of the famous 'Castle' class introduced by Peter Drummond, a number of which were built by Dübs & Co., at their Glasgow Locomotive Works. The 1916 engines were ordered from NBL by the Highland's new Locomotive Superintendent, Christopher Cumming, and possessed larger boilers, greater fuel capacity in the tenders, and 6ft, compared with the original 5ft 9in driving wheels. Cumming's other order on NBL at this time, the 4-4-0 design, were more of the David Jones 'Loch' class, a type which was first built for the Highland Railway back in 1896. The new locomotives, like their predecessors were built south of the Clyde, at the Queen's Park Works.

Both the 'Loch' class and 'Castle' class, orders L667 and L668 respectively, were ordered in October 1915, with delivery scheduled for June 1916. However, the impact of work for the war effort was impacting locomotive orders for the home railways, and delivery was not completed for both types until August and September 1917. The changes to Peter Drummond's original 'Castle' class design had begun back in 1913, with order L527 for four locomotives (modified from order L365, in 1909), placed with NBL by the railway company in 1912. The modifications included a slightly lengthened wheelbase, extended smokebox, and what have been described as 'deflector chimneys'.

In 1917, the penultimate year of the war, only two orders were received from railways in Britain, since most of the output of all three works was destined for war service, and overseas railways. The two UK orders consisted of 34 goods engines under order L695 for the North British

Railway, and another four 0-6-0 mineral engines, under order L701, for the Furness Railway. These two orders were constructed at the Atlas and Hyde Park works, respectively. The following year was no better on the domestic market for locomotives, with the Ministry of Munitions orders for R.O.D. 2-8-0s forming the bulk of the activity in all three works. In 1918, for the first and only time in the company's history to that date, home orders exceeded the export contracts – albeit by only two orders! The home orders consisted of two for the Great Northern Railway (L705 & L709), one for the Glasgow & South Western (L706), and two for the North British Railway (L716 & L717), with the remaining eight orders in 1918 being placed by the Ministry of Munitions. The total number of engines built for the home companies was 50, whilst that for overseas was only slightly less, at 45 locomotives.

The first of the Great Northern Railway orders was for ten of the new O1 class 2-8-0s, to the specification of that company's Locomotive Superintendent, a certain Mr H. N. Gresley. Order L705, for the first ten, was built at Hyde Park Works, with delivery scheduled between April and June 1919, whilst the second order for five locomotives, L709, was built at Atlas Works. The leading dimensions of these important new freight locomotives were as follows:

Order No	L705	L709
Works Nos	22060–22069	22099–22103
Running Nos	462–471	472–476
Wheel arrangement	2-8-0	
Wheel dia.		
coupled	4ft 8in	
leading	2ft 8in	
Wheelbase		
engine	27ft 2in	
overall	53ft 3in	
Heating surface		
tubes	1,922.00 sq ft	
heaters	570.00 sq ft	
firebox	162.00 sq ft	
total	2,654.00 sq ft	
Grate area	27.60 sq ft	
Cylinders (2, outside)	21in x 28in	
Boiler pressure	170 lb/sq in.	
Weight (in w.o.): total	119 tons 5 cwt	

In both cases, the engines only were built by NBL, the railway company providing the six-wheeled tenders. The 15 engines supplied by NBL were sandwiched between Mr Gresley's experiments with three-cylinder propulsion, and the use of his derived, or conjugated valve gear. GNR engine number 461 had appeared from Doncaster Works in 1918 with this new form of valve gear, which had been produced in order to improve the efficiency of the steam locomotive. Gresley's work in this area, and in particular with the 2-8-0 O1 class was not re-commenced until 1920, when a batch of 3-cylinder 2-8-0s was selected for comparative trials with the 2-cylinder version. The 2-cylinder engine selected for the trials was No.466, one of the batch of ten built by NBL in 1919, at Hyde Park, and from the results of the trials, although the 3-cylinder design became the standard heavy freight engine, NBL contributed in some small way to the establishment of that standard.

An interesting pair of entries appears in the NBL drawing office register for 1st July 1918, showing the Ministry of Munitions ordering 20 2-6-0 locomotives, one for Hyde Park, the other for Queen's Park. In fact these Moguls, again to Mr Gresley's specifications, were required for the war effort on the Great Northern Railway, and the drawings came to NBL from Beyer Peacock in Manchester. Like the

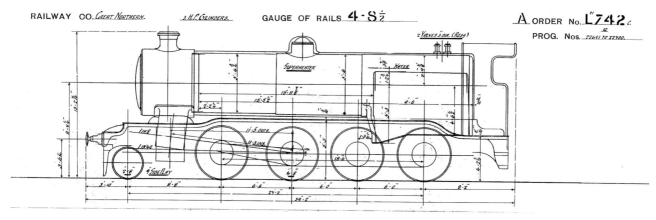

Class O2, 3-cylinder 2-8-0 for the Great Northern Railway, to a Gresley design, and built by NBL to order L742 in 1921.

Mitchell Library Collection

original O1 class 2-8-0s, no tenders were supplied from Glasgow for NBL orders L698 and L699, with the engines carrying works numbers 21971-21990 and GNR running numbers 1660 to 1679. They were curiously described as 'new to BP's drawings', which suggests perhaps that they were a new type of order for NBL from the Great Northern, since they were based on the improved K2 class 2-6-0, built by the railway company at Doncaster. In total, there were 75 of this class of mixed traffic engines on the GNR, and later, LNER.

The following year, 1919, saw a slight resurgence in orders coming in to the company, although only two came from Britain, and no further orders were forthcoming from War Office sources. The two home orders were from the Great North of Scotland Railway (order No. L730), and the Furness Railway (order No. L733), respectively. The total number of engines built was also small, the GN of SR wanted six 4-4-0s, and the Furness another five 0-6-0 goods engines. If such a state of affairs was to continue for any length of time, the future would hardly be promising for the mighty NBL, with its three works, and a multiplicity of erecting shops, foundries, boiler, and machine shops.

By 1920 conditions appeared to improve, and in March of that year, an order came from the North British Railway for a pair of Atlantic types, whilst the Great Northern came back in April for more 2-8-0 heavy freight engines. This time however, following the success of the 3-cylinder locomotive No. 461, H. N. Gresley ordered ten new 3-cylinder 2-8-0s, which were built under NBL order L742 at Atlas Works. Once again, no tenders were supplied, with leading dimensions as follows:

Order No	L742
Works Nos	22691–22700
Running Nos	477–486
Wheel arrangement	2-8-0
Wheel dia.	
coupled	4ft 8in
leading	2ft 8in
Wheelbase	
engine	27ft 2in
overall	53ft 3in
Heating surface	
tubes	1,868.50 sq ft
s/heater	430.50 sq ft
firebox	163.50 sq ft
total	2,462.50 sq ft
Grate area	27.50 sq ft
Cylinders (2 out, 1 inside)	18.5in x 28in
Boiler pressure	180 lb/sq. in.
Weight (in w.o.) total	130 tons 13 cwt

The originally scheduled delivery dates from Atlas

Works for these modified, 3-cylinder 2-8-0s was October 1920, although the first of what became the O2 class did not appear until 1921. NBL were entrusted with the work of building the first of the new Gresley 3-cylinder engines, and in order to prove the economy of operation of the new design over the 2-cylinder arrangement, dynamometer tests were held. The locomotives involved were both built by NBL – No. 466 of Class O1, and recently built Class O2 No. 479. The results confirmed their designer's expectations, and although the earliest builds had the Great Northern cab, later engines of what became class O2 had the LNER side windowed cab. In the same year as the new GNR 2-8-0s were ordered, the same company had placed the largest contract, for 50 new 0-6-2 tank engines, all built at Hyde Park Works, under order L734.

The North British Railway placed a total of three orders with NBL in 1920, the first of which came in March, for 15 of the 0-6-0 goods engines, to order L739. These were broadly similar to the 0-6-0s which were ordered in six batches from the company, beginning with L347 in 1909. The very next order, L740, was for six of the 4-4-2 tank engines, popular at the time for passenger service. The final order from the railway company, was for a pair of the Reid Atlantics, to order L741 for construction at Hyde Park, and which were essentially the same as the first batch of 14 built for the North British Railway back in 1906. The pair which constituted the 1920 order differed in the respect that they were superheated, with the Robinson type of superheater, and sported running numbers 509 and 510. Delivery was by all accounts slow, since although ordered in March 1920, they were recorded as being delivered in March of 1921. Little of this delay could be attributed to the 'new technology' of superheating, since NBL had been applying various forms of superheater since before the First World War.

The apparent improvement in locomotive orders at home was in reality non-existent, and 1921 passed with no orders for home railways at all. In 1922, only two orders were placed, by the Caledonian Railway for steam engines, whilst the only other two orders placed at home, were actually by English Electric, for bodies for an order they had received from Japan. Worse still perhaps, the orders from English Electric were for high powered electric locomotives – both company and the new motive power would eventually climb to a dominant position in the railway world. The Caledonian Railway orders were for twelve more of the renowned 4-4-0 passenger types – order L768 – and eight brand new 4-6-0s, for the heaviest Anglo-Scottish expresses – 'The Corridor'. These latter were a new design, the Pickersgill 60 class, as order L769 from NBL, they were a new design, with two outside cylinders, and were the final locomotives built for home consumption, before the Grouping of railways in 1923. They were

The NBL/LNER 'Sandringham' design did result in an acceptable locomotive type, although a number of changes were made, soon after the class entered service in 1929. Eventually, the class numbered 73, with the majority built by the railway company itself, and a batch of eleven by Robert Stephenson in Newcastle. The NBL built engines survived for almost 30 years, in almost original condition, with only two of their number being radically altered in later years. The design and build contract was awarded on 17th February 1928, for ten locomotives, at a price of £7,280 each, with delivery to be completed in the same year. In fact, so far as the LNER were concerned, all ten were recorded as being on the company's books by December that year.

During the initial design phase, a number of problems were encountered, particularly in respect of Gresley's derived three-cylinder valve gear. The LNER design team originally proposed a drive arrangement with all three cylinders driving the leading axle, similar to the railway's own D49 class 4-4-0s, and some earlier 4-6-0s of Class B16, for the North Eastern Railway. The problems with the design were associated with weight restrictions imposed by the LNER's Civil Engineer, for locomotives working the Cambridge and Southern Area lines. NBL had proposed two alternative designs with their submissions for the contract, and the LNER took up the version with a lighter, 18 tons maximum static axle load. Not suprisingly, NBL used earlier drawings of the Pacifics it had built for the LNER to provide such components as the cab, cylinders, and motion. The boiler design too was within the experience of NBL, and the 'Sandringham' design was based around the K3 2-6-0 and O2 2-8-0.

The major problem encountered by NBL in the design, was the drive. Soon after the contract was settled, NBL proposed dividing the drive between the leading and middle coupled axles, as they had done with the LMS 'Royal Scots'. Changes proposed by the LNER included an increase in cylinder diameter to 17.5 in, longer frames at the rear, and lighter springs. The famed 2 to 1 lever of the Gresley valve gear was carried behind the cylinders, to drive the inside cylinder valves. The changes required by the LNER resulted in a delay in delivery of the 'Sandringhams', and the penalty clause was removed from the contract. Originally, they were scheduled for delivery between August and October 1928.

In service, the Hyde Park engines were run in on stopping trains between Glasgow and Edinburgh, before being despatched south to East Anglia. Soon after their arrival though, cracks developed in the front main frames, resulting in the fitting of stiffening plates. Although this provided a stop gap solution, later in life, completely new front end main frames were substituted for the patched up originals. This particular defect may have resulted as weight reduction meant that hornblocks were only fitted to the middle axles, and not the front and rear axleboxes, which had hornguides only. Having said that, the later batches of this class built by the LNER themselves suffered similar frame fractures, and the problem was never fully resolved. Overall, the 'Sandringhams' were a popular locomotive initially, with the first workings including Manchester to Ipswich boat trains. Two members of the NBL batch were rebuilt with the new Thompson design of boiler, and other modifications, to become Class B2, along with nine others. The rebuilt locomotives were Nos 2803 and 2807, NBL Nos 23806 and 23810, and were the result of a more rigorous standardisation programme under Thompson's motive power policies.

In the year that the new Gresley Pacifics were delivered, 1924, the number of home orders doubled, and one of these included the conversion of the Reid-Ramsay steam-electric locomotive to a geared steam turbine. Once again, the order, L791/GT1 was recorded as being built for 'stock', and allotted the works number 23141, but retained the original running number. The conversion was very extensive, although it retained the 4-4-0+0-4-4 wheel arrangement, described as two eight-wheeled bogies. The use of steam turbines, to improve the efficiency of steam locomotives was becoming popular in the 1920s and the patents for this latest North British Loco. Co. example of innovation were taken out in the names of Sir Hugh Reid and one James MacLeod.

Here, being steamed in the yard at Hyde Park, is the rebuilt Reid-Ramsay-McLeod steam turbine. The plaque on the side is to commemorate the 1924 Empire Exhibition at Wembley.

Mitchell Library Collection

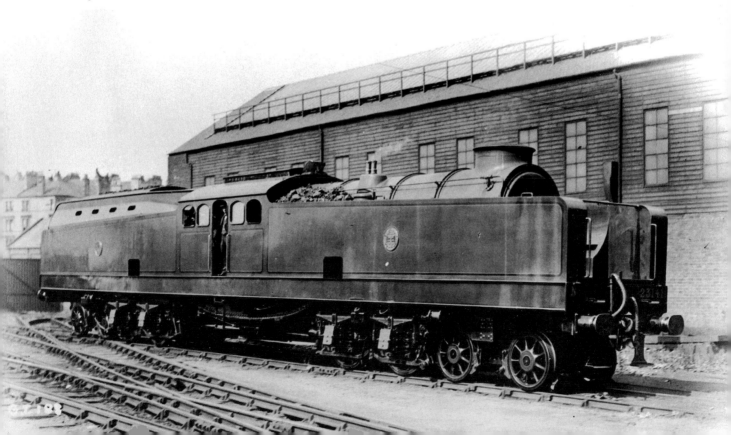

The locomotive was built up on the full length girder frame, which formed the spine of the unit and carried the superstructure. The original 1910 layout was described as having the same running gear layout, however, the original wheels and axles with their armature windings were replaced. In the conversion, the four main axles passed through hollow quill shafts, on which were mounted the driving gears, with the ends of the quill shafts turning the wheels through the wheel spokes. The final drive was accomplished by three springs attached to projections attached to both the wheel spokes, and the ends of the quill shafts. Interestingly perhaps, this quill shaft drive was found on large numbers of electric locomotives throughout Europe, and elsewhere in the world. The outer ends of the axles were carried in axleboxes attached to the 'outside' frames, and supported by leaf springs. The two outer axles on each bogie were there for guidance only, and were not driven, with the low pressure and high pressure turbines carried within the bogie frame at each end of the locomotive.

The boiler was a conventional, superheated, parallel top type, and was coal fired, with bunkers on either side of the firebox. Steam from the boiler passed to a control valve, and admitted to either forward and reverse turbines, with the final exhaust passing from the low pressure turbines at the leading end, into the condenser. The boiler smokebox was actually placed at the trailing end, and of course, a forced draught was provided from a fan, due to the absence of a normal blastpipe arrangement. The condensed steam was returned to a 'hot well', under the centre of the engine, and from there, back into the boiler by means of feed pumps – what we might consider nowadays as an environmentally friendly approach perhaps!

The cab and external appearance of the locomotive was similar to the 1910 version, but in the new Reid-Macleod conversion, appeared more enclosed, with an even more comfortable footplate and driving position. The locomotive was put on display at the British Empire Exhibition at Wembley in 1924, and attracted considerable interest. It was much simpler in design than other, similar types being

Built in 1924, under order L800, was the Southern Railway's N15, or 'King Arthur' class 4-6-0, known as the "Scotch Arthurs", No. 771 *Sir Sagramore* is seen here soon after introduction, in pristine condition, with a Pullman service.

Lens of Sutton

developed, or tested at this time, but the economic recession caused retrenchment of ideas, rather than development, by the railway companies. The contemporary railway press were exhorting the newly formed 'Big Four', LMSR, LNER Southern and Great Western railways to "regard the development of new locomotive types as essential and very practical research work". That indeed is just what they did, but in most cases, the legacy of the different ideas of the previous companies forced the likes of the LMS, LNER, and Southern down a path of consolidation and standardisation, rather than experiment. That same contemporary press also expected that the railway companies would support the innovation from North British Locomotive, and come to the aid of the manufacturer, by running exhaustive trials. This development, like other innovative ideas was not taken up either at home or abroad, and was finally consigned, after some limited testing, to the 'almost but not quite' category of ideas.

Another problem for NBL at this time was the over capacity in its own works, and at the time the new home railways were formed, Atlas Works had not built any locomotives for home use, since 1915. In 1924, out of the total of 14 orders received, only five were for service in the UK. Following orders from the Cardiff Collieries for an 0-6-0 shunting type, and a pair of 4-4-0s for the LMSR's Northern Counties Committee in Northern Ireland, the major orders were from the LMS and Southern railways. The Southern Railway order, L800, was for 20 more of Robert Urie's successful 'King Arthur' 4-6-0s which were first built for the former London & South Western Railway in 1918, as Class N15. The major design change in those built by NBL, was the use of long lap and long travel valve gear, as required by the Southern Railway's CME, R.E.L. Maunsell.

This innovation in mechanical design was first seen on the Great Western Railway between 1900 and 1910, as G. J. Churchward began to assume greater responsibility for the GWR's locomotives. It was also used by the former South Eastern & Chatham Railway, following Maunsell's appointment as Locomotive Superintendent in 1913. This particular technical development was as important as the use of superheating, in improving the performance and efficiency of steam locomotives, although, its adoption and widespread use was quite slow, and the "Scotch Arthurs" as they became known, were the first new engines to be so fitted. The new Southern Railway locomotives had leading dimensions as follows:

The "Scotch Arthurs" were another long-lived NBL built locomotive, with BR Southern Region No. 30790 *Sir Villiars* about to leave Waterloo in July 1957 with a Southampton Boat Train Special. Carrying works number 23286, this example was built at Hyde Park to order L803.

Roger Shenton

Order No	L800
Works Nos	23209-23228
Running Nos	763-782
Wheel arrangement	4-6-0
Wheel dia.	
coupled	6ft 7in
bogie	3ft 7in
Wheelbase	
engine	27ft 6in
overall	58ft 0in
Heating surface	
tubes	1,716.00 sq ft
s/heater	337.00 sq ft
firebox	162.00 sq ft
total	2,215.00 sq ft
Grate area	30.00 sq ft
Cylinders (2 outside)	20.5in x 28in
Boiler pressure	200 lbs/sq. in.
Weight (in w.o.)	
engine	80 tons 19 cwt
tender	57 tons 11 cwt
total	138 tons 10 cwt

Another ten of the "Scotch Arthurs" were ordered from NBL in 1925, to order L803, for the Southern's South Western Section, and again, the engines were built at Hyde Park Works. The running numbers of this second batch were allocated from 783 to 792. The railway company applied names to these famous locomotives, and the 30 built at Springburn carried the following plates:

Order No.	Works No.	Running No.	Name
L800	23209	763	Sir Bors de Ganis
L800	23210	764	Sir Gawain
L800	23211	765	Sir Gareth
L800	23212	766	Sir Geraint
L800	23213	767	Sir Valance
L800	23214	768	Sir Balin
L800	23215	769	Sir Balan
L800	23220	770	Sir Prianius
L800	23221	771	Sir Sagramore
L800	23222	772	Sir Percivale
L800	23223	773	Sir Lavaine
L800	23224	774	Sir Gaheris
L800	23225	775	Sir Agravaine
L800	23226	776	Sir Galagars
L800	23227	777	Sir Lamiel
L800	23228	778	Sir Pelleas
L800	23229	779	Sir Colgrevance
L800	23230	780	Sir Persant
L800	23231	781	Sir Aglovale
L800	23232	782	Sir Brian
L803	23279	783	Sir Gillemere
L803	23280	784	Sir Nerovens
L803	23281	785	Sir Mador de la Porte
L803	23282	786	Sir Lionel
L803	23283	787	Sir Menadeuke
L803	23284	788	Sir Urre of the Mount
L803	23285	789	Sir Guy
L803	23286	790	Sir Villiars
L803	23287	791	Sir Uwaine
L803	23288	792	Sir Hervis de Revel

A few months later, the railway came back to NBL, for a batch of 15, of what is incorrectly described as the railway's Class L in the drawing office register. In fact, Maunsell on the Southern, was under heavy pressure to produce additional locomotives for the London to Folkestone service, then being handled by the seven-year old Wainwright Class L 4-4-0s. There was not the time to produce an entirely new design, so Maunsell opted for improvements to this class, which had appeared in 1919, and entrusted the construction of all 15 to NBL. The design included a much improved front end, smaller cylinders, and a higher boiler pressure, and of course, long lap, travel valves favoured by Maunsell.

In August 1925, order L814 was placed on NBL, with the first delivery scheduled for December, and completion in January 1926. The new locomotives were classified L1, but

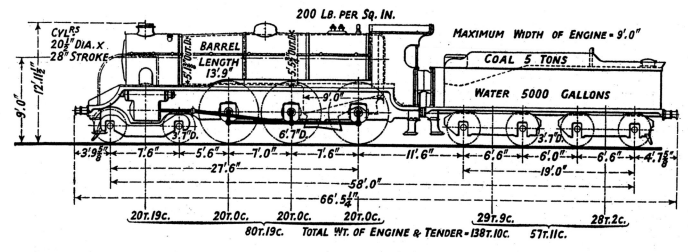

HEATING SURFACE, TUBES—					SUPERHEATER ELEMENTS ... ... 24-1⅞ IN. DIA. OUTS.		
LARGE AND SMALL ... ... 1,716·0 SQ. FT.					LARGE TUBES ... ... 24-5¼ IN. DIA. OUTS. ⎱ 14 FT. 2 IN.		
FIREBOX ... ... 162·0 ,,					SMALL TUBES ... ... 167-2 IN. DIA. OUTS. ⎰ BET. TUBEPLATES		
TOTAL (EVAPORATIVE) ... ... 1,878·0 ,,					GRATE AREA ... ... 30·0 SQ. FT.		
SUPERHEATER ... ... 337·0 ,,					TRACTIVE EFFORT (AT 85 PER CENT. B.P.) ... 25,320·0 LB.		
COMBINED HEATING SURFACES ... ... 2,215·0 ,,							

The Southern Railway 'King Arthur' class N15 4-6-0 was built in two orders (L800 + L803) by NBL, in 1924 and 1925.

Railway Gazette

they were considerably superior in performance to the older L class, and on 80-minute timings from London to the Kent coast, trailing loads could be increased from 225 to 320 tons. They were marginally larger and more powerful than the LMS 4-4-0s which NBL had recently built for the NCC in Northern Ireland, and originally carried the numbers 753-759 and 782-789. All were built at Hyde Park, following on from the "Scotch Arthurs", and carried works numbers 23356-23370. Such ordering demands, for urgent delivery, in very tight timescales were becoming the norm for NBL, but perhaps the most obvious testimony to the company's ability was yet to come, in the shape of a new design for the LMSR – the 'Royal Scot' class 4-6-0.

These locomotives became, perhaps second only to Gresley's Pacifics on the East Coast, the most famous British express passenger locomotives. Their design, construction and success was a lasting testimony to the skills of the North British Locomotive Co., and a fitting end to a review of some of the locomotive types built by the company in its first 25 years.

It has been a tradition that locomotives operated by British railway companies have been associated with the name of the railway's Locomotive Superintendent. In the case of the LMS company's 'Royal Scot' class 4-6-0, they were produced when Henry Fowler was in that seat, and

have been called Fowler's 'Royal Scot' design. In this case, this is, and has always been incorrect, since the greatest proportion of work done on this design, was by the North British Locomotive Co. The order placed by the LMSR was for a locomotive with three cylinders, and a tractive effort of around 30,000 lbs, with all of the detail work to be done by the builder. It was also stated that the locomotives were desperately needed, to take charge of the ever increasing traffic on the railway, and if possible, be in service for the summer of 1927.

The locomotive design was arrived at following experimental runs with a 'Castle class' locomotive from the GWR, and which provided valuable experience on the use of long lap, long travel valve gear. The essential designs were worked out by North British, by borrowing a full set of drawings from the Southern Railway, of the 'King Arthur' class (N15), which NBL had also built for that company. The original leading dimensions of the new LMS 'Royal Scot' class engines were as follows:

The LMSR's Northern Counties Committee operated a stock of the 2P 4-4-0s in passenger service. This is No. 78, one of a batch of five ordered by the LMS in December 1923, for this 5ft 3in gauge network.

Bryan Jackson

The resemblance of the Southern Railway's L1 class 4-4-0s to both the LMSR(NCC), and 2P 4-4-0s is umistakable in this view of No. A759. Fifteen were built for the Southern's Eastern Section at the Hyde Park Works to order L814, with this locomotive carrying works number 23362.

Bryan Jackson

Order No	L833 & L834
Works Nos	23595–23619 (L833)
	23620–23644 (L834)
Running Nos	6100-6149
Wheel arrangement	4-6-0
Length overall*	63ft 2in
	[3,500 gall. tender]
	65ft 2.75in
	[4,000 gall. tender]
Height overall	13ft 2.5in
Width overall	8ft 7.625in
Wheel dia.	
coupled	6ft 9in
bogie	3ft 3.5in
Wheelbase	
engine	27ft 6in
overall	52ft 9.25in*
	[3,500 gall. tender]
	54ft 9in
	[4,000 gall. tender]
Heating surface,	
tubes:	1,892.00 sq ft
s/heater	416.00 sq ft
firebox	189.00 sq ft
total	2,497.00 sq ft
Grate area	31.20 sq ft
Cylinders (2 out, 1 in)	18in x 26in
Boiler pressure	250 lb/sq in
Fuel capacity	
Coal	5.5 tons / 9 tons
Water	3,500 galls. / 4,000 galls.
Weight (in w.o.)	
engine	84 tons 18 cwt
tender	42 tons 14 cwt *
	[3,500 gall. tender]
	54 tons 13 cwt
	[4,000 gall. tender]
total	127 tons 12 cwt
	[3,500 gall. tender]
	139 tons 11 cwt
	[4,000 gall. tender]

* With original Fowler tender.
Original Fowler type 3,500 gallons capacity.

In almost original condition, is NBL built 'Royal Scot' No. 46134 *The Cheshire Regiment*, piloting a rebuilt engine No. 46136 *The Border Regiment*, on the 11.40am from London Euston to Crewe. The semi-fast service is poised to depart from Lichfield Trent Valley station.

Roger Shenton

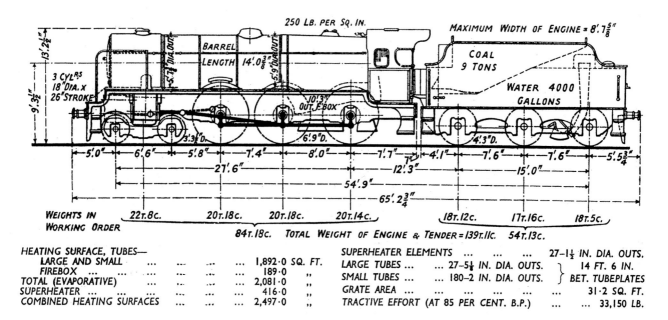

250 LB. PER SQ. IN.

MAXIMUM WIDTH OF ENGINE = 8'. 7⅝"

BARREL LENGTH 14'.0⅜"

COAL 9 TONS

WATER 4000 GALLONS

3 CYL RS 18" DIA. X 26" STROKE

WEIGHTS IN WORKING ORDER	22T.8C.	20T.18C.	20T.18C.	20T.14C.	18T.12C.	17T.16C.	18T.5C.
		84T.18C.			TOTAL WEIGHT OF ENGINE & TENDER = 139T.11C.	54T.13C.	

HEATING SURFACE, TUBES—								SUPERHEATER ELEMENTS	...	...	...	27–1½ IN. DIA. OUTS.	
LARGE AND SMALL	...	...	...	...	1,892·0 SQ. FT.			LARGE TUBES ...	... 27–5¼ IN. DIA. OUTS.	⎫	14 FT. 6 IN.	
FIREBOX	...	...	...	...	189·0	,,		SMALL TUBES ...	... 180–2 IN. DIA. OUTS.	⎬	BET. TUBEPLATES	
TOTAL (EVAPORATIVE)	...	...	...	...	2,081·0	,,		GRATE AREA ...	... ...	...	31·2 SQ. FT.	
SUPERHEATER	...	...	...	...	416·0	,,		TRACTIVE EFFORT (AT 85 PER CENT. B.P.)	...	...	33,150 LB.	
COMBINED HEATING SURFACES	...	...	...	2,497·0	,,							

Most famous of all NBL built engines for the home market in the 1920s, were the LMSR 'Royal Scot' class 4-6-0s.

Railway Gazette

Intriguingly, the Drawing Office Register notes the date of each of the two orders as 25th December 1926, with the first batch of 25 allocated for building at Queen's Park, and the second at Hyde Park. The 50 'Royal Scots' built by NBL were an outstanding success, and in terms of nominal tractive effort were more powerful at the time, than Gresley's A3 Pacifics on the LNER. Whilst speed and power may be a measure of a locomotive's performance, the damage that reciprocating steam engines do to track from vibrations, and the load imposed on bridges, is a major maintenance cost. The NBL built 'Royal Scots' produced the least hammer blow, and did the least damage of any express passenger type of their day, in comparison with GWR 'King' class, LNER A3 class, or the Southern's latest 'Lord Nelson' locomotives.

In late 1927, the new engines were available to work the long distance Anglo–Scottish expresses, in particular, the London–Glasgow 'Royal Scot' service, and the 'Midday Scot'. The new long distance services were scheduled for

Unquestionably NBL's most successful order for the LMSR in the 1920s, was the 'Royal Scot' class designed and built by the Springburn company. No. 6137 was at first named *Vesta*, then given one of the longest names carried by a steam locomotive, *The Prince of Wales's Volunteers, South Lancashire*. The engine is seen here in BR days, outshopped from Crewe Works on the 27th September, 1953, in original conditon. Two years later, No. 46137 was rebuilt with a taper boiler, like others of the class, and withdrawn from service in November 1962. No. 6137 was built to order L834 at Hyde Park Works, and carried works number 23632.

Roger Shenton

only one intermediate stop for engine changes, at either Crewe or Carlisle, and the new 4-6-0s were initially seen to be capable and efficient engines. During extensive tests in late 1927, on the West Coast, the performance of the engines was measured, and the results were seen as a vindication of the design of the locomotive. They were efficient, and powerful engines, and gave the LMSR an opportunity to match its East Coast rivals, the LNER, in capturing the long distance London to Glasgow and Edinburgh passenger traffic. However, despite the initial euphoria over the performance of the type, as mileage travelled built up, in normal service, fuel consumption began to increase, rapidly. This dramatic change in coal consumption with the original design after only moderate mileages was identified, and the adoption of former Midland Railway design practices, was something of a culprit. Use of the Schmidt superheating system had adopted the single piston ring, for the piston valves. It was discovered that this gave rise to considerable leakage, after only moderate mileages. The simple, and effective solution was to provide the piston valves with multiple rings, as in the Ramsbottom design, and restored the 'Royal Scot' class to its pre-eminent position in the LMSR motive power stock. In later years, further changes were made to the original NBL design, including the pairing with larger, 4,000 gallons capacity tenders, and fitting of smoke deflectors. Later still, in William Stanier's day, the class was reboilered with a 'standard' taper boiler design, replacing the original parallel boiler. In this guise, and with other modifications, less dramatic, the class continued in service until almost the end of steam traction in Britain.

Finally, mention must be made of another experimental steam locomotive built by North British Locomotive, using the mechanical portions of a 'Royal Scot' class engine. The project was initiated jointly by The Superheater Co. Ltd, and the LMS Railway, to develop a high pressure steam engine, capable of significantly improving the efficiency of the locomotive in normal service. Order L858, placed in 1928, was for the solitary 4-6-0, initially numbered 6399 in the LMS lists, and was a compound design, for direct comparison with the existing 'Royal Scot' class engines, already in service. The engine was built at Hyde Park, but never entered revenue earning service, following a fatal accident on one of the trial runs conducted in Scotland soon after its completion. In fact, the tragedy occurred as the locomotive, on a test run, was passing through Carstairs station, and one of the tubes in the high pressure steam circuit failed. This in turn, caused a blow back resulting in a fatal injury to one of the testing staff, who was on the footplate at that time. This experiment was stopped immediately, and never resumed. Technically, the differences between the standard NBL 'Royal Scots', and No. 6399 *Fury* were as follows:

Order No	L858
Works No	23890
Running numbers	6399
Cylinders	
(1 – High pressure)	11.5in x 26in
(2 – Low pressure)	18in x 26in
Boiler pressure	
(High)	900 lb/sq. in.
(low)	250 lb/sq. in.
Weight (in w.o.)	
engine	87 tons 2 cwt
tender	43 tons 14 cwt
	[3,500 gall. tender]
total	130 tons 16 cwt
Tractive effort	33,200 lbs

This locomotive was indeed unique amongst British locomotive designs, with a boiler constructed around three distinct components. There was a water tube boiler, with vertical tubes linking a pair of balancing tubes carried roughly at the top outside corners of the firebox, with a lower ring, and a ring forming the base of a combustion chamber. Above and between the upper balancing tubes, was a larger steam drum, within which coiled tubes enabled the high pressure steam from the water tubes to generate steam at a pressure of 900 lb/sq in. The water tube boiler itself, forming a closed circuit, was designed to operate at pressures of between 1,400 and 1,800 lb/sq in. The third component of the steam raising plant was a more or less conventional locomotive boiler, pressed to 250lb/sq in, but

Another ill-fated locomotive to be built at Hyde Park was No. 6399 *Fury* for the LMSR. Under order L858, this locomotive was an experimental high pressure design with a boiler designed by the Superheater Co. The disastrous trial run of the engine is well documented, and the engine was later included as part of the 'Royal Scot' class following rebuilding.

Mitchell Library Collection

reduced in length, to accommodate the rear water tube boiler, and high pressure steam drum. The boiler design was the remit of The Superheater Co. Ltd., and in addition to the expertise of North British Locomotive, John Browns of Sheffield were the providers of the nickel steel pressure vessels. NBL themselves clearly made a considerable contribution to the design, particularly in view of the fact that this complex boiler design was installed on a largely standard 'Royal Scot' chassis.

In operation, the steam generated in the high pressure steam drum, at 900lb, was used, after superheating, in the middle, high pressure cylinder. Following exhaust from the middle cylinder, steam was admitted to a mixing chamber, joining steam generated at 250lb/sq in, in the conventional section of the boiler. From the mixing chamber, steam was then passed to the two outside, low pressure cylinders, before finally being exhausted through the chimney.

This final attempt to secure ever greater economy from the steam locomotive, although undoubtedly highly innovative, was not successful, following the fatal accident on a trial run. However, although the boiler was never used again, nor were any comparisons with the conventional 'Royal Scots' undertaken, this last order in 1928, was not entirely without salvation. The frames built at Hyde Park in

The Fowler F4 class 0-6-0 of the LMSR was built in large numbers in the 1920s, with No. 44057 built to order L802 in 1925, and carrying works number 23254. The photograph was taken in June 1965, and the locomotive was withdrawn in November the same year. The engine itself had outlived its builder, North British, by over three years.

Roger Shenton

1929 were later used in a rebuilt 'Royal Scot' class, becoming No. 6170 *British Legion*.

NBL had, as already described, played a key role in attempting to improve the efficiency of steam locomotive traction, with *Fury* being the final example, for the railways in Britain. But the real success story of the company at the end of the 1920s, was undoubtedly the 'Royal Scot' 4-6-0s, which it designed and built for the LMS. Further examples of the class were built by the railway company itself during the 1930s, at its Derby Works. For 'The Combine', commercial difficulties of survival during the long years of recession continued to dog NBL in the home market through the 1930s too, and resulted in a much reduced workload. The next major orders from home were to come once again as war clouds loomed on the horizon, but the skills, experience, and capacity of the Glasgow locomotive builder were well able to cope with those tasks.

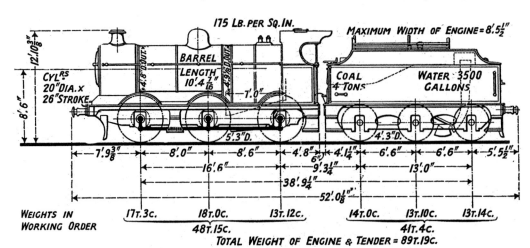

HEATING SURFACE, TUBES—		
LARGE AND SMALL	1,034·0	SQ. FT.
FIREBOX	124·0	,,
TOTAL (EVAPORATIVE)	1,158·0	,,
SUPERHEATER	246·0	,,
COMBINED HEATING SURFACES	1,404·0	,,

SUPERHEATER ELEMENTS ... ... 21—1⅜ IN. DIA. OUTS.
LARGE TUBES ... ... 21—5¼ IN. DIA. OUTS. ⎫ 10 FT. 10½ in.
SMALL TUBES ... ... 146—1¾ IN. DIA. OUTS. ⎬ BET. TUBEPLATES
GRATE AREA ... ... 21·1 SQ. FT.
TRACTIVE EFFORT (AT 85 PER CENT. B.P.) ... ... 24,555 LB.

The humble LMSR Class 4F 0-6-0 was another of the 1920s designs built by NBL. In this case, to order L802 in 1925.

Railway Gazette

Home Orders 1913–1928

Railway	Year	Order No	Works Nos	Qty	Works	Type
Midland & SWJ	1913	L576	20539-40	2	Atlas	4-4-0, same as L479
Furness	1913	L592	20665-66	2	Atlas	0-6-0, similar to L516
Furness	1913	L605	20867-68	2	Atlas	4-4-0, similar to L515
Taff Vale Railway	1914	L647	21156-61	6	Atlas	0-6-2T, similar to Neilson order E811
G&SWR	1914	L649	21172-82	11	Queen's Park	2-6-0, similar to L521
North British	1915	L652	21203-17	15	Atlas	4-4-2T to Yorkshire Eng. Co. design.
North British	1915	L653	21218-29	12	Atlas	0-6-2T, similar to L528
G&SWR	1915	L656	21242-47	6	Queen's Park	0-6-2T, similar to L366
LNWR	1915	L658	21256-65	10	Hyde Park	4-6-0 'Prince of Wales' class
LNWR	1915	L659	21266-75	10	Queen's Park	4-6-0 'Prince of Wales' class
Caledonian	1915	L664	21442-51	10	Atlas	4-4-0
Highland	1915	L667	21456-58	3	Queen's Park	4-4-0 'Loch' class
Highland	1915	L668	21459-61	3	Queen's Park	4-6-0 'Castle' class
Ministry of Munitions	1915	L669	21462-71	10	Hyde Park	2-8-0
Caledonian	1915	L672	21480-91	12	Hyde Park	4-6-2T new
G&SWR	1916	L676	21507-18	12	Queen's Park	0-6-2T, similar to L656
G&SWR	1916	L677	21519-21	3	Hyde Park	0-6-0T new
Consett Iron Co.	1916	L678	21522	1	Queen's Park	0-4-0T, crane engine to Dübs design
Ministry of Munitions	1916	L679	21523-57	35	Atlas	2-8-0, same as L661 for French State Railways
Ministry of Munitions	1917	L689	21768-808	41	Queen's Park	2-8-0, R.O.D. type, same as L496 for Great Central
Ministry of Munitions	1917	L692	21819-68	50	Hyde Park	2-8-0, R.O.D. type, same as L689
Ministry of Munitions	1917	L693	21869-918	50	Queen's Park	2-8-0, R.O.D. type, same as L689
North British	1917	L695	21925-58	34	Atlas	0-6-0, similar to L382
Ministry of Munitions	1917	L698	21971-80	10	Hyde Park	2-6-0 to Beyer Peacock design
Ministry of Munitions	1917	L699	21981-90	10	Queen's Park	2-6-0 to Beyer Peacock design
Furness	1917	L701	21993-96	4	Hyde Park	0-6-0, similar to L592
Ministry of Munitions	1918	L703	22000-29	30	Hyde Park	2-8-0, R.O.D. type, same as L693
Ministry of Munitions	1918	L704	22030-59	30	Queen's Park	2-8-0, R.O.D. type, same as L703
Great Northern	1918	L705	22060-69	10	Hyde Park	2-8-0 O1 class
G&SWR	1918	L706	22070-79	10	Queen's Park	0-6-2T, similar to L576
Ministry of Munitions	1918	L707	22080-93	14	Atlas	2-8-0, R.O.D. type, same as L703/704
Great Northern	1918	L709	22099-103	5	Atlas	2-8-0 O1 class
Ministry of Munitions	1918	L710	22104-15	12	Hyde Park	2-8-0, R.O.D. type, same as L703/704
Ministry of Munitions	1918	L711	22116-27	12	Queen's Park	2-8-0, R.O.D. type, same as L703/704
Ministry of Munitions	1918	L712	22128-77	50	Hyde Park	2-8-0, R.O.D. type, same as L710/711
Ministry of Munitions	1918	L713	22178-227	50	Queen's Park	2-8-0, R.O.D. type, same as L710/711
Ministry of Munitions	1918	L714	22228-57	30	Atlas	2-8-0, R.O.D. type, same as L710/711
North British	1918	L716	22268-77 & 22490-99	20	Atlas	0-6-0, similar to L695
North British	1918	L717	22278-87	10	Atlas	0-6-2T, similar to L653
GN of Scotland	1919	L730	22561-66	6	Hyde Park	4-4-0 F class
Furness	1919	L733	22572-76	5	Atlas	0-6-0, similar to L701
Great Northern	1920	L734	22577-626	50	Hyde Park	0-6-2T, new Class N2 to GNR design
North British	1920	L739	22668-82	15	Atlas	0-6-0, similar to L716
North British	1920	L740	22683-88	6	Atlas	4-4-2T, similar to L652
North British	1920	L741	22689-90	2	Hyde Park	4-4-2, similar to L175 but superheated
G&SWR	1920	L762	22886-91	6	Hyde Park	4-6-4T Class 540, new design
Strain & Robertson (For Chile)	1922	L767	22941-42	2	Hyde Park	0-4-0T, same as L629
Caledonian	1922	L768	22943-54	12	Hyde Park	4-4-0, similar to L664
Caledonian	1922	L769	22955-62	8	Queen's Park	4-6-0 new design
English Elect. Co.	1922	E2	2-27	26	Hyde Park	1200hp Bo-Bo for Japan (mech. parts only)
English Elect. Co.	1922	E3	28-35	8	Hyde Park	1800hp 1Co-Co1 for Japan (mech. parts only)
LMSR(NCC)	1923	L786	23096-100	5	Queen's Park	4-4-0 to railway co's drawings
LNER	1923	L787	23101-20	20	Hyde Park	4-6-2 A3 Pacifics Nos 2563–2582
LMSR	1923	L788	23121-35	15	Queen's Park	0-6-0T Class 3F Nos 7120–7134
NBL – stock	1924	L791	23141	1	Hyde Park	Reid-MacLeod geared turbine
Cardiff Collieries Ltd.	1924	L792	23142	1	Hyde Park	0-6-0T, to NBL design
Strain & Robertson (For Chile)	1924	L794	23153-54	2	Hyde Park	0-4-0T for A. Gibbs & Son, Chile
Strain & Robertson (For Chile)	1924	L795	23155	1	Hyde Park	0-4-0T, for Buchanan Jones & Co., Chile
LMSR(NCC)	1924	L797	23171-72	2	Queen's Park	4-4-0 same as L786
Strain & Robertson (For Chile)	1924	L799	23208	1	Hyde Park	0-4-0T, for Buchanan Jones & Co., Chile
SR	1924	L800	23209-28	20	Hyde Park	4-6-0 'King Arthur' Nos 763–782
LMSR	1924	L801	23229-53	25	Queen's Park	4-4-0 compound Nos 1135–1159
LMSR	1924	L802	23254-78	25	Queen's Park	0-6-0
SR	1925	L803	23279-88	10	Hyde Park	4-6-0
SR	1925	L814	23356-70	15	Hyde Park	4-4-0 class L Nos 753–759 & 782–789
Strain & Robertson (For Chile)	1925	L816	23372	1	Hyde Park	0-4-0T, for Reducto Nitrate of Bellavista, similar to L546

LMSR	1926	L819	23396-425	30	Hyde Park	0-6-0T Fowler 3F Nos 16400–16429
LMSR	1926	L820	23426-55	31	Queen's Park	0-6-0T Fowler 3F Nos 16430–16459
LMSR	1926	L821	23456-80	25	Queen's Park	0-6-0 Fowler 4F Nos 4382–4406
Nth British Distillery Co.	1926	L828	23556	1	Hyde Park	0-4-0T
LMSR	1926	L833	23595-619	25	Queen's Park	4-6-0 'Royal Scot' Nos 6100–6124
LMSR	1926	L834	23620-44	25	Hyde Park	4-6-0 'Royal Scot' Nos 6125–6149
LMSR	1927	L835	23646-60	15	Hyde Park	0-6-0 Fowler 4F Nos 4477–4491
LMSR	1927	L836	23661-75	15	Queen's Park	0-6-0 Fowler 4F Nos 4492–4506
LNER	1928	L850	23803-12	10	Hyde Park	4-6-0 class B17 Nos 2800–2809
GWR	1928	L852	23818-42	25	Hyde Park	0-6-0PT 5700 class Nos 5700–5724
GWR	1928	L853	23843-67	25	Queen's Park	0-6-0PT 5700 class Nos 5725–5749
LMSR	1928	L858	23890	1	Hyde Park	4-6-0 'Royal Scot' No. 6399 *Fury*

Railway	No. of orders	No. of engines	Avg. engines/order
North British	8	114	14.3
Caledonian	4	42	10.5
Highland	2	6	3
Great Northern	3	65	21.67
G&SWR	6	48	8
Furness	4	13	3.3
LNWR	2	20	10
Midland & SWJ	1	2	2
GN of Scotland	1	6	6
LMSR	13	239	18.4
LNER	2	30	15
GWR	2	50	25
Southern Railway	3	45	15
Ministry of Munitions	15	434	28.93
Industrial	8	10	1
Others	4	41	3.5
Total	78	1165	14.94

4

Export Orders 1903–1928

Each of the three separate Glasgow steam engine builders had a long tradition of supplying motive power overseas, as outlined earlier. The very first order received officially by the North British Co. came from India, and was constructed at Hyde Park Works. The order L1, was for five 4-6-0 tender locomotives, for the metre gauge lines of the Indian State Railways – Eastern Bengal Railways. These were the first standard, metre gauge types, but were based on an earlier Neilson & Co. order (E874 - E887). South of the River Clyde, Dübs & Co's Glasgow Locomotive Works at Polmadie received the next order for NBL, which came from the other side of the world – two 0-6-2 engines for Kansei Japan. Indian State Railways ordered a pair of 0-6-2s which were also built at Polmadie, whilst the first work undertaken by Atlas Works under the new management, was for the Luataro Nitrate Co., an industrial line in Chile.

In total, in the first year of existence, no less than 51 orders were received from overseas railways, 23 of which were put together at the Hyde Park Works, and 14 each at the Atlas and Glasgow Locomotive Works. It will be recalled that this latter site was located south of the Clyde, in the area known as Little Govan. In the drawing office register, Dübs & Co.'s former works were noted as 'G', for Glasgow, until 1907, when the works were re-christened Queen's Park.

North British built many more locomotives for export than for the home market, with easily the most frequent orders coming from India, Africa and South America. Although most of these were from colonial outposts, European orders were not unknown, and a number of locomotives were supplied to France and Spain especially. In fact, between 1903 and 1928 52 orders for over 500 loco-

Order L69 was built for an Indian railway, in 1904, the East Bengal Railway. Five of these metre gauge 4-8-0s were constructed at Hyde Park, and carried running numbers 151–155 (works numbers 16468–16472), the first shown here. They were amongst the first Indian Standard engines to this design, produced under the guidance of the Standards Committee, in order to improve the quality of locomotives operated on the sub-continent.
Mitchell Library Collection

motives were placed from France, Spain, and Portugal – although Portugal only placed two orders in total. Ironically, when NBL came to begin building diesel and electric types, the Estoril Railway in Portugal provided the first, and sole order for an electric locomotive placed by a railway company outside Britain.

North and South America
In contrast to the home orders, the locomotives for export were frequently larger, and heavier, and in the first year, ranged from small tank engines, through 4-6-0s and 2-8-2s, to a 'Modified Fairlie' 0-6-6-0, for Mexico. The largest number of locomotives in a single order came from the Central South African Railways, and was for 35 2-8-2 types to order L40. In July 1903, Indian State Railways ordered 29 of the 0-6-2 tank engines, and two months earlier, Canadian Pacific had ordered 20 4-6-0s. The Canadian order was L9, and this batch carried works numbers 16034 – 16053, from Hyde Park Works. This was the second order for these 4-6-0s from Hyde Park, although the previous build was carried out under the Neilson, Reid & Co. flag of course. They were classified ST12 by Canadian Pacific, and carried running numbers 981 to 1000, and although originally built as compounds, they were rebuilt as simple expansion in 1921. Leading dimensions of these 4-6-0s were originally as follows:

Order No	L9
Works Nos	16034 – 16053
Running numbers	981 – 1000
Wheel arrangement	4-6-0
Wheel dia.	
coupled	5ft 38in
bogie	2ft 6in
Wheelbase	
engine	25ft 2in
overall	52ft 8 ⅝in
Heating surface	
tubes	2,262.50 sq ft
firebox	158.50 sq ft
total	2,421.00 sq ft
Grate area	32.00 sq ft

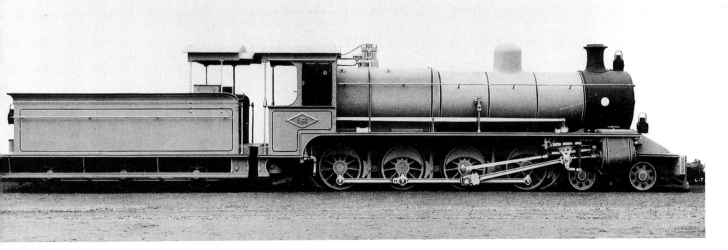

Several Fairlie articulated types were built for Mexico, and this is No. 171, the first of order L6, which carried running numbers 171 to 174. These standard gauge engines had also been built by Neilson, Reid & Co.

Mitchell Library Collection

Cylinders (2 high pressure)	20in x 26in
(1 low pressure)	33in x 26in
Boiler pressure	210 lb/sq in
Weight (in w.o.)	
total	131 tons 12cwt

These locomotives were renumbered and reclassified under the Vaughan system, which was developed in 1905. The original Class ST12 became Class D6B, and were renumbered from 520 – 539, although the rebuilding from compound to simple affected only five engines. Some of the

NBL supplied 4-6-0s, including the earlier Neilson orders, were renumbered more than once, as schemes were devised to enable Canadian Pacific to allocate running numbers to new diesel locomotives. These particular types were amongst the very few that were supplied to North America, and a number were scrapped even before the Second World War.

Still on the American continent, Mexico ordered four Fairlie type 0-6-6-0 locomotives in 1903, to order L6, which were built at Hyde Park Works. In South America, both the Buenos Aires & Pacific, and the Great Western of Brazil came to NBL for a total of 20 locomotives, whilst late in the first year, neighbouring Uruguay ordered a single standard gauge 2-6-0. All of these locomotives were built at the former Dübs & Co.'s Glasgow Locomotive Works. The two Buenos Aires & Pacific orders, L15 and L16, were essentially following on from earlier orders placed with Dübs.

Orders for Central and North America 1903–1928

Railway	Year	Order No.	Works Nos	Qty	Works	Type
Mexican Rly. Co.	1903	L6	16028-31	4	Hyde Park	0-6-6-0T Modified Fairlie Type
Canadian Pacific	1903	L9	16034-53	20	Hyde Park	4-6-0 CPR design, "Class ST12"
Demerara Rly. Co. [British Guiana]	1903	L23	16181	1	Atlas	2-4-2T, similar to Sharp, Stewart No. 4591
Demerara Rly. Co. [British Guiana]	1903	L47	16331	1	Atlas	0-6-0T, similar to Sharp, Stewart No. 23321
Mexican Rly. Co.	1904	L77	16541-42	2	Hyde Park	0-6-6-0T, same as L6
Union Rly. of Havana	1905	L119	16858-59	2	Atlas	4-6-0, same as Sharp Stewart order E1218
Mexican Rly. Co.	1907	L259	18210-11	2	Hyde Park	0-6-6-0T, similar to L6
Mexican Rly. Co.	1907	L272	18313-14	2	Hyde Park	0-6-6-0T, same as L259
Mexican Rly. Co.	1907	L273	18315-16	2	Hyde Park	0-6-6-0T, similar to L272
San Domingo & Santiago	1908	L313	18636-37	2	Hyde Park	2-6-2T
Samana and Santiago Rly.	1912	L549	20295	1	Hyde Park	2-6-2T, similar to L313
San Domingo & Santiago	1913	L549	20295	1	Hyde Park	2-6-2T, similar to L313
San Domingo & Santiago	1914	L614	20936	1	Hyde Park	2-6-2T, similar to L549
San Domingo & Santiago	1920	L744	22706-07	2	Hyde Park	2-6-2T, similar to L614

Country	No. of orders	No. of engines	Avg. engines/order
Canada	1	20	20
Mexico	5	12	2.2
West Indies	8	11	1.38
Total	14	43	3.07

This design dates back to 1904, and was ordered by almost all of the Argentinian railways, this example, No. 65, although carrying 'Central of Argentina' insignia, as order L323 was from a batch of 24 ordered by the Buenos Aires & Pacific in September 1908. All of the order was built at Queen's Park, and carried running numbers 65 to 88.

Mitchell Library Collection

A fifth of all orders received by NBL, and more than a quarter of all engines built between 1903 and 1912, came from South America. In particular, Argentina, from which source, no less than 84 orders were received, resulting in the building of no fewer than 895 locomotives. The railways of that country have been described as vast, and constructed with more than a little involvement from British industry and capital, from the Victorian era, until the railways were nationalised in 1948. There were three principal gauges on lines radiating from Buenos Aires, and elsewhere in South America. The 5ft 6in gauge was adopted on the Buenos Aires Great Southern, Central Argentine, Buenos Aires & Pacific, and Buenos Aires Western, each of which placed substantial orders with NBL. The Buenos Aires Midland had laid its tracks to the standard 4ft 8½in gauge, whilst another odd one out was the Central Cordoba, whose lines were laid to the metre gauge.

In Brazil, the next most common source of orders for NBL, the Sao Paulo Railway was constructed to 5ft 3in gauge, whilst the Great Western of Brazil was a metre gauge line. Occasional orders were taken from Peru, Paraguay and Chile, whose nitrate industry was an extremely profitable undertaking, with which Britain was involved.

The first orders from Argentina, the Buenos Aires & Pacific were again follow on orders from previous contracts placed with Dübs & Co., for 4-6-0 and 0-6-0 tank engines. The years up to the outbreak of World War I saw a large number of 4-6-0 and 2-8-0 tender locomotives supplied, for both passenger and mixed traffic duties. Suburban passenger tanks, such as those built to orders L146 and L161, were provided in quantity for the Buenos Aires Great Southern. The first of these two contracts was an important success for NBL, since Beyer Peacock of Manchester had been the dominant supplier to the railway, and the 22 NBL built outside cylinder tank engines were a success from the start. They were ordered in July 1905, with delivery in the first three months of 1906, and were followed by a second order in November 1905, for delivery in Summer 1906. The leading dimensions of this class were as follows:

The suburban services out of Buenos Aires in Argentina saw a number of NBL built tank engines, including the Class 8A 2-6-2T illustrated here (No. 394). Twenty-two of these were built at Queen's Park Works in 1906, to order L146. At the time these engines were built the works south of the River Clyde was still known as the Glasgow Locomotive Works, as it had been under its former owners, Dübs & Co.

Mitchell Library Collection

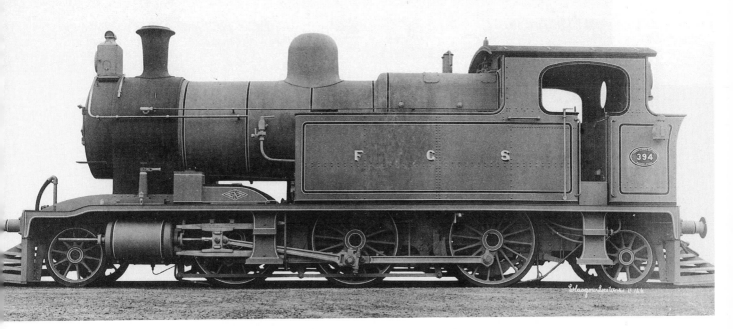

Order No	L146 & L161	
Works Nos	17124–17145 & 17285–17296	
Class	8A	
Running Nos	394–415, 456–467	
	(renumbered, 3321–3354)	
Wheel arrangement	2-6-2T	
Wheel dia.		
coupled	5ft 2in	
Heating surface		
total	1,660.00 sq ft	
Grate area	27.00 sq ft	
Cylinders (2)	18in x 26in	
Boiler pressure	160 lb/sq in	
Weight in w.o. (total)	73 tons 15 cwt	

Originally these locomotives were not superheated, and fitted for burning coal, although in later life they were all superheated, and the original 18in x 26in cylinders were replaced by 19in x 26in, fitted with piston valves, and equipped for oil burning. The Class 8A were a highly successful design for suburban work, and a small number survived until the late 1960s, when they were more than 60 years old ! The 8As were the forerunner of a number of similar designs for the Buenos Aires Great Southern, up to the final class of passenger tank, the Class 8E. These latter though were a 2-6-4 tank, and a three-cylinder design, as the ultimate replacement for the 2-6-2Ts on the Buenos Aires suburban traffic. NBL constructed 15 of the Class 8E, and had built a number of the predecessor 2-6-2T's, in company with Vulcan Foundry, Hawthorn, Leslie, Beyer Peacock, and Robert Stephenson & Co. The first of the NBL builds in Class 8A were never recorded as having spare boilers, and in lasting over 60 years, the quality of NBL's workmanship speaks for itself.

Orders for South America 1903–1912

Railway	Year	Order No.	Works Nos	Qty	Works.	Type
Luataro Nitrate Co.	1903	L5	16027	1	Atlas	0-6-2T, same as Sharp, Stewart order E1031
Great Western of Brazil	1903	L18	16118-27	10	Queens Park	2-6-0
Buenos Aires & Pacific	1903	L15	16103-8	6	Queens Park	4-6-0
Buenos Aires & Pacific	1903	L16	16109-12	4	Queens Park	0-6-0T
Taltal Rly. Co. [Peru]	1903	L33	16209-10	2	Queens Park	2-6-0
Uruguay Northern	1903	L51	16349	1	Queens Park	2-6-0
Buenos Aires & Rosario	1904	L54	16353-67	15	Queens Park	2-8-0 to B.A.&R. designs, "Class C6A"
Buenos Aires & Pacific	1904	L55	16368-69	2	Queens Park	4-4-2T
Buenos Aires & Pacific	1904	L62	16435-42	8	Queens Park	4-6-0, same as L15
Buenos Aires & Pacific	1904	L63	16443-46	4	Queens Park	4-6-0, similar to Dübs order 4399E
Buenos Aires & Rosario	1904	L65	16448-62	15	Atlas	4-6-0, 2-cylinder compound, "Class P7A"
Buenos Aires & Pacific	1904	L72	16512-23	12	Queens Park	4-6-0, same as L62
Great Western of Brazil	1904	L89	16612-26	15	Queens Park	2-6-0, similar to L18
Buenos Aires & Pacific	1904	L96	16673-16676	4	Queens Park	0-6-0T, similar to L16
Buenos Aires & Pacific	1904	L98	16683-85	3	Queens Park	4-6-0, similar to L72
Buenos Aires & Pacific	1904	L99	16686-95	10	Queens Park	4-6-0, similar to L98
Buenos Aires & Pacific	1904	L100	16696-701	6	Queens Park	2-8-0, new design
Buenos Aires Western	1904	L104	16720-25	6	Atlas	2-6-0, compound, similar to Sharp, Stewart order E1217
Buenos Aires & Pacific	1905	L110	16755-60	6	Queens Park	4-4-2T, same as L55
Buenos Aires & Rosario	1905	L117	16833-52	20	Queens Park	2-8-0, same as L54, "Class C6A" compound
Great Western of Brazil	1905	L118	16853-57	5	Queens Park	4-8-0, new design
Buenos Aires & Pacific	1905	L124	16897	1	Queens Park	0-4-0T, crane engine
Buenos Aires Western	1905	L126	16899-902	4	Atlas	4-4-0, similar to Sharp Stewart order E1216
Buenos Aires Western	1905	L127	16903-12	10	Atlas	2-8-0, new design
Buenos Aires Western	1905	L128	16913-27	15	Hyde Park	2-8-0, similar to L127
Buenos Aires & Pacific	1905	L131	16945-48	4	Queens Park	0-6-0T, same as L96
Buenos Aires & Pacific	1905	L132	16949-56	8	Queens Park	4-6-0, same as L99
Buenos Aires & Pacific	1905	L133	16957-62	6	Queens Park	4-6-0, same as L132
Buenos Aires & Pacific	1905	L134	16963-66	4	Queens Park	4-4-2, new design
Buenos Aires Great Southern	1905	L146	17124-45	22	Queens Park	2-6-2T, to new design from railway company, "Class 8A"
Great Western of Brazil	1905	L153	17226-31	6	Queens Park	4-4-0, new design
Buenos Aires Great Southern	1905	L157	17264	1	Queens Park	0-4-0T, crane locomotive
Buenos Aires Western	1905	L159	17266-80	15	Hyde Park	2-8-0, same as L127/L128
Sao Paulo Railway	1905	L160	17281-84	4	Atlas	4-6-0
Buenos Aires Great Southern	1905	L161	17285-96	12	Atlas	2-6-2T, similar to L146, "Class 8A"
Buenos Aires & Pacific	1905	L162	17297-302	6	Queens Park	2-8-0, similar to L100
Buenos Aires & Pacific	1905	L168	17332-35	4	Queens Park	4-4-2, similar to L134
Buenos Aires & Pacific	1905	L169	17336-39	4	Queens Park	2-8-0, same as L162
Buenos Aires & Pacific	1905	L170	17340-45	6	Queens Park	4-6-0, similar to L133
Cordoba Central (Argentina)	1906	L172	17347-57	11	Hyde Park	0-6-2T
Cordoba Central (Argentina)	1906	L173	17358-17367	10	Hyde Park	4-6-2, "Class M2"
Buenos Aires Great Southern	1906	L182	17436-47	12	Atlas	4-6-0, 2-cylinder compound, "Class 12A"
Buenos Aires & Pacific	1906	L183	17448-51	4	Queens Park	0-6-0T
Buenos Aires & Pacific	1906	L184	17452-57	6	Queens Park	4-4-4T, to new NBL/Queens Park design
Buenos Aires & Pacific	1906	L185	17458-17469	12	Queens Park	4-6-0, similar to L170
Buenos Aires & Pacific	1906	L186	17470-78	9	Queens Park	0-6-0T, to Kerr, Stuart designs
Buenos Aires & Pacific	1906	L191	17495-518	24	Hyde Park	2-8-0

Railway	Year	Lot	Works Nos.	Qty	Works	Description
Buenos Aires & Pacific	1906	L192	17519-42	24	Queens Park	2-8-0, similar to L169
Buenos Aires & Pacific	1906	L193	17543-48	6	Queens Park	0-6-0T, similar to L183
Buenos Aires & Pacific	1906	L194	17549-54	6	Queens Park	4-6-0, similar to L185
Buenos Aires & Rosario	1906	L197	17601-40	40	Atlas	2-8-0, to BA&R designs, 2-cyl. compound
Argentine Great Western	1906	L198	17641-44	4	Hyde Park	4-6-0
Cordoba Central (Argentina)	1906	L203	17669-76, 17683-701, & 18332-37	33	Hyde Park	4-8-0, "Class C7"
Cordoba Central (Argentina)	1906	L204	17702-19	18	Queens Park	4-6-2, "Class C5"
Cordoba Central (Argentina)	1906	L205	17720-24	5	Queens Park	4-4-2
Buenos Aires & Pacific	1906	L209	17739-46	8	Queens Park	0-4-4T
Buenos Aires Western	1906	L210	17747-58	12	Queens Park	2-6-2T
Buenos Aires Western	1906	L211	17759-78	20	Hyde Park	4-6-0, 2-cyl. compound
Buenos Aires & Pacific	1906	L214	17802-07	6	Queens Park	4-4-2, similar to L168
Argentine Great Western	1906	L219	17828-39	12	Queens Park	2-8-0, same as L192
Buenos Aires & Pacific	1906	L221	17844-49	6	Queens Park	4-6-0, similar to L194
Great Western of Brazil	1906	L228	17898-903	6	Queens Park	2-8-0, new design
Sao Paulo Railway	1907	L235	17920-23	4	Atlas	4-6-0, same as L160
Sao Paulo Railway	1907	L247	18078-79	2	Atlas	4-6-0, same as L235
Buenos Aires Western	1907	L250	18087	1	Queens Park	0-4-0T, crane engine
Buenos Aires & Pacific	1907	L260	18212-23	12	Queens Park	0-6-0T, similar to L183/193
Buenos Aires & Pacific	1907	L261	18224-33	10	Queens Park	4-6-0, similar to L221
Buenos Aires & Pacific	1907	L262	18234-43	10	Queens Park	4-6-0, similar to L194
Buenos Aires Western	1907	L270	18292-311	20	Queens Park	2-6-0, mixed traffic compound
Luataro Nitrate Co.	1907	L271	18312	1	Atlas	0-6-2T, same as L5
Buenos Aires & Pacific	1907	L276	18324-29	6	Queens Park	2-8-2T, new design
Argentine Government	1907	L278	17677-82	6	Hyde Park	4-8-0, same as L203 for Cordoba Central Rly.
Cordoba Nth. Western (Argentina)	1907	L282	18375-76	2	Atlas	4-6-0, metre gauge
Luataro Nitrate Co.	1907	L283	18377	1	Atlas	0-6-2T, same as L5 and L271
Great Western of Brazil	1907	L287	18387-92	5	Queens Park	2-6-0, same as L89
Buenos Aires & Pacific	1908	L291	18405-16	12	Queens Park	4-4-4T, same as L184
Buenos Aires & Pacific	1908	L292	18417-28	12	Queens Park	2-8-0, similar to L219
Buenos Aires & Pacific	1908	L293	18429-40	12	Queens Park	2-8-0, similar to L292
Chile State Rlys.	1908	L296	18449-63	15	Atlas	4-6-0
Chile State Rlys.	1908	L297	18464-503	40	Hyde Park	2-6-0
Central of Peru	1908	L307	18602-16	15	Queens Park	2-8-0
Central of Peru	1908	L308	18617-19	3	Queens Park	2-8-0, same as L307
Central of Peru	1908	L309	18620-25	6	Queens Park	2-6-2T
Buenos Aires Western	1908	L314	18638-49	12	Hyde Park	2-6-4T
Buenos Aires & Pacific	1908	L323	18711-34	24	Queens Park	2-8-0, similar to L292
Buenos Aires Midland	1908	L324	18735-38	4	Hyde Park	4-6-0
Buenos Aires & Pacific	1908	L326	18745-56	12	Queens Park	4-6-2
Buenos Aires & Rosario	1908	L329	18760-74	15	Hyde Park	0-6-0T
Buenos Aires Midland	1908	L334	18793-802	10	Hyde Park	4-6-0, same as L324
Sao Paulo Railway	1909	L349	18908-17	10	Atlas	2-8-0 to SPR design
Great Western of Brazil	1909	L354	18934-39	6	Queens Park	2-8-0, similar to L228
Buenos Aires & Pacific	1909	L358	18965-70	6	Queens Park	4-4-4T, same as L291
Buenos Aires & Pacific	1909	L373	19034	1	Queens Park	4-6-2, similar to L326, but s/heated.
Buenos Aires & Pacific	1909	L375	19038-47	10	Hyde Park	0-6-0T
Argentine Government	1909	L381	19084	1	Hyde Park	4-8-0
Central Argentine	1909	L383	19095-116	22	Hyde Park	4-6-2, "Class P9A" compound to rly co.'s design
Leopoldina Rly. (Brazil)	1909	L387	19127-32	6	Queens Park	4-6-0
Paraguay Central	1909	L389	19134-43	10	Atlas	2-6-0
Paraguay Central	1909	L390	19144-47	4	Atlas	2-6-0, similar to L389
Buenos Aires Midland	1910	L395	19177-81	5	Hyde Park	4-6-0, similar to L324
Great Western of Brazil	1910	L397	19185-94	10	Queens Park	2-6-0, similar to L287
Entre Rios Rly. (Argentina)	1910	L399	19207-16	10	Atlas	4-6-0, to NBL design
Argentine Government	1910	L410	19298-307	10	Hyde Park	2-8-4T, new design
Great Western of Brazil	1910	L411	19308-13	6	Queens Park	2-6-0, same as L397
Great Western of Brazil	1910	L417	19323-24	2	Queens Park	4-8-0, same as L118
Buenos Aires & Pacific	1910	L428	19360-64	5	Atlas	4-6-2, similar to L373, but s/heated
Buenos Aires & Pacific	1910	L429	19365-70	6	Atlas	4-6-0, same as L428, but non-s/heated
Argentine Government	1910	L432	19378-402	25	Hyde Park	2-8-2, to Henschel designs
Argentine Government	1910	L433	19403-27	25	Queens Park	2-8-2, same as L432
Antofagasta & Bolivia	1910	L434	19428-35	8	Hyde Park	2-8-0, to railway co.'s drawings
Sao Paulo Railway	1910	L439	19499-503	5	Atlas	4-6-2, with Schmidt s/heater
Peru Nth Western	1911	L445	19560-63	4	Atlas	4-8-0, generally to NBL design
Leopoldina Rly. (Brazil)	1911	L449	19587-92	6	Queens Park	4-6-0, similar to L387
Great Western of Brazil	1911	L455	19628-42	15	Queens Park	2-6-0, similar to L411
Great Western of Brazil	1911	L460	19650-54	5	Queens Park	2-6-0, same as L455
Entre Rios (Argentina)	1911	L462	19667-69	3	Atlas	4-6-0, based on L399
Entre Rios (Argentina)	1911	L463	19670-74	5	Atlas	2-8-0, new design

Sao Paulo Railway	1911	L472	19704-06	3	Atlas	2-8-4T, with Schmidt s/heater
Buenos Aires & Pacific	1911	L481	19764-69	6	Queens Park	2-8-2T, similar to L276
Buenos Aires & Pacific	1911	L482	19770-83	14	Queens Park	2-8-0, with 5,500 gallons tender
Leopoldina Rly. (Brazil)	1911	L483	19784-89	6	Queens Park	4-6-0, same as L449
Leopoldina Rly. (Brazil)	1912	L494	19849-53	5	Queens Park	2-8-0 to Beyer Peacock designs
Entre Rios (Argentina)	1912	L495	19854-58	5	Atlas	4-6-0, same as L462
Central Argentine	1912	L499	19922-41	20	Queens Park	4-6-2, "Class PS8" with Robinson s/heater
Entre Rios (Argentina)	1912	L503	19976-80	5	Atlas	4-6-0, same as L495
Leopoldina Rly. (Brazil)	1912	L507	19995	1	Queens Park	2-8-0 to Beyer Peacock designs, same as L494
Paraguay Central	1912	L519	20082	1	Atlas	2-6-0, same as L390
Buenos Aires Great Southern	1912	L534	20186-206	21	Hyde Park	2-6-2T, "Class 8C" similar to L146
Buenos Aires Great Southern	1912	L535	20207-16	10	Hyde Park	2-6-2T, similar to L534
Sao Paulo Railway	1912	L537	20220-24	5	Atlas	2-8-4T, similar to L472
Luataro Nitrate Co.	1912	L540	20236	1	Atlas	0-6-2T, same as L271

Country	No. of orders	No. of engines	Avg. engines/order
Argentina	91	926	10.18
Brazil	24	148	6.17
Chile	2	55	27.5
Peru	5	30	6
Paraguay	3	15	5
Uruguay	1	1	1
Industrial & Others	5	12	2.4
Total	131	1187	9.06

Tank engines were not the only products to be despatched from Glasgow to South America, with a large number of 2-8-0 and 4-6-0 types keeping them company. In the years up to the First World War, the 4-6-0 seemed to be the most popular design, although very few were supplied as fitted from new with superheaters, but a number followed the contemporary fashion for compounding. Amongst the most powerful, and indeed the heaviest, were the 24 2-8-0s ordered in 1909, but whose design ancestry could be traced back to order L100, placed some five years earlier. The total of 82 similar 2-8-0 engines, all of which were built at Queen's Park Works, and including the order L323 from

1909, were used by the Buenos Aires & Pacific, and the Argentine Great Western Railways. The leading dimensions were as follows:

Order No	L323
Works Nos	18711–18734
Class	BA
Running Nos	65-88
Wheel arrangement	2-8-0
Wheel dia.	
coupled	4ft 10in
leading	3ft 1in
Heating surface	
tubes	1,840.00 sq ft
firebox	156.00 sq ft
total	1,996.00 sq ft
Grate area	27.50 sq ft
Cylinders (2)	19.5in x 26in
Boiler pressure	175 lb/sq in
Tractive effort @ 75% b.p.	22,372 lbs
Weight in w.o.	
engine	76 tons 11 cwt
tender	63 tons 15 cwt
total	140 tons 6 cwt

The application of compounding to steam locomotives was very much in vogue, just after the turn of the century. Here, built by NBL at the Atlas Works, in 1906, is No. 544, one of the Class 12A 4-6-0s for the Buenos Aires Great Southern Railway. The compound system used the Von Borries principle, and the locomotive had 19in diameter high pressure cylinders, and 27.5in diameter low pressure cylinders. In this example, the locomotive was from order L182, for twelve locomotives, carrying works numbers 17436–17447 and running numbers 544 to 555. North British constructed a number of Von Borries compounds, mostly for South America and India.

Mitchell Library Collection

These 4-6-2s for the Buenos Aires & Pacific Railway were only the second batch to be built with superheaters. In this case, constructed to order L428 at the Atlas Works in 1910, the design dated back to 1908, when the first non-superheated engines of this class were built for the BA&P. Except that they were built for the 5ft 6in gauge lines of Argentina, there was some similarity with the Pacifics for Western Australia, also illustrated in this chapter.

Mitchell Library Collection

This class was the last 2-8-0 type to be built by NBL for this railway in the period under review. They were originally shipped as non-superheated, but later modified, and equipped for oil-burning. Numerous other 2-8-0s had been built for Argentina in a five year spell, up to 1908, including a large number of two-cylinder compounds. These latter were essentially the same as the engines of the Class 11 series, and which were a common sight all over the Pampas, hauling freight and livestock trains. On the compound front, the Central Argentine ordered a batch of 22 Pacifics (NBL Order No. 383) in 909, to a design produced by the railway, and which were all built at the Hyde Park Works. In 1912, the Central Argentine turned against compounding, in

favour of simple expansion for its Pacific designs, when it placed an order, L499 for 20 locomotives, equipped with the Robinson design of superheater. This was a popular design, reflected in orders for another 30 in 1913, ten of which, to order L571, had larger coupled wheels – at 6ft 2in, compared with the 5ft 8in of previous orders. Pacific types were also ordered by the Buenos Aires & Pacific, some built with Schmidt superheaters, others without, whilst the Sao Paulo Railway in Brazil also ordered a batch of superheated engines, but which were simple expansion types.

In fact, the 'new express passenger' type for the Buenos Aires & Pacific , L373, was ordered in July 1909, and as the sole representative of the class was exhibited at the International Railway & Land Transport Exhibition in Buenos Aires in 1910. It was an impressive looking, heavy and powerful locomotive, fitted with the Schmidt superheater, Walschaerts valve gear, and the then typical bogie tender. The total weight of this engine and tender was over 144 tons, and even at 75% of the rather low (150 lb/sq in) boiler pressure, it was able to develop a tractive effort of a little under 20,000 lb. The Buenos Aires & Pacific was a line where the water quality was not good, and which was a

Orders for South America 1913–1928

Railway	Year	Order No.	Works Nos	Qty	Works	Type
Entre Rios (Argentina)	1913	L559	20389-98	10	Atlas	2-8-0, same as L463
Central Argentine	1913	L570	20491-510	20	Queens Park	4-6-2, "Class PS8" similar to L499
Central Argentine	1913	L571	20511-20	10	Queens Park	4-6-2, "Class PS10" similar to L499
Buenos Aires Great Southern	1913	L575	20529-38	10	Atlas	2-8-0, "Class 11b" to Henschel drawings
Buenos Aires & Pacific	1913	L577	20541-44	4	Queens Park	0-6-0ST, similar to L375
Buenos Aires & Pacific	1913	L578	20545-54	10	Queens Park	4-6-4T
Sao Paulo Railway	1913	L581	20561-65	5	Atlas	4-6-0, new to NBL design
Great Western of Brazil	1913	L590	20649-51	3	Queens Park	4-8-0, similar to L417
Great Western of Brazil	1913	L591	20652-64	13	Queens Park	2-6-0, similar to L411
Central Argentine	1914	L624	20994-21013	20	Queens Park	4-6-2, "Class PS8" similar to L570
Central Argentine	1914	L625	21014-53	40	Hyde Park	4-8-0, "Class CS6" similar to L197
Central Argentine	1918	L718	22288-317	30	Queens Park	4-8-0, "Class CS6A" compound similar to L625
Peruvian Govt. (N.W. Rly.)	1923	L779	23056	1	Hyde Park	4-8-0, similar to L445
Buenos Aires Great Southern	1923	L783	23074-88	15	Queens Park	2-6-4T, "Class 8E" new to Hawthorn Leslie designs
Buenos Aires Great Southern	1924	L796	23156-70	15	Hyde Park	2-6-2T, "Class 8D" similar to L535
Iquique - Buchanan Jones & Co.	1925	L804	23289	1	Hyde Park	0-4-0T, similar to L586 & 670
Chile - A. Gibbs & Son	1925	L805	23290	1	Hyde Park	0-4-0T, similar to L244
Antofagasta & Bolivia	1925	L808	23298-9	2	Queens Park	2-8-2, new to rly co.'s designs

North Western of Peru	1925	L815	23371	1	Hyde Park	4-8-0, same as L779
Cordoba Central	1926	L822	23481-95	15	Hyde Park	4-6-4T, based on Henschel design
Sao Paulo Railway	1926	L823	23496-501	6	Hyde Park	2-8-4T, "Class J", similar to L537
Antofagasta & Bolivia	1926	L830	23562-81	20	Queens Park	2-8-4T, new to rly co.'s designs
Central Argentine	1928	L847	23744-71 & 23816-7	30	Hyde Park	0-6-2T, "Class SS5" based on Beyer Peacock design
Leopoldina Railway (Brazil)	1928	L855	23886-07	2	Queens Park	0-6-0T, new design
Sao Paulo Railway	1929	L864	23946-51	6	Queens Park	2-8-4T, "Class J", similar to L537
Sao Paulo Railway	1934	L895	24299-300	2	Hyde Park	4-6-4T, new NBL design
Sao Paulo Railway	1936	L898	24375-78	4	Hyde Park	4-6-4T, new NBL design, similar to L895
Sao Paulo Railway	1937	L916	24459-62	4	Hyde Park	2-8-4T, "Class J", similar to L864

Country	No. of orders	No. of engines	Avg. engines/order
Argentina	12	219	18.6
Brazil	10	55	5.5
Chile	2	22	11
Peru	2	2	1
Industrials	2	2	1
Total	28	300	10.7

concern not only for the designers and builders, but obviously perhaps, also for the maintenance staff and operators. In this locomotive from Springburn, the boiler was conspicuously large, at 5ft 9in diameter internally, and provided with a larger than normal steam space, to reduce the risk of 'foaming'.

The new Pacifics were constructed at Queen's Park, where the previous, non-superheated versions of the same class had been built. Another five of these superheated Pacifics were ordered under L428 in 1910, and which were complemented by yet another order, L429, for a further six, but without superheaters, at the same time. In fact these were the final orders received by NBL from the Buenos Aires & Pacific for 4-6-2s up to 1928, and only the Central Argentine ordered additional batches of Pacifics, with the final order coming in 1914, just before the outbreak of the First World War.

In neighbouring Brazil, the Sao Paulo Railway ordered its first NBL built, superheated Pacifics in December 1910, to order L439, five of which were constructed for the 5ft 3in gauge, at Atlas Works. Although they were the only Pacific order from that railway for NBL, the locomotives were of similar proportions to the orders from Argentina, with the same equally 'modern technical innovations'. The principal dimensions were as follows:

Order No	L439
Works Nos	19499-19503
Running Nos	92-96
Wheel arrangement	4-6-2
Wheel dia.	
coupled	5ft 6in
leading	3ft 0in
Heating surface	
tubes	1,435.00 sq ft
s/heater	430.00 sq ft
firebox	164.70 sq ft
total	2,029.70 sq ft
Grate area	28.50 sq ft
Cylinders (2)	21.5in x 26in
Boiler pressure	200 lb/sq in
Weight in w.o., total	118 tons 6 cwt

The first of the superheated Pacifics for the Buenos Aires & Pacific was built at Atlas Works in late 1910. Five engines were built under order L428, and equipped with a Schmidt superheater, whilst a second order (L429), was for a further six Pacifics, but without a superheater.

Mitchell Library Collection

Above: The Pacific types built for Sudan Government Railways 3ft 6in gauge lines, and to order L419, were completed in 1911. The non-superheated boiler was carried on bar frames, and the inverted leaf springs on the bogie tender were an unusual feature. In appearance it could be said they were almost typically British, a feature not inconsistent with the sales of NBL products to the colonies of the British Empire.

Mitchell Library Collection

Below: The solitary Class 11 2-8-2, built to order L31 at Hyde Park Works in 1903, carried works number 16207 and running number 700 of the Central South African Railways. Here was one of the earliest of a steady stream of orders from South Africa for the Springburn company, for the 3ft 6in gauge.

Mitchell Library Collection

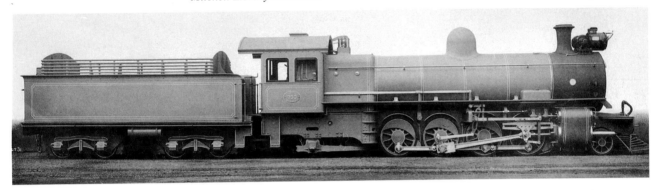

African Orders

At this time of course, NBL had no single headquarters, and each of the three sites continued with their respective design, construction and administrative facilities. Orders were being received in rapid succession in these early years, with the order number having reached L308 by the end of 1908. Significantly most orders came from South America, Africa and India, where the British colonial influence was clearly a factor in the winning of contracts. In Africa, all the colonies placed large orders, but especially strong, were the contracts received from Natal, Rhodesia and South Africa, with 15 Pacific types and 36 2-8-2s being built to orders L29, L30, L37 and L40 in the first year alone. Each of these four orders was constructed at Hyde Park, and became classes 10 (4-6-2s), and 11 in South Africa. The Pacifics were considered to be of *"remarkable power and dimensions"*, and important enough to merit an official photograph being taken of works number 16226, together with the directors of NBL. The leading dimensions of the 4-6-2s for the Central South African Railways were as follows:

Order No	L29 & L37
Works Nos	16194–16203 & 16226–16230
Running Nos	650–659 & 660–664
Wheel arrangement	4-6-2
Wheel dia.	
coupled	5ft 2in
bogie	2ft 4 1/2in
trailing	2ft 9in
Wheelbase	
engine	10ft 10ins
Heating surface	
tubes	1,724.00 sq ft
firebox	128.00 sq ft
total	1,842.00 sq ft
Grate area	33.00 sq ft
Cylinders (2 outside)	18.5in x 26in
Boiler pressure	200 lb/sq. in.
Weight (in w.o.): total	119 tons 19cwt

The Class 10 Pacifics for the 3ft 6in gauge should have represented the high water mark for some years to come after 1903, and were certainly a powerful and impressive type. In fact CSA Railways never placed another order with NBL in the first five years. The "11th class" engines, ordered as L31 and L40, and with only one engine ordered under L31, the remaining 35 were covered by order L40, placed two months later, in November 1903. These 2-8-2 engines were a freight type, and very similar in general appearance to the Pacifics, with the same bogie tender. The leading dimensions were as follows:

Order No	L31 & L40
Works Nos	16207 & 16250–16284
Running Nos	700 & 701–735
Wheel arrangement	2-8-2
Wheel dia.	
coupled	4ft 0in
leading	2ft 6in
trailing	2ft 6in
Heating surface	
tubes	2,136.00 sq ft
firebox	142.00 sq ft
total	2,278.00 sq ft
Grate area	37.00 sq ft
Cylinders (2 outside)	20in x 26in
Boiler pressure	200 lb/sq. in.
Weight (in w.o.)	total: 128 tons 3cwt

Orders for Africa 1903–1912

Railway	Year	Order No.	Works Nos.	Works	Qty	Type
Natal Rly.	1903	L12	16060-84	Queens Park	25	4-8-2T, improved Dübs design
Rhodesia Rly.	1903	L13	16085-94	Hyde Park	10	4-8-0, modified '7th Class'
Cape Government	1903	L14	16095-102	Hyde Park	8	2-8-0, new design to rly co.'s drawings
Cape Government	1903	L21	16161-70	Hyde Park	10	4-8-0 Class 8, similar to Neilson order E872
Rhodesia Rly.	1903	L22	16171-80	Hyde Park	10	4-8-0, modified '7th Class', same as L13
Natal Rly.	1903	L28	16192-93	Queens Park	2	4-6-2 Class 2
Central South African Rlys.	1903	L29	16194-203	Hyde Park	10	4-6-2 Class 10, new design
Central South African Rlys.	1903	L31	16207	Hyde Park	1	2-8-2 Class 11, new design
Rhodesia Rly.	1903	L36	16216-25	Hyde Park	10	4-8-0, Class 8
Central South African Rlys.	1903	L37	16226-30	Hyde Park	5	4-6-2 Class 10, same as L29
Central South African Rlys.	1903	L40	16250-84	Hyde Park	35	2-8-2 Class 11, same as L31
Egypt (War Office)	1903	L43	16290-301	Hyde Park	12	4-6-0, to rly co.'s sketched design
Egypt (War Office)	1903	L44	16302-16	Hyde Park	15	4-6-0, to rly co.'s sketched design
New Cape Cent. Rly.	1903	L50	16348	Hyde Park	1	4-8-0, similar to Neilson order E903
Natal Govt. Rly.	1904	L56	16370-94	Hyde Park	25	4-8-0 Class 1
Natal Govt. Rly.	1904	L61	16395-419	Queens Park	25	4-8-0 Class 1, same as L56
Egyptian State Rly.	1904	L75	16524-38	Hyde Park	15	0-6-0
Cape Government	1904	L90	16227	Atlas	1	0-4-0, railmotor
Egyptian State Rly.	1904	L93	16644	Hyde Park	1	4-4-2
Egypt (War Office)	1905	L109	16753-54	Hyde Park	2	4-6-0, similar to L44
Egypt Delta Lines Rly.	1905	L120	16860-65	Atlas	6	0-6-4T, new design
Egyptian State Rly.	1905	L121	16866	Hyde Park	1	4-4-2, similar to L93
Egyptian State Rly.	1905	L122	16867-81	Hyde Park	15	0-6-0, generally to NBL drawings
Egyptian State Rly.	1905	L123	16882-96	Hyde Park	15	4-4-0, generally to NBL drawings
Cape Government	1906	L196	17600	Hyde Park	1	4-4-2, 3-cyl. compound
Egypt (War Office)	1906	L224	17853-62	Hyde Park	10	4-6-0, KHOR Class passenger engines
Egypt Delta Lines Rly.	1907	L239	18017-22	Atlas	6	0-6-4T, similar to L120
Egyptian State Rly.	1907	L242	18047-46	Atlas	10	4-4-2T Class F, to NBL design
Egyptian State Rly.	1907	L245	18053-62	Hyde Park	10	4-6-0 Class B
Nthn. Nigeria Rly.	1908	L300	18511-15	Hyde Park	5	4-8-0, "Emir" Class, to NBL design
Sthn. Nigeria Rly.	1908	L317	18658-61	Hyde Park	4	4-8-0, "Emir" Class, to NBL design
Natal Govt. Rlys.	1908	L339	18829-33	Queens Park	5	4-8-2 Class 3, to Natal Rly. design
Central South African Rlys.	1909	L359	18971-80	Hyde Park	10	4-6-2, "10th Class"
South African Rlys.	1909	L378	19051-71	Queens Park	21	4-8-0 Class B, for Natal, the first order after amalgamation
South African Rlys.	1910	L398	19195-206	Hyde Park	12	4-6-2, modified 'Hendrie Class C'
South African Rlys.	1910	L400	19217-41	Hyde Park	25	4-8-2, similar to L339
South African Rlys.	1910	L401	19242-43	Atlas	2	4-8-2 Class 4
Nthn. Nigeria Rly.	1910	L404	19262	Hyde Park	1	4-8-0, "Emir" Class, to NBL design
Sthn. Nigeria Rly.	1910	L405	19263-65	Hyde Park	3	0-6-0T Class 31, to rly. co.'s design
Rhodesia Rly.	1910	L414	19317-19	Hyde Park	3	4-8-0, 8th Class, similar to L36
Sudan Government	1910	L419	19328-31	Hyde Park	4	4-6-2, to rly co.'s designs
Sudan Government	1910	L420	19332-34	Hyde Park	3	4-6-0, to rly co.'s designs
Sudan Government	1910	L422	19338-42	Hyde Park	5	4-6-2, to rly co.'s designs
Benguela Railway	1910	L424	19348-52	Atlas	5	4-6-0, "6th Class", similar to Neilson order E777
Sthn. Nigeria Rly.	1910	L425	19353-54	Hyde Park	2	0-6-0T Class 31, to rly co.'s design
South African Rlys.	1910	L426	19355	Hyde Park	1	2-6-6-2 "Class ME", high pressure Mallet
Rhodesia Rly.	1910	L427	19356-59	Hyde Park	4	4-8-0, 8th Class, same as L414
South African Rlys.	1911	L448	19577-86	Queens Park	10	2-6-6-0, "MC Class", Mallet compound
South African Rlys.	1911	L450	19593-96	Atlas	4	4-8-2, 12th Class, with Schmidt s/heater
South African Rlys.	1911	L451	19597-601	Atlas	5	4-8-2, "D" Class, with Schmidt s/heater
Sudan Government	1911	L452	19602-3	Hyde Park	2	4-6-2, same as L419
Nthn. Nigeria Rly.	1911	L456	19643	Hyde Park	1	4-8-0, "Emir" Class, to NBL design
Uganda Railway	1911	L459	19648-49	Queens Park	2	0-6-6-0, modified Fairlie, similar to L384
Nthn. Nigeria Rly.	1911	L465	19677-78	Hyde Park	2	2-6-2, to rly co.'s designs
South African Rlys.	1911	L468	19684-87	Atlas	4	4-8-2, 12th Class, similar to L450
South African Rlys.	1911	L469	19688-92	Atlas	5	4-8-2, "D" Class, with Schmidt s/heater
Rhodesia Rly.	1911	L478	19743-54	Hyde Park	12	4-8-0, "9th Class", with Schmidt s/heater
Transvaal	1911	L484	19790	Queens Park	1	0-6-0T, same as L64
Rhodesia Rly.	1911	L488	19818-23	Hyde Park	6	4-8-0, "9th Class", with Schmidt s/heater
Gold Coast Rly.	1912	L504	19981-82	Atlas	2	4-6-4T, new design
Uganda Railway	1912	L506	19989-94	Queens Park	6	0-6-6-0, modified Fairlie, similar to L449
Rhodesia Rly.	1912	L508	19996-20002	Hyde Park	7	4-8-2, 10th Class
Sudan Government	1912	L510	20008-09	Hyde Park	2	4-6-2, to rly co.'s designs, as L419
Nigerian Rlys.	1912	L523	20134-37	Hyde Park	4	4-8-0, new design, with Schmidt s/heater
South African Rlys.	1912	L529	20173-80	Atlas	8	4-8-2 "12th Class", similar to L468
New Cape Central Rly.	1912	L536	20217-19	Hyde Park	3	4-8-0, "7th Class", similar to Neilson order E868
South African Rlys.	1912	L538	20225-34	Hyde Park	10	4-8-2 "Class 4A", similar to L401
Uganda Railway	1912	L543	20272-81	Queens Park	10	0-6-6-0, modified Fairlie, similar to L506

Indian State Rly. – East Bengal	1908	L294	18441-46	6	Hyde Park	4-6-0, standard type
H.H. The Nizam's Rly.	1908	L299	18508-10	3	Atlas	4-6-0, "Class A", to rly co.'s drawings
Indian State Rly. – North Western	1908	L301	18516-51	36	Hyde Park	2-8-0, "Class HG"
Indian State Rly. – North Western	1908	L302	18552-56	5	Atlas	4-4-0, "Class SP"
Indian State Rly. – North Western	1908	L303	18557-86	30	Atlas	0-6-0, "Class SG"
Indian State Rly. – North Western	1908	L305	18593-98	6	Hyde Park	2-6-2T, same as L115
Indian State Rly. – North Western	1908	L306	18599-601	3	Atlas	0-6-0, "Class SG", same as L303
Indian State Rly. – North Western	1908	L311	18628-31	4	Atlas	4-4-0, "Class SP"
Indian State Rly. – East Bengal	1908	L312	18632-35	4	Hyde Park	4-6-0, standard type
Samana and Southern Rly.	1908	L313	18636-37	2	Hyde Park	2-6-2T, similar to Neilson E873, but 2-4-2T
Bengal Nagpur Rly.	1908	L315	18650-53	4	Atlas	2-8-2, "Class B", to rly co.'s design
Bengal Nagpur Rly.	1908	L316	18654-57	4	Atlas	4-6-2, "Class C", similar to L218
Indian State Rly. – East Bengal	1908	L318	18662-71	10	Hyde Park	4-6-0, standard type
Indian State Rly. – North Western	1908	L320	18675-78	4	Hyde Park	2-8-0, "Class HG"
Indian State Rly. – East Bengal	1908	L321	18679-83	5	Hyde Park	4-6-0, standard type
Indian State Rly. – North Western	1908	L322	18684-710	27	Atlas	0-6-0, "Class SG", same as L306
Bhavnagar G. J. P.	1908	L325	18739-44	6	Hyde Park	4-6-0, "Class P", similar to L251
Ceylon Railways	1908	L331	18778-81	4	Atlas	4-6-4T, to rly co.'s drawings
Indian State Rly. – North Western	1908	L332	18782-90	9	Hyde Park	2-6-2T, same as L305
East India Rly. Co.	1908	L337	18809-16	8	Hyde Park	4-4-2
East India Rly. Co.	1908	L338	18817-28	12	Hyde Park	4-6-0
Bengal Nagpur Rly.	1909	L341	18836-40	5	Atlas	4-6-0, "Class GM", similar to L244
Bengal Nagpur Rly.	1909	L342	18841-50	10	Queens Park	2-8-0, "Class H", similar to L246
Bengal Nagpur Rly.	1909	L343	18851-55	5	Hyde Park	2-6-4T, "Class FT", similar to L189
Bengal Nagpur Rly.	1909	L348	18890-907	18	Atlas	2-8-2, "Class B", to rly co.'s design
Bombay, Baroda & C.I.	1909	L351	18920-9	10	Hyde Park	4-6-0, standard type, "Class H"
Bombay, Baroda & C.I.	1909	L352	18930-31	2	Hyde Park	4-6-0, standard type, "Class H"
Bombay, Baroda & C.I.	1909	L353	18932-33	2	Hyde Park	2-8-0, "Class HG", similar to L320
South Indian Rlys.	1909	L360	18981-90	10	Hyde Park	4-6-0, standard type
Madras & Southern Mahratta Rly.	1909	L363	18999-19004	6	Atlas	4-4-0, similar to L311
Madras & Southern Mahratta Rly.	1909	L364	19005-10	6	Hyde Park	0-6-0, similar to L322
South Indian Rlys.	1909	L371	19022-25	4	Queens Park	0-8-2T, 'Abt' rack & adhesion, "Class P"
South Indian Rlys.	1909	L372	19026-33	8	Hyde Park	4-4-0, "Class T"
Bombay, Baroda & C.I.	1909	L374	19035-7	3	Hyde Park	4-6-0, standard type, "Class H"
Indian State Rly. – East Bengal	1909	L380	19080-83	4	Hyde Park	4-4-2
Bengal Nagpur Rly.	1909	L385	19121-23	3	Atlas	2-8-2, "Class B", to rly co.'s design
Bengal Nagpur Rly.	1909	L386	19124-26	3	Atlas	2-8-2, "Class B", to rly co.'s design
Rohilkund & K. Rly.	1909	L392	19152-54	3	Queens Park	0-6-0, modified "Class F"
Rohilkund & K. Rly.	1909	L393	19155-58	4	Queens Park	4-6-0, standard type
Indian State Rly. – North Western	1910	L396	19182-84	3	Atlas	2-6-2T, similar to L332
Bhavnagar G. J. P.	1910	L403	19259-61	3	Hyde Park	4-6-0, "Class P", same as L325
Indian State Rly. – North Western	1910	L407	19267-71	5	Queens Park	4-4-0, "Class SP"
Indian State Rly. – North Western	1910	L408	19272-85	14	Queens Park	0-6-0, "Class SG"
Indian State Rly. – OR Rly.	1910	L409	19286-97	12	Queens Park	0-6-0, similar to L302
Madras & Southern Mahratta Rly.	1910	L418	19325-27	3	Queens Park	0-6-6-0, modified Fairlie type
Ceylon Rlys.	1910	L423	19343-47	5	Queens Park	4-4-0
H.H. The Nizam's Rly.	1910	L435	19436-45	10	Queens Park	4-6-0, standard type
Great Indian Peninsula	1910	L438	19466-98	33	Atlas	2-8-0, "Class H/3"
Indian State Rly. – North Western	1911	L457	19644-45	2	Atlas	2-8-2, "Class B", to rly. co.'s design
Indian State Rly. – North Western	1911	L458	19646-47	2	Atlas	4-6-2, "Class C", similar to L316
Indian State Rly. – East Bengal	1911	L466	19679-82	4	Atlas	0-6-0, standard type
Bengal Nagpur Rly.	1911	L467	19683	1	Atlas	2-6-2
Ceylon Rlys.	1911	L470	19693-702	10	Hyde Park	4-4-0, new design
Bombay, Baroda & C.I.	1911	L476	19729-41	13	Atlas	0-6-0, standard type, with Schmidt s/heater
Madras & Southern Mahratta Rly.	1911	L480	19757-63	7	Hyde Park	4-6-0, standard type, "Class P"
South Indian Rlys.	1911	L485	19791-92	2	Hyde Park	4-4-0, "Class T", same as L372
Indian State Rly. – North Western	1911	L486	19793-805	13	Atlas	0-6-0, "Class SG", same as L322
Indian State Rly. – North Western	1911	L487	19806-17	12	Hyde Park	2-8-0, "Class HG", similar to L353
H.H. The Nizam's Rly.	1912	L490	19825-26	2	Atlas	4-6-0, "Class A", same as L299
Ceylon Rlys.	1912	L491	19827	1	Queens Park	0-6-0T
Indian State Rly. – North Western	1912	L498	19912-21	10	Atlas	4-4-0, "Class SP", same as L407
Assam Rly. & Trading Co.	1912	L502	19974-75	2	Hyde Park	4-6-0, "Class H", similar to L233
H.H. The Nizam's Rly.	1912	L505	19983-88	6	Atlas	4-6-0, "Class A", similar to L490
East India Rly. Co.	1912	L509	20003-7	5	Hyde Park	4-6-0, also built by Vulcan Fdry.
Great Indian Peninsula	1912	L511	20010-25	16	Atlas	0-8-4T, "Class Y/3", new design
Great Indian Peninsula	1912	L512	20026-30	5	Atlas	0-8-4T, "Class Y/4", new design, similar to L511
Indian State Rly. – North Western	1912	L513	20031-67	37	Queens Park	0-6-0, "Class SG", similar to L408
Indian State Rly. – North Western	1912	L514	20068-70	3	Queens Park	0-6-2T "Class ST", similar to L83
Bengal Nagpur Rly.	1912	L524	20138-42	5	Hyde Park	4-4-2, "Class K", similar to L217
Darjeeling–Himalaya Rly.	1912	L525	20143-44	2	Atlas	0-4-0T, "Class B", to redrawn Sharp, Stewart design
Gondal Porbander State Rly.	1912	L530	20181	1	Hyde Park	0-6-0, "Class F", similar to Neilson's order E604
Madras & Southern Mahratta Rly.	1912	L539	20235	1	Hyde Park	4-6-0, standard type, "Class P"
East India Rly. Co.	1912	L541	20237-56	20	Hyde Park	2-8-0, to rly co.'s design, similar to L176
East India Rly. Co.	1912	L542	20257-71	15	Queens Park	4-6-0, also built by Vulcan Fdry.

Jodhpur & K. Rly.	1912	L547	20289-91	3	Hyde Park	4-6-0, standard type, similar to L318
Jodhpur & K. Rly.	1912	L548	20292-94	3	Hyde Park	4-6-0, standard type, similar to L435

Country	No. of orders	No. of engines	Avg. engines/order
India	151	1462	9.68
Ceylon	4	20	5
Total	155	1482	9.56

The Bengal to Nagpur Railway placed its first orders in 1904, for 20 Class H 2-8-0s, and ten Class G 4-6-0s. The Class H 2-8-0s were also built for the railway by Robert Stephenson & Co., whilst the 4-6-0s were largely the same as previous Atlas Works engines for this railway. More Class H 2-8-0s were built by Hyde Park Works under order L92, in early 1905. A year or so later, both the Bengal to Nagpur, and Great Indian Peninsula railways were seen to be following the British fashion for Atlantic types in passenger service. Under order L212, the Class E/1 4-4-2s were produced for the G. I. P. R, and under order L217, a pair of Class K 4-4-2s were built for the Bengal–Nagpur Railway. The B. N. R. engines were four-cylinder compounds, with two inside, low pressure cylinders, and two high pressure cylinders, outside the frames. The earlier Class E/1 type for the G. I. P. R. was a simple expansion design, and totalled 19 in the batch built at Atlas Works. The principal dimensions of this class were:

Order No	L212
Works Nos	17779-17797
Running Nos	921-939
Class	E/1
Wheel arrangement	4-4-2
Wheel dia.	
coupled	5ft 6in
bogie	3ft 6in
trailing	4ft 3in
Heating surface	
tubes	1,880.00 sq ft
firebox	157.00 sq ft
total	2,037.00 sq ft
Grate area	32.00 sq ft
Cylinders (2 outside)	19.5in x 26in
Weight (in w.o.): total	126 tons 15cwt

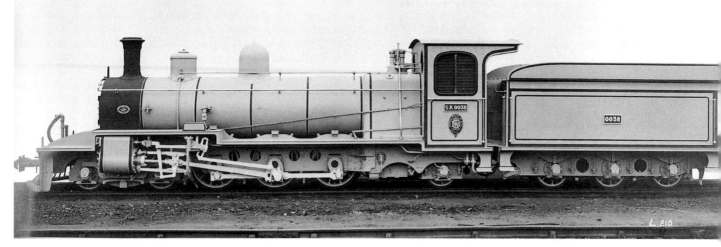

Above: Officially logged as order L218 for the Bengal–Nagpur Railway, these outside framed Pacifics were built for the 2ft 6in gauge Satpura Railway, operated by the BNR. In this case, No. S.R.0038 was the last of the batch of nine, built in 1906/07, at the Atlas Works. They were noted as Class C, and the coupled wheels were only 3ft 6in in diameter.

Mitchell Library Collection

Below: These large Pacific types for the Bengal–Nagpur Railway were built to order L854, and 18 in all were constructed at Hyde Park. Still popular in India was the compound system, in this case, these 4-6-2s were 4-cylinder 'De Glehn' compounds. The two inside, high pressure cylinders were 16.5in diameter, whilst the two outside, low pressure cylinders were 25in diameter, with a common stroke of 26in. In service, they were "Class M", and carried running numbers 792 to 809; this is the first of the class.

Mitchell Library Collection

NORTH BRITISH LOCOMOTIVE CO., LTD., GLASGOW.
PASSENGER LOCOMOTIVE FOR THE BENGAL NAGPUR RAILWAY.
4 CYLINDER TYPE "DE GLEHN" COMPOUND.

Gauge of Railway, 5ft. 6in.

TYPE. 4-6-2	ENGINE.				TENDER.		
4 Cylinders ... { Dia. 2 H.P. ... 16½ in. / 2 L.P. ... 25 in. / Stroke ... ... 26 in.	Heating Surface { Tubes ... ... / Firebox ... ... / Total		2,228 sq. ft. / 211 „ / 2,439 „		Wheels, Dia. ... ... 3 ft. 7 in.		
					Wheel Base ... ... 22 ft. 3 in.		
Wheels ... { Front Bogie, Dia. 3 ft. 0 in. / Coupled ... 6 ft. 2 in. / Hind Bogie ... 3 ft. 7 in.	Do do. { Superheater / Total		637 „ / 3,076 „		Tank Capacity ... 4,750 gallons		
					Fuel Space (10 tons) ... 450 cub. ft.		
	Firegrate Area		51 „		Weight, Full ... 65 tons 12 cwts.		
Wheel Base ... { Rigid ... 13 ft. 2 in. / Total ... 36 ft. 1 in.	Tractive Force at 60% of Boiler Pressure		28,700 lbs.				
Working Pressure ... 250 lbs. per sq. in.	Weight { In Working Order 105 tons 0 cwts. / On Coupled Wheels 64 „ 7 „				ENGINE & TENDER.		
Boiler Feed, 2 No. 10 Injectors					Wheel Base, Total ... ... 67ft. 10in.		

Boiler Plates, Steel.	Boiler Tubes, Steel.	Steam Brake on Engine.
Firebox „ Copper.		Vacuum Brake on Tender.

Another view of the massive 4-cylinder Class M compound Pacifics for the Bengal–Nagpur Railway in India.

Author's Collection

Wheel arrangement	4-6-2
Class	C
Wheel dia.	
coupled	3ft 6in
Bogie	2ft 3in
trailing	2ft 3in
Heating surface	
tubes	898.00 sq ft
firebox	66.00 sq ft
total	964.00 sq ft
Grate area	17.50 sq ft
Cylinders (2 outside)	14.5in x 18in
Boiler pressure	160 lb/sq. in.
Weight (in w.o.): total	52 tons 11cwt

Whilst following the British fashion for Atlantics, the new NBL built engines reinforced the 'British in India' presence in the names they carried, which ranged from *Lord Clive*, through *Sir Donald Stewart*, to *Tweeddale*. In service, the new locomotives replaced the C/5 class 4-4-0s on fast passenger duties, in particular, the Bombay to Poona "Race Specials" – a 191 km run the 4-4-2s were scheduled to make in three hours.

The Bengal–Nagpur Railway placed the largest number of orders with NBL, some of which were repeats, clearly a sign of faith in the quality of the products. Orders L79, L244, L277 and L315 were examples of this, covering 2-8-2s and standard mixed traffic 4-6-0s. Order L79 was in fact a follow on order from Class G 4-6-0s built by Sharp, Stewart at Atlas Works, and to specification E1209. In total, the 15 Bengal–Nagpur orders covered 106 locomotives, and whilst the majority were built to the Indian standard 5ft 6in gauge, others, like the six 2-8-2s from orders L277 and L315, were narrow (2ft 6in) gauge types. Also built for the 2ft 6in gauge lines were 13 Pacific types, to orders L218 and L316, whose appearance, with rather commodious, and well protected footplate, was typical of locomotives built for India at this time. NBL's Atlas Works built the 2ft 6in gauge Class C Pacifics, continuing the works' association with the country, begun under Sharp, Stewart's ownership. The main dimensions of these locomotives were:

Order No	L218 & L316
Works Nos	17819-17827 & 18654-18657
Running Nos	0033-0038, 0039C-0041C, 005C

Into 1909, the Bengal–Nagpur continued to place regular orders – three were received in January alone – which once again included repeats of previous orders. Up until the outbreak of the First World War, 94 out of 329 orders went to India, although the last orders – for Bengal–Nagpur, Ceylon, and Nizam's State Railway – were received after the hostilities had started. In fact, 1913 and 1914 witnessed, respectively, 61 and 55 orders in total from overseas railways.

A dramatic reduction in overseas orders was recorded from 1915, and NBL never again reached the pre-war production peaks achieved in 1914. Only three orders came from India in 1915, although one of these, a pair of 0-4-0 tank engines for the Darjeeling & Himalaya Railway was cancelled. Similarly, in 1916, Bengal–Nagpur ordered another batch of the Class H 2-8-0 engines but no further orders were received by NBL from India until 1917, when the Madras & Southern Mahratta ordered six 4-6-0s and six 4-8-0s. Both of these classes were built for the metre gauge, and the last mentioned, as order L697 was a fairly old design, which had been built by Hyde Park back in 1904, to order L69, for the East Bengal Railway. A modified version of this 4-8-0 was supplied to the Assam–Bengal Railway in 1905/6, whilst the Southern Madras Railway ordered five of the Class G 4-8-0s in 1906. The six locomotives ordered under L697 in 1917 were constructed by Atlas Works.

In 1918 no orders were placed by the Indian railways at all, but in 1919, this was more than compensated for in the shape of nine out of the 15 orders placed with NBL from all sources. Again, in the following year 1920, from a total of 19 orders placed, no fewer than ten came from India, including the Bengal–Nagpur, Madras & Southern

Mahratta, and the North Western Railway. In the ensuing eight years, up until the 25th anniversary of NBL's formation, the company received only 96 orders in total, of which a quarter – 24 orders – came from the subcontinent. This dramatic decline in the company's order books following the end of the First World War, reflected the severe economic depression that afflicted industry at this time. In fact, 1921 was the worst year to that date for the company, with only four orders, and none at all from the home market, and all four orders placed, came from India.

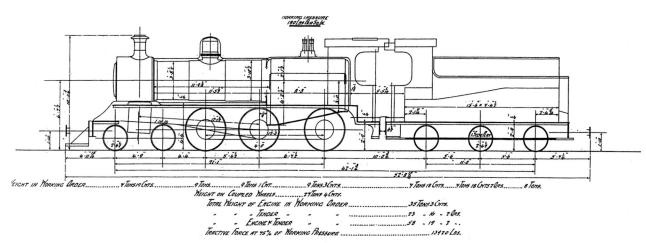

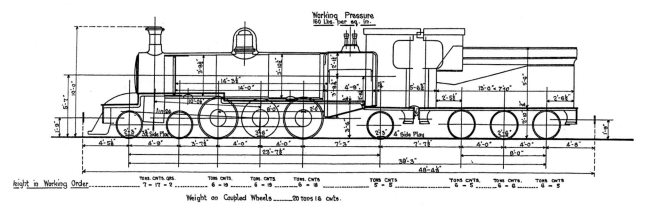

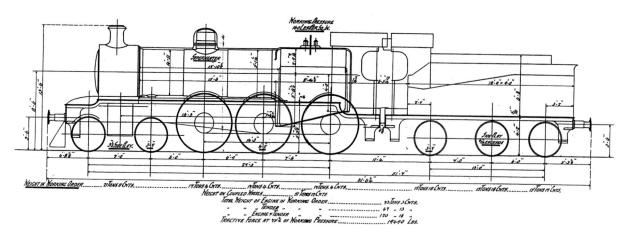

Top: The Indian Standard 4-6-0 for metre gauge lines is represented in this design for Assam-Bengal Railways and built under various orders, including L279.
Mitchell Library Collection

Middle: This diagram shows the general arrangement of the Class C Pacifics for the 2ft 6in gauge lines of the Bengal-Nagpur Railway, built in 1905, to order L144.
Mitchell Library Collection

Bottom: Another Indian Standard design, was this 4-6-0 for the 5ft 6in gauge lines of the Great Indian Peninsula Railway. In this case, in superheated form, and built by NBL to order L593 in 1913.
Mitchell Library Collection

Orders for India and Ceylon 1913–1928

Railway	Year	Order No.	Works Nos	Works	Qty	Type
Indian State Rly. - North Western	1913	L550	20296-325	Queens Park	30	0-6-0, "Class SG", similar to L513
Indian State Rly. - North Western	1913	L551	20326-45	Hyde Park	20	2-8-0, "Class HG", similar to L487
Indian State Rly. - North Western	1913	L552	20346-55	Atlas	10	4-4-0, "Class SP", similar to L498
Indian State Rly. - North Western	1913	L553	20356-58	Queens Park	3	0-6-2T "Class ST", similar to L514
Indian State Rly. - OR Rly.	1913	L554	20359-63 & 20427-29	Atlas	8	0-6-0, similar to L409
South India Rly.	1913	L556	20374-80	Hyde Park	7	4-6-0, "Class B", similar to L180 drawings
South India Rly.	1913	L557	20381-85	Hyde Park	5	4-6-0, "Class M", to Vulcan Fdry. drawings, with modifications
Bengal Nagpur Rly.	1913	L558	20386-88	Hyde Park	3	4-4-2, "Class K", similar to L524
Bengal Nagpur Rly.	1913	L561	20404-13	Atlas	10	2-8-0, "Class HM", similar to L342
Bengal Nagpur Rly.	1913	L562	20414-18	Atlas	5	2-8-0, "Class HS", similar to L561
Bengal Nagpur Rly.	1913	L563	20419-23	Atlas	5	2-8-0, "Class HS", similar to L562
Madras & Southern Mahratta Rly.	1913	L564	20424-26	Hyde Park	3	4-6-0, standard type, "Class P"
East India Rly. Co.	1913	L567	20457-71	Hyde Park	15	2-8-0, to rly co.'s design, similar to L541
East India Rly. Co.	1913	L568	20472-74	Queens Park	3	4-6-0, also built by Vulcan Fdry.
East India Rly. Co.	1913	L569	20475-90	Hyde Park	16	0-6-4T, new type, to Vulcan Fdry. drgs.
South India Rly.	1913	L572	20521-24	Hyde Park	4	4-4-0, "Class T", similar to L485
Gondal P. State Rly.	1913	L573	20525-26	Atlas	2	0-6-0, "Class F", similar to L530
Indian State Rly. - JB Rly.	1913	L582	20566	Hyde Park	1	4-6-0, standard type, similar to L548
Darjeeling–Himalaya Rly.	1913	L586	20638-40	Atlas	3	0-4-0T, "Class B", same as L525
Darjeeling–Himalaya Rly.	1913	L587	20641-42	Atlas	2	4-6-2, to NBL type S713
ISR Delhi Construction Co.	1913	L589	20646-48	Atlas	3	2-8-2, same as L457, for North Western Rly.
Great Indian Peninsula	1913	L593	20667-74	Hyde Park	8	4-6-0, "Class D/4" similar to L46/L142
Great Indian Peninsula	1913	L594	20675-752	Hyde Park	78	2-8-0, "Class H/4", similar to L438
Bengal Nagpur Rly	1913	L596	20756-72	Atlas	17	2-8-0, "Class HS", similar to L563
H.H. The Nizam's Rly.	1913	L597	20773-76	Atlas	4	4-6-0, "Class A", similar to L505
East India Rly. Co.	1913	L598	20777-811	Queens Park	35	0-6-0, standard type, similar to L466
South India Rly.	1913	L603	20861-64	Hyde Park	4	4-6-0, "Class B", same as L556
East India Rly. Co.	1913	L606	20869-98	Queens Park	30	0-6-0, standard type, same as L598
Bengal Nagpur Rly.	1913	L608	20903-12	Atlas	10	4-6-2, "Class C", similar to L316
Bengal Nagpur Rly.	1913	L609	20913-17	Queens Park	5	4-4-2, "Class K", similar to L558, De Glehn compound
Indian State Rly. - North Western	1913	L611	20922-31	Hyde Park	10	4-6-0, standard type, "Class HP"
Indian State Rly. - North Western	1913	L612	20932-34	Queens Park	3	0-6-2T "Class ST", similar to L553
Bombay, Baroda & C.I.	1914	L616	20939-48	Hyde Park	10	4-6-0, standard type, "Class H", similar to L351
Indian State Rly. - North Western	1914	L618	20952-55	Atlas	4	2-8-2, "Class G", similar to BNR Class B
Indian State Rly. - OR Rly.	1914	L621	20963-70	Queens Park	8	0-6-0, similar to L554
Madras & Southern Mahratta Rly.	1914	L628	20172-5 & 21153	Hyde Park	5	4-6-0, similar to L267
Madras & Southern Mahratta Rly.	1914	L630	21077-78	Hyde Park	2	4-6-0, similar to L628, "Class MH"
Indian State Rly. - North Western	1914	L632	21083	Atlas	1	2-8-2, "Class G", same as L618
Indian State Rly. - North Western	1914	L633	21084	Atlas	1	4-6-2, "Class P", similar to L458
Bengal Nagpur Rly.	1914	L634	21085-92	Atlas	8	2-8-0, "Class HS", similar to L596
Bengal Nagpur Rly.	1914	L635	21093-99	Atlas	7	2-8-2, "Class BS", similar to L386
Bengal Nagpur Rly.	1914	L636	21100-04	Atlas	5	4-6-2, "Class CS", similar to L608
Bhavnagar Rly.	1914	L642	21142-44 & 21198-21200	Hyde Park	6	4-6-0, "Class P", similar to L403
East India Rly. Co.	1914	L643	21145-46	Queens Park	2	0-6-0, standard type, similar to L598
Bengal Nagpur Rly.	1914	L644	21147-48	Atlas	2	2-8-0, "Class HS", same as L634
Ceylon Rly.	1914	L645	21149-52	Queens Park	4	0-6-0T, similar to L491
Jodhpur Bik. Rly.	1914	L646	21154-55	Atlas	2	4-6-0, standard type, "Class P", similar to L582
H.H. The Nizam's Rly.	1914	L648	21162-71	Queens Park	10	4-6-0, standard type, similar to L611
South India Rly.	1915	L651	21201-02	Hyde Park	2	4-4-0, "Class T", similar to L572
Great Indian Peninsula	1915	L665	21452-55	Atlas	4	2-8-2, "Class B1", similar to L635
Darjeeling–Himalaya Rly.	1915	L670	21472-73	Atlas	2	0-4-0T, "Class B" – order cancelled
Bengal Nagpur Rly.	1916	L675	21506	Atlas	1	2-8-0, "Class HS" – order cancelled
Assam–Bengal Rly.	1917	L694	21919-24	Hyde Park	6	4-6-0, standard mixed traffic type, based on L279
Madras & Southern Mahratta Rly.	1917	L696	21959-64	Atlas	6	4-6-0, "Class P", based on Nasmyth Wilson drgs.
Madras & Southern Mahratta Rly.	1917	L697	21965-70	Atlas	6	4-8-0, "Class G", similar to L208
Indian State Rly. - North Western	1917	L700	21991-92	Atlas	2	2-8-2, "Class G", similar to L632
Great Indian Peninsula	1919	L719	22318-47	Queens Park	30	2-10-0, new "Class N/1", to NBL designs
Bengal Nagpur Rly.	1919	L721	22418-47	Hyde Park	30	2-8-0, "Class HS", similar to L675
Madras & Southern Mahratta Rly.	1919	L722	22448-79	Hyde Park	32	4-8-0, "Class G", similar to L697
Great Indian Peninsula	1919	L723	22480-89	Hyde Park	10	0-8-4T, "Class Y/4", similar to L512
Bengal Nagpur Rly.	1919	L724	22500-4	Atlas	5	2-8-2, "Class BS", similar to L635
Great Indian Peninsula	1919	L728	22348-77	Queens Park	30	2-8-0, "Class H/4", similar to L594
Great Indian Peninsula	1919	L729	22378-407	Queens Park	30	2-8-0, "Class H/4", similar to L728
South India Rly.	1919	L731	22567-69	Atlas	3	4-4-0, "Class O", similar to L149
South India Rly.	1919	L732	22570-71	Atlas	2	4-4-4T, "Class E", similar to L181
Bengal Nagpur Rly.	1920	L736	22634-48	Hyde Park	15	2-8-0, "Class HS", same as L721

Bengal Nagpur Rly.	1920	L737	22649-53	Atlas	5	4-6-0, "Class GS", similar to L341
Bengal Nagpur Rly.	1920	L738	22654-67	Queens Park	14	2-8-2T, "Class L", to Robt. Stephenson's drgs.
Indian State Rly. - North Western	1920	L749	22766-72	Atlas	7	2-8-2, "Class GS", similar to L700
Junagad State Rly.	1920	L750	22773-4	Hyde Park	2	4-6-0, "Class P", same as L403
South India Rly.	1920	L752	22782	Atlas	1	4-4-4T, "Class E", same as L732
Madras & Southern Mahratta Rly.	1920	L754	22793-95	Queens Park	3	0-6-6-0, "Class IM", similar to Burma Rly. order L743
Bengal Nagpur Rly.	1920	L756	22802-26	Hyde Park	25	2-8-0, "Class HS", same as L736
Bengal Nagpur Rly.	1920	L757	22827-30	Queens Park	4	2-8-2T, "Class L", same as L738
South India Rly.	1920	L758	22831-35	Atlas	5	4-6-0, "Class M", similar to L557
Bombay, Baroda & C.I.	1921	L763	22892-911	Hyde Park	20	4-6-0, standard type, "Class H", similar to L616
Madras & Southern Mahratta Rly.	1921	L764	22912-17	Atlas	6	4-6-0, standard type, "Class W", similar to L763
Great Indian Peninsula	1921	L765	22918	Atlas	1	2-8-2, "Class B1", similar to L665
East India Rly. Co.	1921	L766	22919-40	Queens Park	22	2-8-0, similar to L728
Bhavnagar Rly.	1922	L770	22963-64	Hyde Park	2	4-6-0, "Class P", similar to L642
South India Rly.	1922	L772	22972-88	Atlas	17	4-6-0, "Class B", similar to L603
Great Indian Peninsula	1922	L773	22989-23004	Queens Park	16	4-6-0, "Class D/5" similar to L593
Great Indian Peninsula	1922	L774	23005-19	Queens Park	15	4-6-0, "Class D/5" similar to L773
East India Rly. Co.	1923	L775	23020-32	Hyde Park	13	2-8-0, "Class GS", similar to L766
South India Rly.	1923	L776	23033-38	Atlas	6	4-6-0, "Class B", same as L772
East India Rly. Co.	1923	L778	23044-55	Hyde Park	12	2-8-0, "Class GS", similar to L775
South India Rly.	1923	L781	23067-8	Queens Park	2	4-6-0, "Class SP", new type to Vulcan Fdry. drgs.
South India Rly.	1923	L782	23069-73	Queens Park	5	0-6-0, "Class K", new type to Kitson's drgs.
Junagad State Rly.	1924	L789	23136-39	Queens Park	4	4-6-0, similar to L207
Darjeeling–Himalaya Rly.	1925	L806	23291-3	Queens Park	3	0-4-0T, "Class B", similar to L586
Darjeeling–Himalaya Rly.	1925	L809	23300-304	Queens Park	5	0-4-0T, "Class B", similar to L806
Bhavnagar Rly.	1926	L826	23542-3	Hyde Park	2	4-6-0, "Class P", similar to L770
Madras & Southern Mahratta Rly.	1926	L827	23544-55	Hyde Park	12	2-6-4T, "Class F/5", new design
Indian State Rly. - East Bengal	1926	L829	23557-61	Hyde Park	5	2-6-4T, similar to L827
Madras & Southern Mahratta Rly.	1927	L838	23676-7	Hyde Park	2	2-6-4T, similar to L827
Darjeeling–Himalaya Rly.	1927	L839	23678	Queens Park	1	0-4-0T, "Class B", same as L806
Jamnagar & Dwarka Rly.	1927	L846	23742-43	Hyde Park	2	4-6-0, "Class P", similar to L826, s/heater fitted
Bhavnagar Rly.	1928	L851	23813-5	Hyde Park	3	4-6-0, "Class P", similar to L826, not s/heated
Bengal Nagpur Rly.	1928	L854	23868-85	Hyde Park	18	4-6-2, "Class M", new design, De Glehn compound

Country	No. of orders	No. of engines	Avg. engines/orders
India	98	911	9.3
Ceylon	1	4	4
Total	99	915	9.31

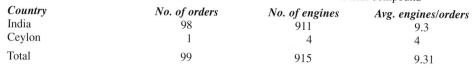
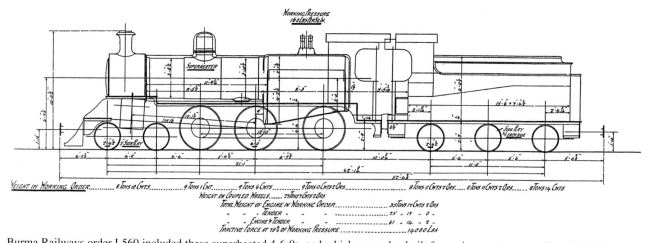

Burma Railways order L560 included these superheated 4-6-0s, and which were also built for various metre gauge lines in India.

Mitchell Library Collection

In 1914, NBL built these Indian Standard 4-6-0s for H.H. The Nizam's Railway, to order L648.

Mitchell Library Collection

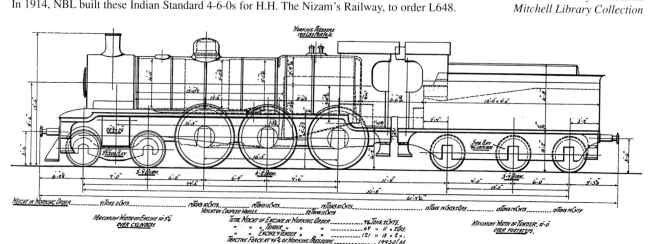

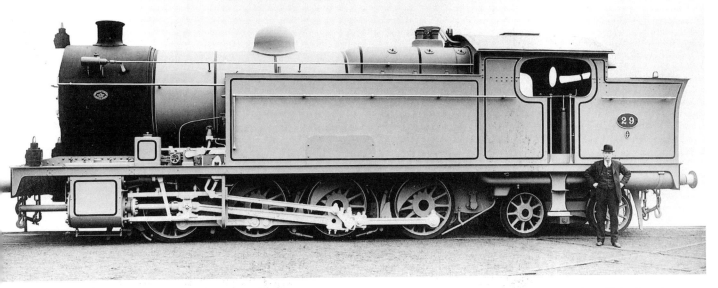

At the height of the British Empire, India was, like South America, perhaps the most lucrative source of locomotive orders at Springburn. Amongst the most prolific railways was the Great Indian Peninsula Railway (GIP), and in May 1912, two separate orders for these massive 0-8-4 tank engines were received. Five were built under order L512 and 16 under order L511. The engine shown, No. 29, is one of order L512, and classified as Y/4, they carried running numbers 29 to 33, and were built at the Atlas Works.

Mitchell Library Collection

The Great Indian Peninsula Railway, who had also placed numerous orders with NBL in its first five years, did not come back with any more contracts until 1910, when 33 Class H3 2-8-0s were ordered. The GIPR, along with the South Indian Railway, had been placing some locomotive orders with the likes of Krauss-Maffei and Henschel of Germany, who were major competitors for NBL in many countries. An interesting couple of orders from the GIPR in 1912, L511 and L512, were for 0-8-4 tank locomotives to a new design, and the second order of this pair included modifications to provide piston valves, and Schmidt superheaters. The leading dimensions were:

Order No	L511 & L512
Works Nos	20010-20035 &
	20026-20030
Running Nos	34-49 & 29-33
Wheel arrangement	0-8-4T
Class	Y/3 & Y/4
Wheel dia.	
coupled	4ft 3in
trailing	3ft 0in
Heating surface	
tubes	1,552.00 sq ft
s/heater	436.00 sq ft
firebox	172.00 sq ft
total	2,160.00 sq ft
Grate area	32.00 sq ft
Cylinders (2)	20" x 26"
Boiler pressure	160 lb/sq. in.
Weight (in w.o.): total	102 tons 1cwt

These engines were built in Atlas Works, and being intended for working on the steep gradients of the 'Ghats', they were designed for that purpose by the Locomotive Superintendent of the railway company. They were certainly an impressive design for what was essentially a banking locomotive. In 1910, the GIPR placed a large order with NBL, for 78 of the Class H4 2-8-0 locomotives, which were a follow on from earlier orders for the same type. This design was re-ordered after the war, another 60 in fact, in 1921, to orders L728 and L729, along with 20 of the NBL designed 2-10-0s, under order L719. These latter were for heavy freight duties, with trains of more than 1,600 tons, running between Bombay and Bhusaval, up and over the severe Ghat Inclines.

India of course was not the only country placing orders with NBL, but it was certainly the most profitable marketplace for the company up to the outbreak of the First World War. A contemporary press report for 1915 stated that *"the Scottish locomotive trade has been good for the past year"*. However, it was also noted that prospects were not so bright for the future, and *"one manufacturing firm"* made an entry in its order book to the effect that the order received was to *"replace engines sunk by the enemy"*.

China and the Far East

Further east, through Burma and into China, NBL secured some important orders in the years up to the First World War. Amongst the more interesting of the early orders were the standard gauge Mallet compounds for the Peking–Kalgan railway. Only three of these articulated types were built at the Queen's Park Works, and no tenders were supplied. Unconventional steam locomotives were not new to NBL, with Mexico repeating orders it had placed for the 0-6-6-0 'Modified Fairlie' engines, on a number of occasions. The Chinese engines were placed to order L274 in September 1907, by the railway's agents, J. Whittall & Co. Ltd, and they were delivered in May and June the following year. The main dimensions of the locomotives were:

Order No	L274
Works Nos	18317–18319
Running Nos	21–23
Wheel arrangement	0-6-6-0
Wheel dia., coupled	4ft 3in
Heating surface, total	2,591.00 sq ft
Grate area	45.10 sq ft
Cylinders (2 low press.)	28.75in x 28in
(2 high press.)	18in x 28in
Weight (in w.o.): total	96 tons

These three locomotives were constructed at Queen's Park Works, and were the first such engines built by NBL. The boiler and rear set of coupled wheels were fixed to the main frames, with a forward extension of the frames carrying the second set of coupled wheels, driven by the low pressure cylinders. The boiler was rigidly mounted to the rear portion of the frames, with the smokebox supported on a saddle attached to the front extension, on a sliding bolster.

The Far East was the source of a large number of orders until the late 1920s, due to the British colonial presence in China. In this case, No. 21 was the first of three Mallet compounds for the Peking–Kalgan Railway, built at the Queen's Park Works in 1908. These locomotives were supplied to the railway without tenders, and amongst the obvious details in this broadside view is the use of slide valves in the Walschaerts type valve gear.

Mitchell Library Collection

The articulated joint between front and rear frames was formed by cast steel cross stays, with lateral movement of the whole front section controlled by springs attached to the underside of the smokebox. The Walschaerts valve motion included Richardson type, balanced slide valves. None of these engines was superheated. Although the original order was for only three locomotives, the tenders of which were built in China, a fourth Mallet was ordered and built in 1909, to the same design.

Other oriental orders came from the Imperial Taiwan Railway, for 2-4-2 and 4-4-0 types, whilst the Manila Railway in the Phillipines ordered 0-6-2 and 4-6-2 types for the 3ft 6in gauge lines. In the same year as the extra Mallet

was ordered, the Tientsin–Peking Railway ordered eight standard gauge Moguls, to an NBL design, which were built in the Atlas Works. This was noted as being design No. 551, and included six-wheeled tenders. A similar 2-6-0, of NBL design, No. 552, incorporated a bogie tender, and was the specification for order L361, for a batch of four engines for the recently opened Kowloon–Canton Railway. The British Section of this line was opened on 1st October 1910 and was the subject of later electrification schemes in the 1980s, following the completion of the Hong Kong Metro. The railway on which the new NBL built locomotives were put to work formed part of the 'New Territories', leased for a period of 99 years, by the British Government in 1898. The 2-6-0s and newly opened railway formed an important artery, linking Hong Kong, Canton and the Chinese border. More of these 2-6-0s were ordered in 1911, for both the Kowloon–Canton Railway, and the Tientsin–Peking line in China.

Another view of the unusual 0-6-6-0 Mallet compounds for China, three of which were ordered under L274 in 1907.

Mitchell Library Collection

REFERENCE NO. L 274   4'-8½' GAUGE.
4 MALLET TYPE LOCOMOTIVES FOR CHINA
BUILT BY THE NORTH BRITISH LOCOMOTIVE COMPANY, LIMITED.
1907 - 1909
96 TONS IN FULL WORKING ORDER. (WITHOUT TENDER)

Above: Engine No. 161 was the second of order L602, and supplied to the Manila Railway in the Phillipines in 1914, just before the outbreak of war. This order was in fact for ten locomotives, seven of which went to South Africa, and the remaining three to the Far East.
Mitchell Library Collection

Below: This NBL publicity photograph shows the typically British lines of these 4-6-4 tank locomotives for the Manila Railway in the Phillipines. As the legend shows, this type was also built for South African Railways, under NBL order L602.
Author's Collection

NORTH BRITISH LOCOMOTIVE CO., LTD., GLASGOW.
TANK LOCOMOTIVE FOR S.A.R. AND THE MANILA RAILWAY CO. (1906) LTD.

Gauge of Railway, 3 ft. 6 in.

TYPE 4-6-4   TANK ENGINE.

CYLINDERS	Diameter	17 in.	HEATING SURFACE	Tubes	844 sq. ft.	
	Stroke	24 in.		Firebox	118 ,,	
				Total	962 ,,	
WHEELS	Front Bogie Dia.	2 ft. 7½ in.	Do. do.	Superheater	257 ,,	
	Coupled ,,	4 ft. 0 in.		Total	1219 ,,	
	Hind Bogie ,,	2 ft. 7½ in.				
WHEEL-BASE	Rigid	12 ft. 3 in.	FIREGRATE AREA		18·4 ,,	
	Total	32 ft. 10½ in.				

WORKING PRESSURE - 160 lbs. per sq. in.

TRACTIVE FORCE at 75% of Boiler Pressure 17,340 lbs.

BOILER FEED - 2 Injectors No. 9 {1 Combination {1 Exhaust Steam

WEIGHT {In Working Order - 70 tons 18 cwt {On Coupled Wheels 36 ,, 0 ,,

TANK CAPACITY - 2,350 gallons.

FUEL SPACE - 180 cub. ft.

Boiler Plates, Iron.
Firebox ,, Copper.

Boiler Tubes {5¼-in. dia. COPPER. {1¼ in. dia. BRASS.

Vacuum and Hand Brake.
Reversing Gear, Screw and Steam

This 2-6-0 was designed by NBL, and built to order L379 for the standard gauge Tientsin to Pukow Railway in China, in 1909. Eight were built at Atlas Works, and carried works numbers 19072–19079 (running numbers 7–14). Compare the style of this design with that of the Pacific locomotives built by NBL for the same railway almost 25 years later, and illustrated in Chapter 7. Still almost typically a British design.

Mitchell Library Collection

In Burma, another British colony, NBL supplied a new design of Mallet locomotive, but this time, complete with tenders, working over some very severe gradients, on the 1,530 route miles of metre gauge network. At the time, the Burma Railways were expanding quite rapidly, with ever increasing passenger and freight traffic. Although, at the time NBL delivered its new locomotives, under order L384, Rangoon station was still under construction! The metre gauge Mallets had the following dimensions:

Order No	L384
Works Nos	19117-19120
Class	N
Wheel arrangement	0-6-6-0
Wheel dia., coupled	3ft 3in
Heating surface, total	1,513.00 sq ft
Cylinders (2 low press.)	24.50in x 20in
(2 high press.)	15.5in x 20in
Boiler pressure:	180 lb/sq in
Weight (in w.o.): total:	89 tons 17cwt

Locomotives of this design were also supplied to the Uganda Railway in Africa late in 1911, whilst a further four engines were completed for Burma in 1913. They were once again a compound type, and all were built at Queen's Park Works, together with further batches of six and ten, for the Uganda Railway.

Orders for China and Far East 1903–1912

Railway	Year	Order No.	Works Nos	Qty	Works	Type
Kansei Rly. (Japan)	1903	L2	16019-20	2	Queens Park	0-6-2T
Burma Rly. Co.	1903	L38	16231-39	9	Hyde Park	4-6-0, "Class J" similar to L30
Burma Rly. Co.	1903	L39	16240-49	10	Atlas	4-6-0, "Class K" similar to L30
Hokkaido Rly. (Japan)	1903	L49	16342-47	6	Queens Park	2-6-0
Shanghai–Nanking	1904	L101	16702-09	8	Atlas	4-6-0, "Class B" to rly. co.'s design
Shanghai–Nanking	1904	L102	16710-11	2	Atlas	4-6-2, "Class A" to rly. co.'s design
Imperial Japanese Rlys.	1905	L108	16735-52	18	Hyde Park	0-6-2T
Imperial Japanese Rlys.	1905	L112	16767-96	30	Hyde Park	0-6-2T, similar to L108
Imperial Japanese Rlys.	1905	L113	16797-816	20	Atlas	0-6-2T, similar to L108
Burma Rly. Co.	1905	L116	16824-32	9	Hyde Park	4-6-0, "Class J" same as L38
Kanson Rly. Co. (Japan)	1905	L129	16928-32	5	Hyde Park	0-6-2T, similar to L112
Imperial Japanese Rlys.	1905	L136	16973-17022	50	Hyde Park	0-6-2T, similar to L112
Imperial Japanese Rlys.	1905	L137	17023-52	30	Atlas	0-6-2T, similar to L136
Imperial Japanese Rlys.	1905	L138	17053-72	20	Queens Park	0-6-2T, similar to L136
Imperial Chinese Rlys.	1905	L143	17104-07	4	Queens Park	4-6-0, no tenders supplied
Manila Railway	1906	L179	17410-14	5	Queens Park	4-4-2, to rly. co.'s design
Imperial Chinese Rlys.	1906	L187	17479-82	4	Queens Park	2-6-2T, to NBL design
Imperial Chinese Rlys.	1906	L199	17645-46	2	Queens Park	4-6-0, similar to L143
Kansei Rly. (Japan)	1906	L206	17725-26	2	Queens Park	2-6-0, "Class 2"
Shanghai–Nanking	1906	L231	17911-12	2	Atlas	4-6-0, "Class B" similar to L101
Shanghai–Nanking	1906	L232	17913-14	2	Atlas	4-4-0, "Class C" to rly. co.'s design
Imperial Chinese Rlys.	1907	L236	17924-29	6	Queens Park	2-6-2ST, same as L187
Imperial Chinese Rlys.	1907	L241	18035-36	2	Queens Park	2-6-2ST, same as L236
Peking–Kalgan Rly.	1907	L274	18317-19	3	Queens Park	0-6-6-0 Mallet compound
Imperial Taiwan	1907	L284	18378-82	5	Queens Park	2-4-2T
Imperial Taiwan	1907	L285	18383-84	2	Hyde Park	4-4-0
Manila Railway	1907	L288	18393-402	10	Queens Park	0-6-2T, "Class B" to NBL design
Burma Mines Ltd.	1908	L319	18672-74	3	Atlas	0-6-0
Imperial Taiwan	1908	L340	18834-35	2	Hyde Park	4-4-0, same as L285
Manila Railway	1909	L355	18940-49	10	Queens Park	0-6-2T, "Class B" same as L288
Manila Railway	1909	L356	18950-54	5	Queens Park	4-6-2T, "Class E"
Kowloon–Canton Rly.	1909	L361	18991-94	4	Atlas	2-6-0, to NBL design

Railway	Year	Order No.	Works Nos	Qty	Works	Type
Burma Railway Co.	1909	L362	18995-98	4	Atlas	2-6-2T, "Class M" similar to L256
Peking–Kalgan Rly.	1909	L367	19017	1	Queens Park	0-6-6-0 Mallet compound, same as L274
Peking–Tientsin Rly.	1909	L379	19072-79	8	Atlas	2-6-0, to NBL design
Burma Railway Co.	1909	L384	19117-20	4	Queens Park	0-6-6-0 "Class N" Mallet compound, same as L274
Manila Railway	1910	L431	19373-77	5	Queens Park	0-6-2T, "Class B" similar to L355
Kowloon–Canton Rly.	1911	L443	19557-59	3	Atlas	2-6-0, "Class A" similar to L361
Imperial Japanese Rlys.	1911	L446	19564-75	12	Queens Park	4-6-0, "Type 8700" to NBL design, but no tenders
Peking–Tientsin Rly.	1911	L454	19624-27	4	Atlas	2-6-0, same as L379
Federated Malay States	1912	L497	19909-11	3	Atlas	0-6-4T, "Class I" to Kitsons designs
Royal Siamese	1912	L501	19962-73	12	Atlas	4-6-0, engine similar to L207
Burma Railway Co.	1912	L517	20077-80	4	Queens Park	0-6-6-0 "Class N" Mallet compound, similar to L384
Peking–Mukden Rly.	1912	L518	20081	1	Queens Park	2-6-2T

Country	No. of orders	No. of engines	Avg. engines/order
Burma	7	43	6.14
Malaya	1	3	3
Siam (Thailand)	1	12	12
China/Hong Kong	16	56	3.5
Phillipines	5	35	7
Japan	11	195	17.73
Taiwan	3	9	3
Total	44	353	8.02

Back in 1903, Burma Railways ordered its first mixed traffic 4-6-0s for the metre gauge, under orders L38 and L39. The last mentioned was originally scheduled for building at Hyde Park, but was transferred to Atlas Works after the drawings were completed. Some 19 engines were ordered initially, but the Class K 4-6-0s were not supplemented until ten years later, in 1913. Interestingly the first orders were referred to as being similar to order L30, which was a batch of three 4-6-0s built at Hyde Park, for the metre gauge East Bengal Railway in India. No less than 13 orders were placed by Burma Railways between 1903 and 1928, totalling 70 locomotives. The majority of these were the 0-6-6-0 N class compounds, and the K Class 4-6-0s, with a handful of 2-6-2 tank engines and an 0-6-0 design for Burma Mines Ltd.

Although the most orders came from China/Hong Kong and Burma, by far the greatest number of locomotives were built for Japanese railways, 195 in all, between 1903 and 1912. These were mainly built for the 3ft 6in gauge, and for the most part they were 0-6-2 tank engines, except for a 2-6-0 design for the Kansei Railway, and in 1911, a 4-6-0 type to an NBL design for the Imperial Japanese Railways. This class, known as type 8700, was for 3ft gauge lines, to the NBL design designated S561A, and were supplied without tenders, from Queen's Park Works.

Orders for China and Far East 1913–1928

Railway	Year	Order No.	Works Nos	Qty	Works	Type
Burma Rly. Co.	1913	L560	20399-403	5	Queens Park	4-6-0, "Class K" same as L39
Kowloon–Canton Rly.	1913	L588	20643-45	3	Atlas	2-6-0, "Class A", engine as L443, tender as L361
Manila Railway	1913	L602	20851-53	3	Atlas	4-6-4, South African Rlys design
Shanghai–Nanking	1913	L610	20918-21	4	Atlas	4-4-2, "Class E" new type
Burma Rly. Co.	1914	L631	21079-82	4	Queens Park	0-6-6-0, "Class N" similar to L517
Burma Mines Ltd.	1914	L637	21105-07	3	Atlas	0-6-0, similar to L319
Royal Siamese	1914	L641	21137-41	5	Hyde Park	4-6-0, "Class E" similar to L501
Royal Siamese	1916	L686	21758-62	5	Hyde Park	4-6-0, "Class E" similar to L641
Royal Siamese	1917	L691	21809-18	10	Hyde Park	4-6-0, "Class E" same as L686
Burma Rly. Co.	1917	L702	21997-99	3	Hyde Park	4-6-0, "Class K" similar to L560
Royal Siamese	1918	L715	22258-67	10	Hyde Park	4-6-0, same as L686
Federated Malay States	1919	L725	22505-20	16	Queens Park	4-6-2, "Class P" new to Kitson & Co. designs
Shanghai–Nanking	1919	L726	22521-26	6	Atlas	4-6-0, "Class B" similar to L231
Shanghai–Nanking	1920	L735	22627-33	7	Atlas	4-6-0, "Class B" same as L726
Burma Rly. Co.	1920	L743	22701-05	5	Queens Park	0-6-6-0, "Class N" similar to L631
Peking–Mukden Rly.	1920	L753	22783-92	10	Queens Park	2-6-2T, similar to L518
Burma Rly. Co.	1922	L771	22965-71	7	Atlas	4-6-0, "Class K" similar to L702
Federated Malay States	1927	L840	23679-81	3	Hyde Park	4-6-2, "Class S" new design
Shanghai–Nanking	1930	L870	24026-33	8	Hyde Park	4-6-2, new design
Peiping–Liaoning Rly.	1930	L876	24080-05	6	Queens Park	2-8-2, to railway company's drawings

Country	No. of orders	No. of engines	Avg. engines/order
Burma	6	27	4.5
Malaya	2	19	9.5
Siam (Thailand)	4	30	7.5
China/Hong Kong	7	44	6
Phillipines	1	3	3
Total	20	123	6.06

Also sold to Australia, were these standard gauge Class K 2-8-0s, eight of which were built at Hyde Park in 1915, under order L654. They were given running numbers K.27 to K.34, and were similar to order L500, built for New South Wales as Class T, in 1912.

Mitchell Library Collection

Australia and New Zealand

On the opposite side of the world to Glasgow, the countries of Australia and New Zealand placed only 19 orders for 290 locomotives with NBL during its first 25 years. However, there were a number of interesting and important designs from amongst these orders. Overall, they ranged from a pair of four-cylinder 0-6-0T rack locomotives for Queensland, to the legendary Class AB Pacifics for New Zealand. Only Australia placed orders with NBL until after the First World War, with the majority of these for Western Australia's 3ft 6in gauge lines. The first order to come to NBL from the other side of the world was from New South Wales, as order L48, at the beginning of December 1903, for a batch of ten standard gauge 2-8-0s. These locomotives were built at the Glasgow Locomotive Works (formerly Dübs & Co.), and followed on from similar orders supplied by Dübs, and Neilson, Reid & Co. before the amalgamation.

The majority of locomotives supplied to Australia up to the outbreak of war were 2-8-0 types, with most of the orders shared between Western Australia and New South Wales. In addition, some 42 larger 4-8-0 types were built for the Western Australian Government Railway, all before

1914, but none afterwards. Some Pacific types were also built, again mostly for Western Australia, the last of which, in 1924 to order L793, was for ten Class P engines. In total though, no less than 103 Consolidation types were built for Australia by NBL, which averaged out to about four each year for the first 25 years of the company's existence. Queensland Government Railways placed an order for a pair of four-cylinder 0-6-0 side tank engines in 1905, equipped with the gearing necessary to engage in a central Abt rack, for working steep inclines. This order was repeated almost ten years later, when two more, similar locomotives were supplied. Other than the single 4-8-0 locomotive for the Emu Bay Railway Co. in Tasmania, the 2-8-0s were the mainstay of NBL's work for Australia at this time. With the exception of order L48 for New South Wales, orders L471, 500, 585, 654 and 655 completed the ordering, between 1911 and 1915, when 83 engines were built, at an average of more than 20 a year.

The initial order, for a single non-superheated locomotive, was L471, which in its turn was to all intents and pur-

Built by NBL in 1913 for South Australia Government Railways, to order L526 for 15 locomotives, all were built at the Atlas Works. The photograph shows No. 207, as now preserved by the Australian Railway Historical Society, at Mile End. The Rx class locomotive is still in use, on steam excursions and more than 80 years old.

Phil Butler

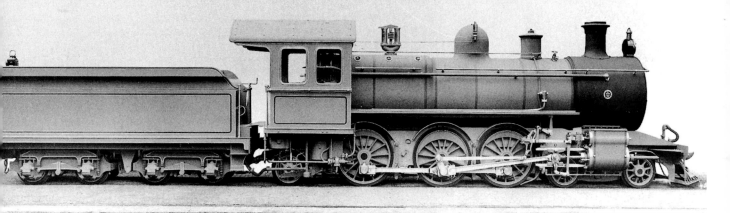

Western Australia, like most of Africa, built its railways to 3ft 6in gauge. In 1910, 20 of these new Class E Pacifics were ordered for the State Government. The design was new as well, produced in Australia, but like many others, with details worked out by the drawing offices in Springburn. Hyde Park Works built the locomotives, which carried works numbers 19604–19623, to order L453.   *Mitchell Library Collection*

poses the same as order E757, built by Neilson, Reid & Co. for Western Australia. Order L654 though, constructed in 1915 for the Commonwealth Railways, epitomises the 2-8-0 design for Australia from Glasgow at this time, with leading dimensions as follows:

Order No	L654
Works Nos	21230-21237
Class	K
Running Nos	27-34
Wheel arrangement	2-8-0
Wheel dia.	
coupled	4ft 3in
leading	2ft 9.5in
Heating surface	
tubes	1,660.00 sq ft
s/heater	300.00 sq ft
firebox	172.00 sq ft
total	2,132.00 sq ft
Grate area	30.00 sq ft
Cylinders (2)	22in x 26in
Boiler pressure	150 lb/sq in
Weight in w.o.	
engine	68 tons 10 cwt
tender	48 tons
total	116 tons 10 cwt

This particular example was fitted with the Robinson superheater, with its short return loops and pressure relief valves, as also was order L655 for New South Wales, and which represented the last of the type. Both of these orders, for eight and four locomotives respectively, were completed at Hyde Park Works. Across in New Zealand, it was not until 1920 that NBL received its first order, for 25 of the new Class AB Pacifics. Having said that, Glasgow had been building engines for New Zealand for some time, such as those supplied by Sharp, Stewart's Atlas Works in 1901, when a batch of ten Class UC 4-6-0s were built. Sharp, Stewart had also provided a number of 4-8-0 freight locomotives, designated Class B, and which underwent various modifications in service. Perhaps the most unusual change was the conversion of two of the class into 4-6-4 tank engines, at NZR's Addington Workshops, for working the famous Rimutaka Incline.

In general, New Zealand Railways imported locomotives from various sources, including Baldwin and Alco in the USA, but it was not without its own workshops and locomotive building industry. The eventual NBL built Class AB Pacifics had their ancestry in the completion of the North Island main line, from Auckland to Wellington in the early 1900s, and the entry into service of the four-cylinder Class A compound Pacifics. These locomotives have been described as the most elegant steam types to operate in New Zealand, and in their original, unsuperheated form, were built by the railways themselves, and A. & G. Price, in New

One of the most famous and successful exports to New Zealand were the Class AB Pacifics. This view shows the first of this new design, built at the Queen's Park Works in 1921. These early ABs were fitted with the Robinson superheater
                    Mitchell Library Collection

The Class AB Pacifics for New Zealand Railways were ordered from NBL in 1923, to order L777. This view is of No. 804 (works number 23039), built in 1925, and still at work in June 1962, shunting at Burnside.

New Zealand Rly & Loco. Society (Inc.) Archives Collection

Zealand. Subsequent modifications to the Class A included superheating, and the conversion from the De Glehn compound system, to simple expansion.

The next step towards the Class AB, was the appearance of a report on the inadequacies of New Zealand's locomotive stock in 1915, whereupon orders were placed with Baldwin for a two-cylinder Pacific type. These were the Class AA engines, which were a successful development towards answering New Zealand's motive power problems. Even more success was just around the corner, as NZR's design staff and workshops built the first Class AB, two-cylinder Pacifics, with their Vanderbilt tenders. Whilst the ravages of the First World War were a mitigating factor, and the inability of NZR's workshops to satisfy the railway's demands, it was not until October 1920, that NBL began work on a batch of 25 of these new locomotives. Order L759 was constructed at Queen's Park Works, and the original dimensions were as follows:

Order No	L759 & L761
Works Nos	22836-22860 (L759)
	22866-22885 (L761)

Class	AB
Running Nos	718-742 (L759)
	743-762 (L761)
Overall length	62ft 5in
Overall height	11ft 5.875in
Overall width	8ft 0in
Wheel arrangement	4-6-2
Wheelbase	
engine	27ft 1in
tender	14ft 0in
Wheel dia.	
coupled	4ft 6in
leading	2ft 6in
trailing	2ft 2.5in
Heating surface	
evaporative	1,148.00 sq ft
superheater	204.00 sq ft
total	1,352.00 sq ft
Grate area	33.00 sq ft
Cylinders (2)	17in x 26in
Boiler pressure	180 lb/sq in
Tractive effort @ 80% b.p.	20,030 lb
Fuel capacity	
coal	4 tons 10 cwt
water	3,500 gallons
Weight in w.o.	
engine	51 tons 6 cwt
tender	33 tons 8 cwt
total	84 tons 14 cwt

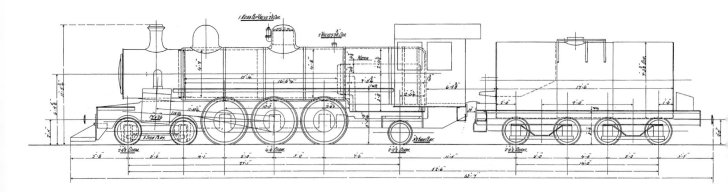

The famous Class AB Pacifics for New Zealand were built by NBL to three orders; L759, 761, and 777.

Mitchell Library Collection

Almost immediately after this order was received, a further contract was placed by New Zealand Railways for 20 more Class AB Pacifics, as order L761. All 45 engines on these two orders were delivered during 1921 and 1922, with Nos 718 to 732 in service on South Island, and 733 to 762 on the North Island main lines. During delivery however, two locomotives were lost with the wreck of the ship, the *Wiltshire,* off the New Zealand coast, and in 1923 the drawing office register records a third order for 'ABs', L777. In fact, New Zealand Railways had increased the original contract with NBL by three engines, with a further two engines to replace those lost at sea. The new engines were to be numbered 773 to 775 (NBL Works Nos 23039-23041), and the two replacements were for engine numbers 732 and 762, with the replacements carrying NBL numbers 23042 and 23043. All of the AB class Pacifics were built at Queen's Park Works, and were a great success from the word go, and were widely used all over the railway system, on both North and South Island routes. North British built a total of 85 of these famous engines, with a second contract, and the fourth and final order being received at Flemington

Street, in 1924, for 35 locomotives, under order L798. The additional engines were ordered following the completion of the Midland line on South Island, and the link to Whangarei on North Island, which resulted in increased traffic. They were an economical design to operate, and well received by the engine crews, although during the 1920s, the maintenance costs were found to be quite high, as a result of flaws in the design. Some of these faults, highlighted during G. S. Lynde's early years as CME, included the frequent failures of crossheads, and numerous breakages of the engine and tender coupling. Other design defects were found with the tender itself, and locomotive's firebox stays, piston valves, and aspects of the superheater design. Despite these concerns about the design, and its effect on locomotive maintenance, they were popular locomotives, and well suited to their work. So popular were these engines, that no fewer than four have been rescued from the breaker's torch, including one of those built by NBL, (NZR number 832), preserved at the Museum of Transport and Technology in Auckland.

Orders for Australia and New Zealand 1903–1928

Railway	Year	Order No.	Works Nos	Qty	Works	Type
New South Wales Govt.	1903	L48	16332-41	10	Queens Park	2-8-0, "Class T"
Metro. Coal Co., Sydney	1903	L52	16350	1	Hyde Park	0-4-0T
Queensland Govt.	1905	L152	17224-5	2	Queens Park	0-6-0T, 'Abt' rack engines
New South Wales Govt.	1907	L249	18086	1	Queens Park	0-4-0T, crane engine
Emu Bay Rly. Co.	1911	L447	19576	1	Queens Park	4-8-0
Western Aust. Govt.	1911	L453	19604-23	20	Hyde Park	4-6-2, new WAGR design, "Class E"
Western Aust. Govt.	1911	L461	19655-66	12	Hyde Park	4-8-0, "Class F"
Western Aust. Govt.	1911	L471	19703	1	Hyde Park	2-8-0, similar to Neilson order, E757
Western Aust. Govt.	1911	L475	19709-28	20	Hyde Park	4-6-4T, new design, "Class D"
Millar's K&J Co. (West. Aust.)	1911	L477	19742	1	Queens Park	4-6-0, "Class G", similar to Dübs order 3413E
New South Wales Govt.	1912	L500	19942-61	20	Hyde Park	2-8-0, to NSWR design, "Class T"
Western Aust. Govt.	1912	L520	20083-20112	30	Hyde Park	4-8-0, "Class F", similar to order L461
South Aust. Govt.	1912	L526	20145-59	15	Atlas	4-6-0, to new SAGR design, "Class Rx"
New South Wales Govt.	1913	L585	20588-637	50	Hyde Park	2-8-0, similar to order L500, "Class T"
Queensland Govt.	1914	L615	20937-38	2	Queens Park	0-6-0T, 'Abt' rack engines, similar to L152
Commonwealth of Austr.	1915	L654	21230-37	8	Hyde Park	2-8-0, similar to order L500, but "Class K"
New South Wales Govt.	1915	L655	21238-41	4	Hyde Park	2-8-0, similar to order L585, "Class T"
New South Wales Govt.	1915	L669	21462-71	10	Hyde Park	2-8-0, similar to order L655, "Class T" **
New Zealand Govt.	1920	L759	22836-60	25	Queens Park	4-6-2, new 'Ab' class to NZR design
New Zealand Govt.	1920	L761	22866-85	20	Queens Park	4-6-2, new 'Ab' class to NZR design, same as L759
New Zealand Govt.	1923	L777	23039-43	5	Queens Park	4-6-2, new 'Ab' class to NZR design, similar to L761
Western Aust. Govt.	1924	L793	23143-52	10	Queens Park	4-6-2, to NBL design, designated 'Class P'
New Zealand Govt.	1924	L798	23173-207	35	Queens Park	4-6-2, new 'Ab' class to NZR design, similar to L777

** Ordered under Ministry of Munitions contracts

Country	No. of orders	No. of engines	Avg. engines/order
Australia	19	218	11.47
New Zealand	4	85	21.25
Total	23	303	13.17

Compared with the engines of this class built by A. & G. Price, and NZR's own Addington Workshops, the NBL built engines showed minor variations in construction. Perhaps one of the most obvious features being the chimney, which on the first NBL built engines was typically British, whilst those built later, had a much simpler tapered, almost stovepipe, chimney. Another characteristic of the NBL built engines was the use of countersunk rivets on the locomotive headstock, compared with the home built engines. Following the appointment of G. S. Lynde as CME, a major overhaul of NZR locomotive stock and its design was undertaken. Lynde's appointment followed an investigation into NZR locomotive practice by Sir Sam Fay and Sir

Vincent Raven, in the early 1920s. Out of these changes, although design and construction problems were noted with the AB class engines, they were one of the few existing designs that were to be kept under the new regime.

The initial design of the AB dated back to the war years of 1914–1918, with the first engine built in 1915, in New Zealand, at the railway's Addington Workshops. The most obvious initial change in design practice from previous work was the adoption of the Vanderbilt type of tender, with its cylindrical water tank. This design was also used in the later Class J, and JA 4-8-2s built in Glasgow, at the outbreak of World War II.

In service, the ABs lasted for more than 35 years, with

In 1911, NBL built 30 of these 4-6-0s for the French State Railways, to order L442. They were noted in the drawing office register as being similar to the Highland Railway's Castle class engines – a fact which is obvious in this broadside view of No. 230–321.

Mitchell Library Collection

the first NBL built engine being put to work in 1921, and the last withdrawal taking place in 1969. Even after the arrival of the superb Class J 4-8-2s and the 4-8-4 Class Ks built in New Zealand, the Abs continued to provide excellent service. It was only the completion of dieselisation that put an end to their careers, and North British were once again associated with a highly successful steam locomotive design.

European Orders

Across Europe, North British had been supplying orders to industrial networks, and a smaller number of main line railway locomotives. Before the outbreak of the First World War, the majority of the 17 orders for industrial types were for the Tharsis Sulphur & Copper Co. and the Rio Tinto Co., and were almost invariably tank engines. Interestingly perhaps, only eight of the 52 European orders were built at the Hyde Park Works, with the remainder almost evenly distributed between Atlas and Queen's Park works. Having said that, order L105, which may be considered as the first for a European main line railway – the Great Southern of Spain – was for six 2-6-0s, and was built at Hyde Park.

Prior to the formation of NBL, all three companies had, as referred to earlier, built locomotives for almost all of the Continental railways, and north to Scandinavia and Russia. France though was the most profitable source of orders for NBL in the period under review, and between 1911 and 1917, no less than 410 locomotives were built. The first orders for France came in 1911, for 50 4-6-0 locomotives, in two orders – L442 (30) and L444 (20) – which were described in the contemporary press as being 'similar to the Highland Railway's Castle Class engines'. This design was originally built by Dübs & Co. for the Highland Railway back in 1900, and all the subsequent examples, including the 50 for France, were constructed at Queen's Park Works. The main differences were modifications to suit the Continental loading gauge, and inclusion of air brake equipment, to fit with the standard practices in France.

The most important period, so far as European railway orders arriving at Springburn was concerned, came during the first couple of years of the First World War. The twelve orders placed between 1915 and 1917 included the 0-4-4-0 'Pechot' type for the French War Office, conventional 4-6-0 and 2-8-0 tender engines, and a 2-8-2T design for

Paris suburban workings. Amongst the most impressive were perhaps the De Glehn compound Pacifics, ordered by French State Railways in 1915, of which no fewer than 40 were built at Queen's Park. In fact, these locomotives were similar in almost all respects to those in service on the Chemins de Fer de L'Etat, and were large, complex locomotives. The De Glehn compound principle was used on locomotives for a number of railways around the world, including those of British colonies, in India, and South America, but apart from the solitary experiment on the GWR, never caught on in Britain.

Under NBL order numbers L660 and L661, 40 De Glehn compound Pacifics, and 80 2-8-0 Consolidation types were built during 1915 and 1916. Hyde Park built the 2-8-0s, whilst the Pacifics came from Queen's Park Works. A further 50 Pacifics were to have been built at Queen's Park in late 1916 and 1917, under order L680, but this order was cancelled, and NBL built only another five of these engines during the First World War. Ordering of the 2-8-0s by the French Government continued up until 1917, when 25 were built under order L690. This order became the last main line steam type built by North British for France, and only Spain placed another order with the company for steam, but not until after World War II.

The main dimensions of the Pacifics and 2-8-0s for France were:

Order No.	L660 & L687
Works Nos	21276-21315 (L660)
	21763-21767 (L687)
Wheel arrangement	4-6-2
Wheel dia.	
coupled	6ft 4.37in
bogie	3ft 1.7in
trailing	4ft 0.4in
Heating surface	
evaporative	2,281.64 sq ft
superheater	683.51 sq ft
total	2,965.15 sq ft
Grate area	45.962 sq ft
Cylinders (4)HP	16.53in x 25.60in
LP	25.19in x 25.60in
Boiler pressure	227.5 lb/sq in
Tractive effort @ 50% bp	20,760 lb
Fuel capacity	
coal	5.9 tonnes
water	4,840 gallons
Weight in w.o.	
engine	95 tons 1 cwt
tender	51 tons 13 cwt
total	146 tons 14 cwt

In construction, these locomotives were not a simple design, naturally, with the outside, high pressure cylinders operated by piston valves, and the inside, low pressure cylinders, by balanced slide valves. The drive, with Walschaerts valve gear, was divided, with the low pressure cylinders driving the leading axle, and the high pressure, the centre axle. Under the De Glehn-Bousquet system, these engines could operate as four-cylinder simple, with an air operated servo motor actuating an intercepting valve, to provide maximum traction. The bypass valves for the high pressure cylinders were also operated by a pneumatic servo motor. The Fives-Lille air-compressors were carried alongside the smokebox, and in addition to the control valves, supplied air for the Westinghouse type brake system. The boiler was described in the contemporary press as being of 'great size', with a distance between tubeplates of over 19ft, and an internal diameter of more than 5ft 6in. The firebox, with its large rocking grate was 6ft wide at the rear, extending over the frames, but narrow at the front, to fit between them. The design gave a large grate area, without over complicating construction, and originally appeared on the Paris–Orleans Railway. North British supplied both locomotives and tenders, with the latter carried on a pair of four-wheeled bogies, and the locomotive and tender weighing in at almost 150 tons.

The freight locomotives ordered at the same time, were simple expansion engines, which was not then standard practice in France, where the majority of steam types were of compound design. There were many similarities with the

Pacific types, especially with the boiler fittings, and aspects of the general design. In all, NBL built 180 of these 2-8-0s, with most constructed at Hyde Park, but 25 were built at Atlas Works in 1917, under order L688. The main dimensions were:

Order No.	L661, L681, L688 & L690
Works Nos	21316-21395 (L661)
	21608-21657 (L681)
	21558-21582 (L688)
	21583-21607 (L690)
Wheel arrangement	2-8-0
Wheelbase	
coupled	16ft 8.8in
total	24ft 11.2in
Wheel dia.	
coupled	4ft 8.6in
leading	2ft 9.4in
Heating surface	
evaporative	1,843.96 sq ft
superheater	394.00 sq ft
total	2,237.96 sq ft
Grate area	34.01 sq ft
Cylinders (2)	23.23in x 25.60in
Boiler pressure	170.6 lb/sq in
Tractive effort @ 75% bp	31,140 lb
Fuel capacity	
coal	5.0 tonnes
water	3,960 gallons
Weight in w.o.	
engine	73 tons 17 cwt
tender	34 tons 6 cwt
total	118 tons 3 cwt

The boiler itself was slightly larger in diameter, at 5ft 7in, than on the Pacifics, and fitted with the Robinson type superheater. The main difference in appearance though, was

Orders from European railways were less frequent after the First World War, and these complicated looking 4-6-0s were built at Atlas Works (L662) in 1916. No less than 40 locomotives were delivered to the Paris–Orleans Railway, but the tenders were not part of the order, and were built in France.

Mitchell Library Collection

the use of a round topped firebox, narrowed in to fit between the engine's frames. The tender was again similar to the Pacific locomotives, though smaller in size.

Whilst the French State Railways provided most work for NBL at this time from Europe, the Paris–Orleans Railway placed three orders. The first was for a batch of 40 4-6-0 locomotives, in 1915, to order L662, constructed at Atlas Works, but supplied without tenders. A second order for the 2-8-2 suburban tank engines, as mentioned earlier, was placed in 1916, but construction and delivery was suspended due to the hostilities. These 50 2-8-2 tank engines, as order L682, do not appear again in the company's records, even after the end of the war. The 4-6-0 design was produced by the railway company, and built at Atlas Works. The boiler, with a Belpaire type firebox, was fitted with a Schmidt type superheater, carrying 21 elements, and two 500mm diameter cylinders, with piston valves operated by Walschaerts valve gear. The main dimensions were as follows:

Order No.	L662
Works Nos	21396-21435
Wheel arrangement	4-6-0
Wheelbase [total]	25ft 3.19in
Wheel dia.	
coupled	5ft 9.31in
bogie	2ft 9.88in
Heating surface	
evaporative	1,429.00 sq ft
superheater	423.00 sq ft
total	1,852.00 sq ft
Grate area	29.3 sq ft
Cylinders (2)	19.69in x 25.60in
Boiler pressure	170.0 lb/sq in
Tractive effort @ 75% b.p.	18,220 lb
Weight in w.o. [engine]	67 tons 17 cwt
Axle load (max)	16 tons 7 cwt

In common with the other orders for France, the dimensions were of course metric, although they are quoted here in imperial standards, for comparison with other NBL built locomotives. The 2-8-2T for Paris suburban duties had the following main dimensions:

Order No.	L666
Works Nos	21246A-21275A
Wheel arrangement	2-8-2T
Wheelbase [total]	31ft 10in
Wheel dia.	
coupled	4ft 7.13in
bogie	2ft 9.88in
Heating surface	
evaporative	1,459.00 sq ft
superheater	423.00 sq ft
total	1,882.00 sq ft
Grate area	29.3 sq ft
Cylinders (2)	23.63in x 25.56in
Boiler pressure	170.0 lb/sq in
Tractive effort @ 75% bp	33,000 lbs
Weight in w.o. [total]	91 tons 4.5 cwt
Axle load (max)	17 tons 13 cwt
Fuel	
coal	4 tons
water	2,200 gallons

Looking at the leading dimensions, the cylinder diameter of more than 23 inches was certainly unusually large for a simple expansion locomotive. This design was produced by the railway company, and was similar, generally, to the 4-6-0 types, but with a larger boiler, and greater tractive effort. As was standard practice on the Paris–Orleans Railway, the new suburban tanks were equipped with Walschaerts valve gear. All 30 locomotives were constructed at the Queen's Park Works, alongside the De Glehn compound Pacifics.

Orders for Europe 1903–1912

Railway	Year	Order No.	Works Nos	Qty.	Works	Type
Medina del Campo [Spain]	1903	L8	16033	1	Atlas	0-8-0, same as Sharp, Stewart order E1214
Tharsis Sulphur & Copper Co.	1903	L32	16208	1	Queens Park	0-6-0T, "Class E", new design
Santander & Bilbao Rly.	1903	L41	16285	1	Atlas	4-4-0T, similar to Sharp, Stewart order 4869
Rio Tinto Zinc	1904	L81	16590-02	3	Queens Park	0-6-0T
Santander & Bilbao Rly.	1904	L86	16606	1	Atlas	4-4-0T, similar to L41
Great Southern of Spain Rly.	1905	L105	16726-31	6	Hyde Park	2-6-0
Tharsis Sulphur & Copper Co.	1905	L107	16733-34	2	Queens Park	0-6-0T, "Class E", same as L32
Rio Tinto Zinc	1905	L139	17073-78	6	Queens Park	0-6-0T, same as L81
Rio Tinto Zinc	1905	L163	17303-4	2	Hyde Park	2-8-0, similar to L100, for Argentina
San Martin (Spain)	1905	L140	17079-81	3	Queens Park	4-4-0T, similar to Dübs order 4345E for Vasco Asturiania
Vasco Asturiania Rly. (Spain)	1905	L158	17265	1	Queens Park	4-4-0T, similar to L141
Sierra Minera Rly. [Spain]	1906	L178	17401-09	9	Atlas	4-8-0
Medina del Campo [Spain]	1906	L200	17647-48	2	Atlas	4-6-0, to Sharp, Stewart drawings
Tharsis Sulphur & Copper Co.	1906	L222	17850-51	2	Queens Park	0-8-0T, "Class F", new design
Medina del Campo [Spain]	1906	L234	17919	1	Atlas	4-6-0, to Sharp, Stewart drawings, same as L200
Rio Tinto Zinc	1907	L240	18023-34	12	Queens Park	0-6-0T
Sierra Minera Rly. [Spain]	1907	L252	18093-97	5	Atlas	4-8-0, same as L174 for metre gauge
Rio Tinto Zinc	1907	L275	18320-23	4	Queens Park	0-6-0T, similar to L193 for Argentina
Vasco Asturiania Rly. (Spain)	1908	L295	18447-48	2	Queens Park	2-6-2T
Rio Tinto Co.	1908	L304	18587-92	6	Queens Park	0-6-0T, similar to L240
Rio Tinto Co.	1908	L310	18626-27	2	Hyde Park	0-6-0T, similar to L163
Medina del Campo [Spain]	1908	L330	18775-77	3	Atlas	4-6-0, similar to L234
Sierra Minera Rly. [Spain]	1909	L350	18918-19	2	Atlas	0-6-6-0 Mallet compound (4-cylinders)
Sierra Minera Rly. [Spain]	1909	L368	19018	1	Atlas	0-6-2T, similar to Sharp, Stewart order E1192
Rio Tinto Co.	1909	L370	19020-21	2	Queens Park	0-6-0T, similar to L240/L304
Rio Tinto Co.	1909	L391	19148-51	4	Queens Park	0-6-0T, similar to L240/L304
Sierra Minera Rly. [Spain]	1910	L416	19323-24	2	Atlas	0-6-6-0 Mallet compound (4-cylinders), similar to L350

Railway	Year	Order No.	Works Nos	Qty	Works	Type
Portuguese State Rly.	1910	L421	19335-37	3	Queens Park	2-8-0, 4-cyl. compound to NBL design
Vasco Asturiania Rly. (Spain)	1910	L441	19506	1	Queens Park	2-6-2T, similar to L295
French State Railways	1911	L442	19507-36	30	Queens Park	4-6-0, similar to Highland Rly "Castle" class
French State Railways	1911	L444	19537-56	20	Hyde Park	4-6-0, same as L442
Rio Tinto Co.	1911	L464	19675-76	2	Queens Park	0-6-0T, similar to L391
Tharsis Sulphur & Copper Co.	1912	L489	19824	1	Queens Park	0-8-0T, "F Class", same as L222
Sierra Minera Rly. [Spain]	1912	L531	20182-83	2	Atlas	4-8-0, same as L252
Tharsis Sulphur & Copper Co.	1913	L583	20567	1	Queens Park	0-6-0T, "Class E", same as L107
Tharsis Sulphur & Copper Co.	1914	L623	20993	1	Queens Park	0-8-0T, "F Class", same as L489
Tharsis Sulphur & Copper Co.	1930	L871	24034-37	4	Hyde Park	2-8-0T, to Hohenzollern drawings

Country	No. of orders	No. of engines	Avg. engines/order
France	2	50	25
Spain	17	43	2.53
Portugal	1	3	3
Industrial	17	55	3.24
Total	37	151	4.08

Orders for Europe 1913–1928

Railway	Year	Order No.	Works Nos	Qty	Works	Type
Silla a Cullera Rly.	1914	L613	20935	1	Atlas	2-4-0T
French War Office	1915	L650	21183-97	15	Atlas	0-4-4-0 'Pechot Type' for 600mm gauge war service
French State Railways	1915	L660	21276-315	40	Queens Park	4-6-2 4-cyl. De Glehn compound, to French design
French State Railways	1915	L661	21316-95	80	Hyde Park	2-8-0 to French State Railways design
Paris–Orleans Railway	1915	L662	21396-435	40	Atlas	4-6-0, to Paris–Orleans design, no tenders supplied
Paris–Orleans Railway	1915	L666	21246A-75A	30	Queens Park	2-8-2T to Paris–Orleans Rly. design
French State Railways	1916	L680	21558-607*	0	Queens Park	4-6-2 De Glehn compound – order cancelled
French State Railways	1916	L681	21608-57	50	Hyde Park	2-8-0, same as L661
Paris–Orleans Railway	1916	L682	21658-707	50	Queens Park	2-8-2T, same as L666, but order suspended
French State Railways	1916	L687	21763-67	5	Queens Park	4-6-2, 4-cyl. De Glehn compound, same as L660
French State Railways	1917	L688	21558-82	25	Atlas	2-8-0, same as L681
French State Railways	1917	L690	21583-607	25	Hyde Park	2-8-0, same as L681
Andalous Railway Co.	1918	L708	22094-98	5	Queens Park	2-8-0, similar to L575
Portuguese State Railways	1920	L745	22708-15	8	Queens Park	2-8-0, to railway company's design – new type

* These works numbers were reallocated to order L688 and L690

Country	No. of orders	No. of engines	Avg. engines/order
France	12	360	30
Spain	2	6	3
Portugal	1	8	8
Total	15	374	24.93

The 2-8-0 freight locomotive brought the end of orders to Europe in 1920, when the Portuguese State Railways came to Springburn, for eight engines, under order number L745. Between 1903 and 1928 though, the European markets for NBL built steam locomotives all but disappeared, with the company delivering 6.8% of its output to the Continent. Compared with India, taking 38.4% of that output, or South America taking 23.2%, the European railway market was small. Of course, NBL had to compete not only with the European railways themselves, but also, the major builders. Overall, up to the company's silver jubilee year, 1928, a review of the sources of the company's orders confirms its then dependence on the British Empire, and its railway systems. The mid 1920s though marked the beginning of a long, slow decline, with the production peaks much less marked than the troughs. From the mid 1920s, to the very early post Second World War years, the company closed the Atlas Works, and built only a small number of steam locomotives. However, many of those locomotives were amongst the most famous products of the North British Locomotive Co., and have been preserved for posterity around the world.

5

Growth and Development to 1953

Having established the new company, partly as a trade protection measure, and partly to counter the expansion of the foreign competitors like Baldwin of the USA, how did NBL fair in its first 50 years? The new organisation that emerged in 1903 inherited the experience and reputation of three famous locomotive building concerns, but it had somehow to weld these separate organisations together to continue to survive. That it was in fact able to do so quite early on, and retain a good market share, was at once a tribute to employers and employees alike, and testimony of the importance of the former British Empire to the new company's fortunes.

The headquarters of the new organisation were set up in the heart of Glasgow's Springburn District, synonymous with locomotives and railways. In Springburn, the North British Railway established its works, at Cowlairs, whilst the Caledonian Railway's plant was at St Rollox. Added to this, by 1903 were the Hyde Park Works of Neilson, Reid & Co., and across the North British Railway's tracks from Springburn station, was Sharp, Stewart & Co.'s Atlas Works. All in all a formidable array of locomotive building talent, and railways dominated the social and economic life of the area. To the people who lived in Springburn, and to the thousands of railway workers, the new company was forever known as 'The Combine'. In terms of the overall performance of 'The Combine', there were in the first 50 years, four clearly identifiable phases. The first phase was the pre-First World War period, the second included the war years and immediately after, whilst the third included the

economic depression, and lasted from the mid 1920s to the outbreak of World War II. The fourth, and final phase in this half century review, began with the increase in production for the war effort in 1939–1945, and the complete change of direction that took place in the industry from the late 1940s to 1953.

The Early Years – 1903 to 1914

Throughout the decade which followed the company's formation, the total output, numbers of employees, and profits, continued to be sustained at a high level. In the first five years, the trading profit never fell below £150,000, reaching a peak of £206,394 in 1905. In that year, 572 steam locomotives were delivered, with an average value of just less than £3,000 each. Also in that same year, NBL employees reached a total of 7,363, with an average weekly wage that varied from 26s 11d to 29s (£1.33 to £1.45), depending on which works was paying the wage. Apart from the fact that wages varied according to skills, responsibilities, and other factors, the three works paid at different rates. It was curious too, that, even a decade after its formation, this anomaly still applied. Back in the 1890s, when Sharp, Stewart & Co. moved to Glasgow from Manchester, one of the compelling reasons for the move, was the lower rates of pay to workmen in Glasgow, compared with Manchester. Ironically, back in 1905, workers at Atlas Works, across the railway line from Hyde Park, average weekly pay was 1s (5p) a week more, and no less than 2s 1d (10p) more than the average paid out at the former Dübs works south of the Clyde!

The total number of employees on the books at all three works peaked in 1907, when 7,854 were recorded. The maximum numbers employed at Hyde Park reached a peak in that year, with 3,474 on the books, whilst Glasgow (later Queen's Park), reached its maximum peak in 1908, with 2,424, and Atlas in 1906, when 1,970 were at work there. In Govan, the outbreak of war in 1914 brought a sudden and

A scene typical of British Empire days, showing one of the bar-framed Pacifics built for Sudan Railways in 1911. North British locomotives were at work all over the world, and this view shows one of the locomotives built at Hyde Park Works in the prosperous years before the First World War. The photograph was taken in the Sudan soon after delivery.

Mitchell Library Collection

The massive MH class, articulated locomotives, were built to order L620 at Queen's Park, and this was the second order received from South African Railways in March 1914. These five 2-6-6-2 Mallets carried works numbers 20958–20962, and were given running numbers 1661–1665 by SAR. They were massively proportioned 4-cylinder compounds, with a pair of 20in high pressure, and a pair of 31.5 in low pressure cylinders with a common stroke of 26in. They were of course, not the last articulated locomotives built for SAR.

Mitchell Library Collection

dramatic increase in staff, and in the last year of the period under review, some 3,058 employees were recorded. Employees were not all permanent, and workmen were taken on in gangs, by foremen in order to get the job done, and then dismissed when demand for their skills fell. This common practice throughout the engineering industry, whether railway, shipbuilding, or other heavy engineering, was clearly reflected in the case of NBL, when comparing engines built to numbers employed.

In 1904, Hyde Park employed 3,233, and delivered 210 locomotives, at an average value of £3,611 per engine. The 3,474 employed in the peak year of 1907, produced 250, at an average value of £3,915 per locomotive. The 1,865 strong workforce of the neighbouring Atlas Works constructed some 128 engines, with an average value of £2,946 each. By 1907, curiously, the same number of locomotives were delivered, but from a workforce that had grown to 1,966, and with the average value of locomotives built reaching £3,967. South of the river, the Glasgow Locomotive Works in Govan produced 154 locomotives with a workforce of 2,366 in 1904, and 167 engines in 1907, with a workforce of 2,414. In 1907, the Glasgow

Locomotive Works had become NBL's Queen's Park Works, and the average value of its output had risen to £3,733, from £3,618 in 1904. In terms of the average number of employees needed to build the locomotives, for Hyde Park, these had changed from eleven per engine in 1905, to 14 per engine in 1907. For the remaining works, Atlas required an average of 13 to build each engine in 1905, and 15 in 1907, whilst Queen's Park needed 14 in 1907, compared with 15 in 1905. On the basis of these simple statistics, it would seem that the Atlas and Hyde Park works were less productive in manpower terms than the Queen's Park Works. 1907 was also the year that NBL consolidated its administrative activities in Springburn, and initiated the construction of the Flemington Street headquarters building.

The wages bills for each of the three sites, as noted earlier was different, and in 1905, was £4,400 for Hyde Park, £3,175 for Queen's Park, and £2,708 for Atlas Works. By 1907, the bills had increased to £5,315, £3,548 and £3,067 per week respectively. For the year, this averaged out to a total of £534,716, or a little over 25% of the total value of locomotives delivered in 1907, back in 1905 it had been a little under 32%, so there had been some overall improvement in productivity. Between 1907, and 1914, average wages paid fell to a low of just over 25s a week in 1909, but climbed again to more than 31s a week in 1914. The value of NBL's output fluctuated in a similar way, but was con-

These Class N 0-6-6-0 Mallet locomotives were built to order L517 in 1912/13, for Burma Railways. They were metre gauge compounds, and carried works numbers 20077–20080.

Mitchell Library Collection

Another unusual order for NBL, were these 2ft gauge 0-4-0 saddle tanks, for the Darjeeling to Himalaya Railway. This example builder's No. 20144, dates from 1913, but the design was originally built by Dübs & Co. before the turn of the century. Happily at least, one of the Darjeeling tanks is preserved, at the Indian National Railway Museum, in New Delhi.

Mitchell Library Collection

sistently totalling more than £1.25 million annually, and frequently more than £1.5 million. NBL, in this early phase was what would nowadays be described as a 'blue chip' company, and few better places could be found for investment capital in manufacturing industry in the UK.

The products of NBL were, as described elsewhere, used all over the world, and on many, and indeed most home railways. Between the formation of 'The Combine', and the outbreak of war, no less than 4,862 engines were constructed in Glasgow, and the company employed an average of 7,257 people. The company did not establish its own overseas offices until many years later, but continued to sell its locomotives through agents, just as the three predecessor companies had done. In 1912, the London agents and office was at Messrs Browning & Bertram, 17 Victoria Street, Westminster, and for overseas orders included the following representatives:

Argentina—   Franklin & Herrera Ltd, Buenos Aires
Australia —   Gilbert Lodge & Co., Sydney
West. Australia —John Denny, Perth
China —   Jardine Matheson & Co., Hong Kong &
                   Shanghai
Chile —   Don Domingo Merry Del Val, Santiago
Spain —   Sheldon Goenaga & Co., Bilbao
Portugal —   A.W. Paterson, Lisbon

It is interesting to note of course that India and Africa are excluded from the above list, where, perhaps with the exception of South America, NBL supplied the largest number of steam locomotives.

Back in 1907, the new company notified the commercial world that it was planning to build its new offices, and selected six architects to submit plans with accompanying

costs, for the proposed new office building. The company provided initial design parameters, including sketch plans, and stated that all proposals submitted by the short-listed architects would need to be constrained within a £50,000 budget. In addition, the company would pay 50 guineas to each of the architects who submitted their designs, but were not successful. All of the designs were to become NBL property, and the architect whose plans were the most suitable would get 100 guineas if he was not appointed to complete the task. The successful architect received a commission on the cost of the work, after those costs were agreed by the company.

The chief features of the building, which was constructed around a central quadrangle, were steel framing, fireproof floors, walls and roof, and the walls facing the central quadrangle faced with white, glazed bricks. The main purpose was to provide a well lit ventilated building, which the NBL directors emphasised in their invitation to tender document. They were also at pains to point out that, with the main frontage being only on Flemington Street, the remaining wings of the building should be in the plainest style. The entire top floor was given over to drawing offices, where the maximum possible light was available, and daylight was reflected off the white painted walls, ceilings and support pillars. The building also contained the board room, shipping and general administrative offices.

Bringing all the drawing office and administrative staff together under one roof had taken more than six years, with construction of the new building completed in the summer of 1909. To mark the occasion, the building, with its impressive, but not elaborate Flemington Street facade, was opened on 10th September 1909 by the Rt Hon. The Earl of Roseberry. A garden party was held within the building's internal quadrangle, and on such an occasion NBL was feeling justifiably proud of its achievements. The atmosphere has been described as being typically a family one, with strong ties of company loyalty from all levels of the workforce. In view of the fact that NBL was only in 1909 bringing those staffs together, from that time on, this was perhaps marking a change in loyalties, rather than reinforcing those that existed. Certainly the state of the locomotive industry still looked relatively bouyant, with little sign of the problems to come.

In 1909 and 1910, the number of locomotives built was less than 400, and in 1910, the workforce fell by more than 1,300. Profits were down in the five years from 1909 to 1913 too, from an average of more than £180,000 between 1903 and 1908, to an average of just over £120,000 between 1909 and 1913. 1910 and 1911 were the worst years in this pre-war era, with profits down to £92,000 and £90,000 respectively, and output at 299 and 339 locomotives. The value of deliveries had fallen too, as had wages, which had been cut from the highs of 1906/7, to between 25s and 26s a week in 1909/10. 'The Combine' had built on the reputation of its predecessors during the first decade of its existence, and continued the reputation for quality engineering that made Springburn and Glasgow legendary. Although individual works were still churning out their engines with different builders' plates attached, the railway companies around the world were now dealing with North British Locomotive Co.

There is an interesting analogy with the development of the iron and steel industry at this point, which has a direct bearing on why the company began losing its market share before the First World War. In the iron and steel business, production was much less efficient in sites based in and around the Lanarkshire coalfields, taking considerably more coal to produce every ton of steel, than elsewhere in the industry. With locomotives, NBL had certainly built large numbers of locomotives every year, but they were not so cheaply, or quickly built as those of say, Baldwins in the USA. The growth of this company had been one of the driving forces behind the formation of NBL. Similarly, the strength of the pound (sterling) was to prove difficult, and although there might be a political advantage in supplying locomotives for the British Empire from Britain, they were not the cheapest, neither were they delivered as quickly.

It was becoming a difficult time for NBL, leading up to the war, and the success of the American built locomotives in India in 1903 had not been satisfactorily addressed. Both North American and German locomotive builders had succeeded in taking major orders from countries where, it was expected, that NBL would be the preferred supplier. The company to some extent was shooting itself in the foot on an occasion just before the war, when it reviewed and discussed plans with two Glasgow engineers for a diesel locomotive. At Hyde Park, the Reid's, Sir Hugh, and brother John, considered the proposal at length over a full day, but the Hyde Park hierarchy, as it has been referred to, could see no future in the diesel!

Improvements in the efficiency of steam locomotives had already been pursued by NBL, with the 'Reid-Ramsay' turbine electric locomotive, but to dismiss the diesel could be seen as a turning point. Hindsight to be fair, is a wonderful thing, but this form of alternative motive power was not resurrected after the hostilities, and that was perhaps the most costly mistake. NBL were not alone in the major steam locomotive builders in being unable to make the transition to diesel or electric traction, since arch rivals in the USA were equally unsuccessful in making the grade.

The final three years leading up to the First World War saw the workforce rise from just over 6,000 to more than 8,000 in 1914, and average wages were over 32s a week. Locomotive output climbed back almost to the boom years of 1905/6, with almost 450 engines delivered every year, the value of which had reached around £2 million by 1914. Company profits were increasing, from the low of £90,000 in 1911, and successive years brought figures of £119,000 in 1912, £147,000 in 1913 and £171,000 in 1914. This pre-war growth was soon to be supplemented in work for the

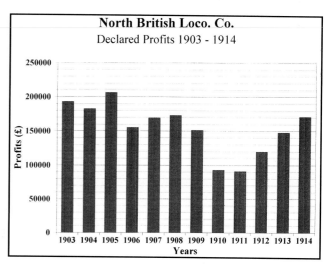

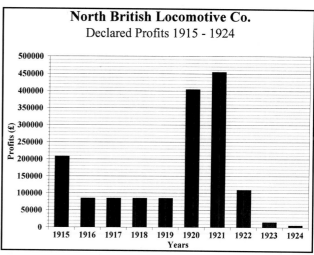

war effort too, and munitions of conflict were constructed in the NBL works at a considerable rate. Sadly too, in 1913, NBL lost another of the links with its famous founders, as J. H. Sharp, Managing Director of the Atlas Works, and formerly with Sharp, Stewart & Co., died.

The War Years and After – 1914 to 1924
In 1914, NBL had been revisiting the application of steam turbines to locomotive traction, always with a view to improving efficiency, and had embarked on two new buildings for specialised locomotive construction. In September 1914, the two new buildings, located within the area of Atlas Works, had only reached foundation level, but with the outbreak of war, it was decided they would be devoted to armaments. In fact, they produced shell cases, shells, mines, and machine gun nests. This latter was known as the

Profit/Loss 1903 to 1924			
Year	Declared Profit	Year	Declared Profit
1903	£193,065.00	1914	£171,094.00
1904	£182,704.00	1915	£207,835.00
1905	£206,394.00	1916	£84,695.00
1906	£155,520.00	1917	£84,695.00
1907	£169,411.00	1918	£84,694.00
1908	£173,006.00	1919	£84,695.00
1909	£151,166.00	1920	£404,503.00
1910	£92,899.00	1921	£454,741.00
1911	£90,954.00	1922	£109,242.00
1912	£119,561.00	1923	£15,838.00
1913	£147,950.00	1924	£6,081.00

'Hobbs machine gun casemate', or 'pill box', and consisted of a bullet-proof revolving shield over a cage, let into the ground, and with a dug-out alongside it, with space for two men. The new buildings were named the 'Mons' and 'Marne' factories, and the specialised locomotive work for which they had been planned, never fully materialised. Statistically, the two munitions factories within Atlas Works produced a total of 864,551 shells, and during the course of the war 806 women and 275 men were directly employed on these products. Another interesting, non-locomotive product to emerge from the works during the war was a number of two-seater biplanes, for service with the Royal Flying Corps, and assembled at NBL almost as a kit of finished parts.

The traditional foundries, boiler and erecting shops of the Atlas, Queen's Park and Hyde Park works were occupied with the implements of war too. Here, gun carriages, military bridges, machine tools, torpedo tubes and tanks were constructed, whilst among the less usual products of engineering works, were artificial limbs for the disabled. With the devotion of so much of the capacity of NBL's works to the war effort, the company still managed to build an average of just under 250 locomotives annually, between 1915 and 1918.

One of the most interesting developments during the war was the design and construction of Mark VIII tanks for the British Army. Almost every component of these tanks, excepting the engine, was built on NBL premises, and the testing was done on-site at Hyde Park, under the watchful eye of one Winston Churchill. The tanks were constructed in the Tank Shop, just along Flemington Street from the headquarters building, and opposite Hyde Park Works. During the hostilities, the Administration Block was given over to the Red Cross, and the five wards of the Springburn 'Red Cross' hospital cared for 8,000 patients between its opening in December 1914, and May 1918. A bronze plaque commemorated the work of the Springburn Red Cross hospital, and a stained glass memorial window was installed in the main entrance hall, dedicated to the company's employees who died in the services during the war. At the end of the war, in 1918, 'The Combine' lost one of the last links with its oldest constituent company, as J. F. Robinson, son of John Robinson of Sharp, Stewart & Co., died.

The number of employees on the company books between 1915 and 1918 varied between 6,905 in 1915, to 6,192 in 1918, whilst the number of orders received at the same time totalled 69. The largest number of orders, 23, was taken in 1915, although the value of deliveries was much less in 1915, than in 1918, when only 16 orders were received – seven of which were from the Ministry of Munitions, for 241 'ROD' type 2-8-0s. During the war, average wages increased significantly, from 35s to 37s a week in 1915, to more than 60s a week in 1918, but despite the war time allowances, the highest rates paid were not reached until 1920. Company profits were declared annually in 1914 and 1915, at £171,000 and £207,000, respectively, but no more accounts were declared until 1919.

In that year, a cumulative account for the years from 1916 to 1919 was published, and 'The Combine' recorded profits of £338,783 for the four-year period.

Locomotive weights, average per engine, and the numbers of men required to build each engine, could be seen as measures of technological change and productivity. In 1914, at the outbreak of war, a total of 469 engines had been built, from a total combined workforce of 8,151, or a little more than 17 for every locomotive delivered. The average weight of each locomotive delivered had reached 85 tons, a figure which ten years earlier had been 67 tons, when 492 locomotives were built by a workforce of 7,464. Such figures clearly have to be interpreted carefully, though certainly as far as average weights were concerned, the general trend was a move towards heavier, more powerful locomotives. On the other hand, does the fact that the number of men needed to build each engine rose from 15 to 17 accurately indicate a decline in productivity?

In 1915, the first full year of hostilities, locomotive output was down to 268, from a total workforce of 6,905, which averaged out at more than 24 employees per locomotive built. Of course, many of the employees were producing armaments, and the machinery of war, so this is not a true or fair measure of the locomotive productivity of NBL at this time. By 1918, at the end of the war, the workforce had been reduced to 6,192, and had constructed some 252 steam engines. This also averaged out at 24 men employed per locomotive delivered, so it may be said that, given the effort put in on other engineering products, productivity had marginally improved when compared with that of 1915. Locomotive average weights had changed over this time too, from fractionally less than 83 tons in 1915, to almost 95.5 tons in 1918. In the same way, the average value of each locomotive had changed too, from around £5,635 in 1915, to £8,611 in 1918 – an increase of more than 50%! The value of deliveries in these last war years, and immediately afterwards, seemed out of proportion to the number of locomotives built, including duplicates, spares, and other equipment.

Take the example of the Hyde Park Works' output, when from 1915, the number of recorded deliveries was 125 engines, with a total value of £754,019. By 1918, eight less engines (117) were recorded as being delivered, but the value was recorded as £1,019,050. For the neighbouring Atlas Works, 62 engines were built, with a value of £252,814 in 1915, but by 1918, the 55 engines built were valued at £423,357. South of the Clyde, Queen's Park's output had changed little, delivering 81 in 1915, and 80 in 1918, but the value was recorded as £503,425 in 1915, and £727,633 in 1918. At the end of the war, the engines produced by Queen's Park Works had gained the most individual value, at more than £9,000, compared with those of Hyde Park, at £8,700, while Atlas products were a bargain, at an average value of £7,697. Clearly these values are impacted by other work, since only a few years later, average values had come down to their immediate pre-war levels.

At the start of the 1920s, deliveries had not climbed back to pre-war levels, although 1919 gave every indication that prosperity was forthcoming, with 15 orders for 334 locomotives. More than 2,000 workers had been taken on, taking the workforce to its highest ever level, and average wages were more than 72s a week. The NBL employees were amongst the most well paid, as well as the most respected in the locomotive business. Profits were up too, along with the recorded value of locomotives delivered, with the former reaching more than £400,000 in 1920 and 1921. However, all was not good, and although a total of 19 orders were taken in 1920, this fell away dramatically in 1921 to only four.

The company's immediate response to this was a cut in wages and employees, with the workforce falling from its high of 8,262 in 1919, to only just over 4,000 in 1922. This marked a major turning point in the company's fortunes, and the effect was noticed as far away as India, where NBL had recovered its fortunes so well immediately after the war. In Calcutta, in 1922, a press report noted that many men had been discharged from the Atlas Works, as a result of the slump in locomotive orders. The 1922 annual report reflected the growing doom and gloom, commenting on the curtailment of orders, as a result of 'unparalleled trade depression'. In the technical press the company reported

Ordered in 1923 from NBL, there were 15 of these Class 8E 2-6-4 tank engines, built at Queen's Park to order 783. Put to work on the suburban passenger services of the Buenos Aires Great Southern Railway, the design was new, and developed by Hawthorn, Leslie, who supplied the drawings to NBL.

Mitchell Library Collection

that it was arranging the work to support the maximum number of men, although it did not say what it was doing to pursue alternative work, and as happened again in the 1930s, waited for the recession to go away. The years 1921 and 1922 were really bad, with the company receiving only four orders in 1921, and eight in 1922, for a total of 263 and 108 engines. Profits fell from £454,000 to £109,000, and yet the company were still able to declare dividends to shareholders of 10% in both years.

On a lighter note, 9th March 1921 was something of a red letter day for NBL, when the then Prince of Wales, later, and for a short time King Edward VIII, visited the works. NBL was no stranger to visiting dignitaries, having entertained VIP's from as far afield as China and the Far East, where railways had placed orders for steam engines with the company. On the occasion of the Prince of Wales visit, he had been touring various engineering works in and around Glasgow, including John Browns shipyard where, ironically, he launched the steamer *Windsor Castle*. The Prince unveiled the war memorial window in the entrance hall of NBL's Flemington Street headquarters, and during a works tour, took a hand in casting copper commemorative discs. At the same time, one of NBL's most celebrated employees at that time, one Robert Downie, was presented with the Military Medal. As Sergeant Robert Downie, he

was amongst the first NBL employees to enlist in 1914, and had won the Victoria Cross, with which he had been presented by King George V. On the prestigious occasion in March 1921, the Prince, accompanied by the families Lorimer and Reid, amongst others, were photographed in front of a recently completed 0-6-2 tank engine, No. 1759, for the Great Northern Railway – another of Mr Nigel Gresley's stars.

The last two years of the period under review saw some quite dramatic changes, though the company's financial results were bolstered by the regular transfers from the reserves, which had been built up in the more prosperous years. Average wages had been cut by more than 33% in 1922, and although incoming orders had climbed into double figures in 1923 and 1924, the number of engines delivered was down to 133 and 87. The company was not doing well, although financially it was keeping its head above water, and the worsening troubles in British industry generally were adding to the problems.

Of the eight orders received in 1922, two were from English Electric, for the bodies and mechanical parts for 26 1,200hp and eight 1,800hp electric locomotives, for the 3ft 6in gauge railways of Japan. Such sub-contracting work was not repeated for more than 20 years, although NBL was looking to diversify at the time, it apparently did not take

The Wembley Exhibition year – 1924 – also saw NBL receive order L793, for ten of these Class P Pacifics for Western Australia. The designs were produced in conjunction with the railway company, and originally carried running numbers 441 to 450, this being No. 443.

Mitchell Library Collection

this type of business too seriously. Although, two years later, in 1924, the Reid-McLeod geared turbine was selected as the exhibit from NBL for the British Empire Exhibition at Wembley. This innovative work, begun before the First World War was aimed at improving the efficiency of steam traction, and reducing the fuel costs for the railways. Output continued at a low level, and the notice which appeared in the Calcutta newspaper contained the observation that although large numbers of men had been discharged from the Atlas Works, it was not the company's plan to close it completely.

In 1923, the year of the formation of the 'Big Four' railways in Britain, Atlas Works ceased to build locomotives as it had done previously. The last order to be allocated for construction there was L776, a batch of six B class 4-6-0s for the metre gauge South Indian Railway. The works had only built 23 locomotives in that year, all of which were B class for India, the final locomotive bearing works number 23038, was outshopped in May 1923. The men recorded as working at Atlas numbered 649 in 1923, reducing to 206 in the following year, and it marked the end of the Sharp, Stewart and Sharp Brothers tradition of locomotive building. Since the formation of NBL in 1903, the Atlas Works in Springburn had constructed 1,700 locomotives, and the year closed with perhaps more difficult years ahead.

At the opposite end of the African continent, Egypt continued to provide a reasonable source of orders for the standard gauge. These Moguls were ordered in 1925, (L841 and L842), with 20 built at Hyde Park, and another 20 at Queen's Park. Engine No. 547 was one of the Hyde Park batch.

Mitchell Library Collection

Not all of the NBL-built steam types for South Africa were an unqualified success, and the 50 engines of Class 19C fell into the less successful category. This was a new design, ordered in 1934 (L887), and built in 1935 at Hyde Park. These locomotives were fitted with 'RC' poppet valve gear, in place of the conventional Walschaerts type. The cams and rollers proved to wear excessively, and they were not good when working long distances in back gear. They were removed from their original suburban duties to branch line turns, and spent most of their working lives in the Western Cape area.

Mitchell Library Collection

The Great Depression and World War II

Starting the mid 1920s in a depression, NBL continued to reflect the dismal state of the locomotive industry, and the barriers to free trade set up by traditional markets for steam, like Australia, were a great problem. NBL had never effectively countered the prodigious output of Baldwin and other North American locomotive builders, and the high value of the £ sterling gave German locomotive builders a major advantage. They were able to win orders, like the Americans, in many British colonies, since NBL simply could not compete on price. A report in the *Railway Gazette* for 1926 states that contracts were secured at an 'unremunerative level'. The mid 1920s saw dividends to shareholders reduced to 5%, and the financial reserves were being depleted by the transfer of large sums of money, often as much as £80,000 annually, in order to show a profit. Even so, in 1924, NBL's declared profit had sunk to only £6,000, but boosted by the transfers from the reserve funds, increased to £13,000 and £14,000 in 1925 and 1926. By 1927, the position had become very serious indeed, and the company was close to extinction, declaring an average of

North British built the very first of the Great Western Railway's 0-6-0 57XX series pannier tanks, and No. 5718 was one of the first order, L582. It was built at Hyde Park Works, and carried works number 23835. Here seen in the summer of 1954 on shed at Westbury.

Roger Shenton

just over £1,500 profit annually between 1928 and 1931. These profits though were only recorded as a result of transferring huge sums from the reserves, and in fact, most years at this time resulted in trading losses. In common with other builders, in order to retain their market share, NBL were tendering for orders at unprofitable prices. Sadly, worse was to come, and the company was only really rescued by the engineering demands of the Second World War, and a post-war 'boom' in the manufacturing industry.

In 1927, the Atlas Works was in the news again, as it was advertised for sale in the *Glasgow Herald*, but no buyer was found, and the works remained an empty shell for years. The machine tools, once the proud possession of the Sharp Stewart enterprise at the turn of the century, and described at some length in the technical press, were sold off. This was the same year that NBL were building the 'Royal Scots' for the LMSR, but although the annual number of orders placed remained in double figures until 1930, only 153 engines were built on average each year. In 1930, only eight orders were received, and 99 locomotives delivered. Of these, 25 were new 57XX 0-6-0 pannier tanks for the GWR, and the remainder were mainly industrial types for Africa, with the exception of a batch of Pacifics for China. The signs were not good for NBL at the end of the 1920s, with many of the locomotives being built to the designs of German locomotive builders, as well as arch rivals Beyer Peacock, and R. & W. Hawthorn, Leslie.

The NBL board's approach to this dramatic reversal of fortunes by comparison with pre-war years was very limited, rejecting suggestions for consolidation of the British locomotive manufacturing industry. Wm Beardmore & Co., a neighbouring engineering giant in Glasgow, had seen its market share collapse in the 1920s, despite a diverse product base. Beardmore had built steam engines in some numbers, but were not in the same league as NBL, and their lack of success in diesel engine manufacture for marine use and airship propulsion, clearly influenced some opinions on such traction for railways. Beardmore had supplied engines to English Electric for rail service at home and abroad, but the decline of the company in the 1920s prompted intervention to the level of the Bank of England, to support the ailing giant. Meanwhile, competition from outside the UK, in the railway markets of the British Empire, even for Indian orders, was growing, and was successful.

In 1929, the parlous state of British industry, the effects of ongoing depressed markets, and even social unrest was causing a major shift in opinion on how to counter the problems. One school of thought, of which NBL and its board seemed to favour, was that this was simply another of the cyclic downturns in the economy, and it was only a question of waiting until it passed. Other companies, who had not had the enormous financial reserves and standing that NBL had acquired in its specialist market, were not in such a happy position. In 1929, a proposal was made for the rationalisation of the whole British locomotive building industry, including NBL, Vulcan Foundry, Armstrong, Whitworth, Beardmore, Beyer Peacock, Robert Stephenson & Co., Hawthorn, Leslie, and others. This radical move, included plans to close down the less profitable plants, and concentrate the structure along similar lines to the now giant Baldwin company in the USA. By the summer of 1929, the

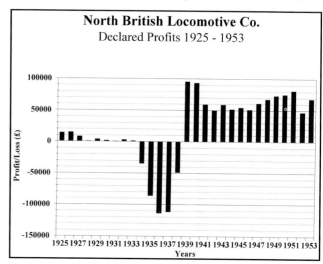

North British Locomotive Co.
Declared Profits 1925 - 1953

major builders, including Vulcan Foundry and Beyer Peacock, had agreed to the proposals, but NBL declined to consent. A watered down version of the original scheme was prepared, and Sir Hugh Reid was offered the position of chief executive in the new holding company that was to be formed. It was believed that the rationalisation of the UK locomotive industry could not have been satisfactorily completed without the participation of NBL.

The views of Sir Hugh Reid have a considerable bearing on the direction of NBL policy, and were in some ways justifiable, but the lack of co-operation in this scheme may well be seen to have had fatal consequences. The proposal for rationalisation, rejected by NBL's chairman, had been supported by the Chancellor of the Exchequer, but the meeting at which the suggestions were put to Sir Hugh Reid was described as a 'disaster'. The discussions with Sir Hugh were cited as being long and friendly, but hopeless, with the NBL chairman giving the impression of forever looking to the good old days before the war. His opposition to the rationalisation plan was perhaps curious, since his company already had one idle plant, which it had been trying to sell, but he had not been in the fortunate position of Beardmore, where the Bank of England had a special responsibility. Some locomotive builders, like Beardmore had increased their capacity to build engines, and the massive over capacity in the UK industry was stretched still further by such actions. NBL's market share potential was not helped by such actions, but by the mid-1930s, Beardmore had gone altogether from the locomotive business.

The events of the 1929/30 period set the seal on the fate of not only Beardmore, but, further into the future, NBL as well. It was apparent that diversification into diesel engine manufacture had not helped the company at all, and gave at least some justification to Sir Hugh Reid, and the NBL's view that there was no long term future, and the major business successes ahead lay with steam traction. The markets had gone by the 1930s, and the neglected new forms of electric and diesel traction were already being adopted by railways in NBL's traditional marketplaces. The adoption of the new forms of traction in massive numbers in the late 1930s and through the 1940s, proved to be the only spur to NBL's involvement.

An interesting exercise in diversification in 1930, was the acquisition of Halley Motors Ltd, a Glasgow firm, specialising in road vehicles, also based in Springburn. It was a curious, and perhaps unlikely development, although Halley Motors were referred to as one of the 'longest established commercial motor manufacturers'. If the intention was to compete with the likes of Leyland Motors, Scammell, and others, it was singularly unsuccessful, and had no impact on NBL's declining locomotive orders.

The already bad situation that had developed in the 1920s, got much worse in the 1930s, as a worldwide economic recession began to bite. Between 1930 and 1935, NBL received only 29 orders – less than five a year – and built no more than 340 locomotives. The Atlas Works were building no locomotives at all, but were still part of the NBL assets, whilst Queen's Park constructed only 52 locomotives in the five years from 1931 to 1935, and none at all in 1932 and 1933. Even the extensive resources of Hyde Park produced no locomotives in 1932, despite scheduled delivery of five engines for the Nizam's State Railway, and eight for the Tientsin–Pukow Railway in China. There are no locomotive deliveries recorded in the official NBL 'Output & Statistics' books for the year.

The effect on men and materials of the trade depression of the 1920s, and the ongoing depression of the 1930s was equally dramatic. Between 1925 and 1928, just over 200 men were still working over at the Atlas Works, but none at

all from 1929 onwards. The massive laying off of workers in the 1930s brought the workforce down, in 1932, from the record level of 8,262 in 1919, to only 389. Of these, 48 were employed at Queen's Park, and 341 at Hyde Park, at an average wage of 45s. Employment levels at the two works continued to remain low until 1939, when the gearing up for war work increased numbers. Locomotive orders had actually increased in 1936 and 1937, although Queen's Park was not officially recorded as delivering any locomotives between 1936 and 1942, while Hyde Park Works was noted as supplying all 571 locomotives built during this time. In fact, the Queen's Park site had not been allocated any locomotive orders since 1934, when order L888, a single locomotive for ICI in South Africa was produced by the former Dübs & Co. works. The next major locomotive order to be allocated directly to Queen's Park, was part of the batch of new War Department 'Austerity' 2-8-0s in 1942.

Company profitability during the 1930s took a disastrous turn, and further drawing on reserves could not halt the decline of the balance sheet into deficit. Given that orders were not coming through in any volume, and massive losses were being recorded year after year, it is little short of miraculous that this specialist steam locomotive builder survived the great depression. By far the worst year was 1936, when the company declared a loss of £113,779, although the average loss for the period 1934 to 1938 was just slightly under £80,000.

Most of the orders in the mid 1930s for service abroad were predominantly industrial and tank types, with some curiosities, such as the Sentinel geared locomotives for Egypt, and an experimental 2-10-4 for South Africa. At home, further orders were received for important new locomotives for the LMSR and LNER, such as the 4-6-0 'Jubilee' class, highly successful 2-6-4 tank engines, and new K3 class 2-6-0s. All of these were built at Hyde Park, whilst, although Queen's Park was no longer constructing engines, the delivery books recorded increasing manufacture of shells for the military in 1936 to 1938. In fact the orders being received fom 1936 onwards included work for the War Department, covering the production of light tanks.

The outbreak of war in 1939 found NBL with 2,333 employees at Hyde Park, and 431 in Queen's Park, although only eight orders for locomotives were received in that year, and 77 locomotives delivered. Prices had clearly recovered, at least on the basis of the assigned value to locomotives built, which was sustained at more than £1 million annually from 1938 onwards. Wages at the outbreak of war showed a significant recovery too, reaching 64s 5d per week for Hyde Park, and 69s 9d for Queen's Park. The latter's

Profit/Loss 1925 to 1953

Year	Declared Profit	Year	Declared Profit
1925	£113,807.00	1940	£93,262.00
1926	£14,288.00	1941	£59,296.00
1927	£7,622.00	1942	£50,145.00
1928	£317.00	1943	£59,036.00
1929	£3,641.00	1944	£51,830.00
1930	£1,668.00	1945	£54,721.00
1931	£463.00	1946	£51,340.00
1932	£2,895.00	1947	£61,185.00
1933	£1,172.00	1948	£67,810.00
1934	(£34,656.00)	1949	£73,552.00
1935	(£86,007.00)	1950	£75,150.00
1936	(£113,779.00)	1951	£81,230.00
1937	(£111,833.00)	1952	£47,008.00
1938	(£48,696.00)	1953	£68,190.00
1939	£95,602.00		

Locomotives Delivered
1904 to 1948

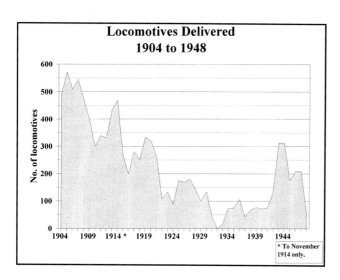

No. of locomotives

1904 1909 1914 * 1919 1924 1929 1934 1939 1944

* To November 1914 only.

Total Weight of Locomotives Delivered
1904 to 1948

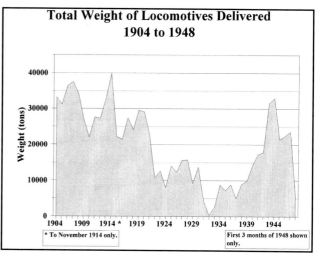

Weight (tons)

1904 1909 1914 * 1919 1924 1929 1934 1939 1944

* To November 1914 only.

First 3 months of 1948 shown only.

North British Locomotive Co.
Weight of Engines Delivered

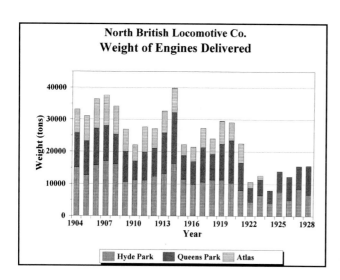

Weight (tons)

1904 1907 1910 1913 1916 1919 1922 1925 1928

Year

Hyde Park   Queens Park   Atlas

North British Locomotive Co.
Weight of Engines Delivered

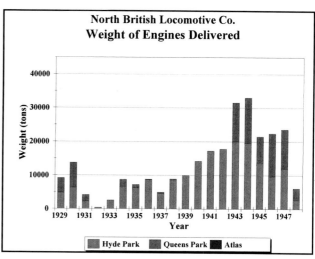

Weight (tons)

1929 1931 1933 1935 1937 1939 1941 1943 1945 1947

Year

Hyde Park   Queens Park   Atlas

Employees 1904 to 1948
Distribution Across Works

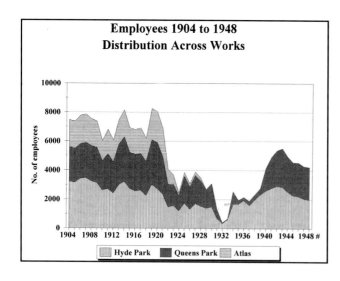

No. of employees

1904 1908 1912 1916 1920 1924 1928 1932 1936 1940 1944 1948 #

Hyde Park   Queens Park   Atlas

Average Number of Employees
1904 to 1948

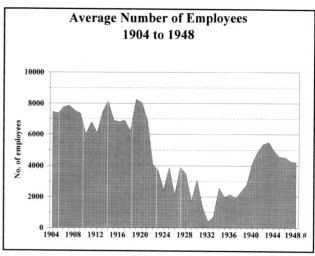

No. of employees

1904 1908 1912 1916 1920 1924 1928 1932 1936 1940 1944 1948 #

The metre gauge Pacifics for the Federated Malay States Railway, ordered in 1939 included some quite 'modern' design features, including the use of poppet valve gear. There had been two previous orders for the Class O.1 locomotives, in 1937 and 1938, but with conventional Walschaerts valve gear.

Mitchell Library Collection

employees were being paid wartime rates from 1940, and a differential of almost £1 a week existed between Hyde Park and Queen's Park. This differential was maintained throughout the war, although it was cut back slightly towards the end of hostilities. From a recorded workforce of none, Queen's Park personnel levels rose to equal, and eventually surpass those of Hyde Park, when the war ended.

The reported profits of this Second World War period were fairly consistent at just over £50,000 annually, with the company engaged in similar activities to the First World War. The most important orders were of course for locomotives, and in 1939, the Ministry of Supply decided that the locomotives to be used would be the Stanier 8F 2-8-0, which had been so successful on the LMSR. North British delivered the first of these WD versions in July 1940, and a further 132 were built by the company. However, on the locomotive front, traditional designs, such as the Stanier 8F were more complicated, costly, and in comparison with later work, slow to build. The later work that again saw the reputation of 'The Combine' returning to its former status, was the Riddles 'Austerity' design of 2-8-0 and 2-10-0. These locomotives, described elsewhere in detail, were built in huge numbers, and took advantage of different design and construction techniques, making them simpler, cheaper, and quicker to build than more traditional designs. They were extremely versatile too, and their reliability earned them years of peacetime service on British Railways and elsewhere.

The more specialist work for the war effort between 1939 and 1945 by NBL has already been mentioned, and the light tank deliveries had reached 143 by 1940. From 1940 onwards, the new 26-ton Matilda tanks were built in large numbers – 619 in all, up to 1942. The Matilda tanks were designed and developed at the Vulcan Foundry in Newton-le-Willows, and at the outbreak of war they were the heaviest tanks in service with the British Army. In both the Matilda tank and 'Austerity' locomotive production, there was a good example of the co-operation between two of the most famous steam locomotive builders. NBL's 619 Matildas kept the workforce busy until 1942, when the Ministry of Supply ordered no fewer than 545 of the newly designed 2-8-0 engines. As a result of this huge order, and subsequent orders for 150 of the 2-10-0 variety, large scale tank production was stopped. The Ministry of Supply designs were highly successful, and demanded in such numbers that Vulcan Foundry were asked to build hundreds of the 2-8-0s, before the end of the war. In total some 1,200 locomotives were supplied, along with considerable numbers of spare parts and boilers.

On pure statistics alone, the NBL contribution to the war effort was very significant, and apart from the tanks and locomotives, 1,600,000 bombs and shells were produced, along with 13,000 naval mines. NBL also constructed an armoured locomotive to War Office designs, in an effort to protect men and machine from attack from enemy aircraft. Again, as in the First World War, NBL produced some more unusual items, unusual at least for a locomotive builder – these were the 800 dough mixing bowls for the Royal Navy!

In 1945 NBL's declared profit was still over £50,000, and 4,544 men and women were employed, whose average wage had risen to an average of 116s 4d (£5.80) weekly. The 175 steam locomotives delivered in that year weighed more than 21,500 tons – an average of 122 tons each. Ten new orders were received by the company in that year too, all for steam locomotives, including 100 of the new Thompson B1 class 4-6-0s for the LNER, and 100 of the massive Class 15F 4-8-2s, and 50 of the Class 19D 4-8-2s for South Africa. This looked like an upturn in orders on a large scale, and given that the effects of the recent war were considerable, there was a potential for considerable growth. Indeed, there was a minor 'boom' in the post-war economy, which may have been seen by NBL as an indication that the waiting for the economic upturn, was over. Still, NBL was not committed to building non-steam locomotives, despite the explosive growth in diesel traction seen in the USA, whose economy had a profound effect on post-war Europe.

The North British Locomotive Co. had survived until 1945 through periods of growth and devastating depression, but its status had changed from a world leader, to a less prominent position. The pre First World War prosperity was never repeated, and the company's financial reserves were depleted rapidly in an effort to keep the company afloat during the 1930s. Its works and workforce were never fully employed until the Second World War, but its direction was never shifted completely away from steam locomotives. By the end of 1945, the writing was clearly on the wall for steam traction, although moving into the new era, the companies that were to become major players in diesel and electric traction were well established. The conversion of a steam locomotive specialist builder, to one who could build all forms of railway locomotives of every type would not be easy. NBL was not unique by any means in this aspect, and its major competition, from Baldwin and Alco in the USA, and the German builders came to experience similar problems. Here too, the lack of realisation that steam traction for railways was coming to an end was to prove a very costly mistake.

In the five years from 1946 to 1951, the company's profitability improved from declared profits of £60,000 to £81,000, and the order books were healthy. The first full year of peace however, brought the retirement of William Lorimer as Chairman, on health grounds, with the company in an optimistic mood.

On the production front, despite the difficulties of the post-war economy, NBL had begun to manufacture only locomotives before the end of hostilities, and this was to prove of some benefit. The 1946 annual meeting however optimistic sounding, indicated some of the problems to come, with statements such as 'it is hoped' that the skilled workforce on active service would return to NBL's shops. The shortage of materials and men, despite the major orders from the LNER, South Africa and India brought its own problems.

The company were not particularly enamoured of the nationalisation process, brought in with the change of government in 1945, seeing it as a 'somewhat academic creed'. The annual meetings of 1947 and 1948 brought similar reflections on commercial progress, with annual dividends of 2.5% on preference stock, and 5% on ordinary stock.

In 1947, NBL opened a South African subsidiary company – the North British Locomotive Co. (Africa) Ltd – which emphasised the importance of this market to NBL. It also followed the government's export or die approach to economic regeneration, but the potential order for 1,000 locomotives for Russia never materialised. Had this happened, then it would have been possible to re-open parts of the Atlas Works, which had been closed for more than 20 years. The other notable event of 1947, was the signing of the agreement with GEC, for the construction of diesel and electric locomotives. The mining locomotives, for which

numerous sales were made, and for which there was considerable potential, also began to appear from the works.

In the following year, and throughout 1949, orders were coming in regularly, but especially for export, and the company's financial results were very good, with dividends maintained at 5% on ordinary shares. There were further board changes in 1950, and some disappointment in the year's work, although the declared profit at more than £75,000, was a good sign. The then chairman of the board, Sir Frederick Stewart stood down, and his place was taken by J. B. Mavor, who was in turn succeeded by T. A. Crowe at the 1954 annual meeting. Mavor came from Mavor & Coulson, and in addition to his chairmanship of NBL, he was also chairman of South West Scotland Electricity Board, amongst other responsibilities. He came to the company at a time when taxation and inflation were considered by industry to be a major problem. Overall though, NBL's position looked good, but diversification was clearly in the board's mind, as they took on Henry Pels & Co., the machine tool company during 1950.

NBL's main UK competitors, Robert Stephenson & Hawthorns, and Beyer Peacock & Co. declared better results in 1950 than NBL, and provided improved returns for shareholders. NBL again in 1950 and the following year, 1951, declared a 5% dividend, but reflected on the growing competition, rising costs, and shortage of materials. The dividend policy was based on the 'need for restraint', but the disappointment in returns for 1950/51, was followed by

The Southern's Class N15 4-6-0 'King Arthur' class had a long and successful career, and lasting well into BR days. Here, as BR No. 30786, *Sir Lionel* is seen going through an overhaul at Eastleigh Works in August 1957. Comparing this with the earlier photograph, in Chapter 3, the smoke deflectors alongside the smokebox were the most obvious modification.

Roger Shenton

cially finished for the occasion. This was in fact not the real 5552, which had been built in 1934, but engine number 5642, which was the latest member of the class. The two engines had swapped running numbers especially for the event, and the new 5552 was turned out in a shiny black livery, with raised, silver coloured letters and numbers.

Curiously, in the same year that NBL was delivering its batch of 5XP's, no locomotives were ordered from the home market at all, and even the solitary 2-6-2T for ICI was destined for overseas service, in South Africa. However, in January 1935, the LNER came back to Springburn for steam locomotives, with an order for 20 of the new Gresley designed Class K3 2-6-0s. Having said they were new, the design had appeared many years earlier, in 1920, as a Mogul for the old Great Northern Railway, and subsequently developed by Gresley for work on the LNER. In 1929, modifications to the engine's suspension were introduced, forming a subclass, K3/3, although the NBL batch was included in subclass K3/2, which formed the bulk of these 2-6-0s.

Order L890, for 20 K3s was almost the last of these three-cylinder 2-6-0s for the LNER, and all were constructed at Hyde Park. The principal dimensions of these NBL built Moguls were as follows:

Order No.	L890
Works Nos	24225-24244
Class	K3
Running Nos	2425/26/27/28/38/39/40/42
	2443/47/48/49/50/51
	2459/61/63/66/67/68
Wheel arrangement	2-6-0
Wheel dia. (coupled)	5ft 8in
Wheel dia. (bogie)	3ft 2in
Heating surface	
tubes	1,719.00 sq ft
firebox	182.00 sq ft
superheater	407.00 sq ft
total	2,308.00 sq ft

Grate area	28.00 sq ft
Boiler pressure	180 lb/sq in
Cylinders(3)	18.5in x 26in
Tractive effort	30,031 lb
Weights	
engine	72tons 12cwt
tender	52tons
total	124tons 12cwt

Equipped with the renowned Gresley 'conjugated' valve gear, these engines were the last to be built for the LNER in Gresley's day, and coincidentally, the last member of the class was withdrawn in the same year that saw the demise of NBL. Including the ten built in Great Northern Railway days, there were some 192 of these 2-6-0s, with one of their number converted to two-cylinder propulsion in 1945, and reclassified K5.

The final order for steam locomotives for the home railways before World War II, came in 1935, again from the LMSR, but this time for passenger tank engines. When Stanier came to Crewe as Chief Mechanical Engineer, he found, as mentioned earlier, that the railway had a great many different locomotive designs, not all of which were suitable for their purpose. The increasing traffic demands for the LMS had already forced them to order a major express passenger type from NBL, and during Stanier's reign, the rationalisation of the motive power stock gathered considerable pace. Standardisation on a range of similar designs, from passenger, through freight, to suburban tank types was imposed, similar in some ways to the process that the Indian railways had gone through before the First World War. NBL had already designed and built the 'Royal Scot' class 4-6-0s, and had built some of Stanier's new three-cylinder 'Jubilees', and in December 1935, an order for 73 two-cylinder suburban tank engines was placed. Once again, Stanier's motive power modernisation programme had outstripped the railway workshops' own capacity, and this new 2-6-4 tank engine, first built by the LMSR in 1935, recorded more than a third of the total coming from NBL.

Under order No. L896, all 73 were constructed at Hyde Park Works in 1936, and were soon at work as general purpose motive power, throughout the LMS system. An earlier, three-cylinder version had been designed and built by the LMSR in 1934, specifically for the London, Tilbury & Southend line services. The new two-cylinder variety started with LMS running numbers 2425, and the

Typically LMS, and typically Stanier perhaps, but this 2-6-4 tank engine was built by North British in 1936, to order L896, and carried works number 24342. Equally of interest in this view, with the engine on an excursion from Wolverhampton to Alton Towers in 1956, is the train itself. The vehicles are actually ex-LMS heavyweight articulated stock, but running in British Railways colours.
Roger Shenton

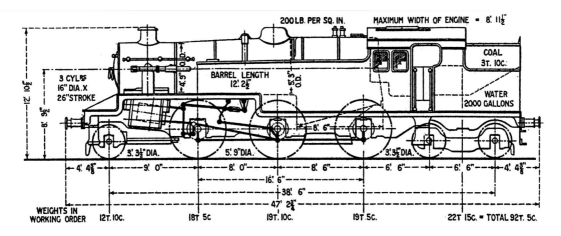

73 of these LMSR Stanier Class 4P 2-6-4 tank engines were built by NBL to order L896.

Railway Gazette

Springburn built engines carried running numbers from 2545 to 2617. The leading dimensions of this class were:

Order No.	L896
Works Nos	24301-24373
Class	4P
Running Nos	2545-2617
Wheel arrangement	2-6-4T
Wheel dia.	
(coupled)	5ft 9in
(bogie)	3ft 3.5in
Heating surface	
tubes	1,223.00 sq ft
firebox	143.00 sq ft
superheater	230.00 sq ft
total	1,596.00 sq ft
Grate area	26.70 sq ft
Boiler pressure	200 lb/sq in
Cylinders (3)	19.625in x 26in
Tractive effort	24,670 lb
Weights, total	87tons 17cwt

Stanier's designs improved the railway's ability to compete for all types of traffic with the other main line railways, and this particular tank engine design was so successful that it was later adapted as part of the standard range for British Railways. It was in turn the last order from the LMS though, and the last to be received by NBL from the home market before the outbreak of the Second World War. In fact, even at the time these locomotives were being delivered, part of the NBL works was already given over to the construction of light tanks and production of munitions. However, although as in 1914–1918, much of NBL's output was for the war effort, from 1939 to 1945, Hyde Park Works built more Stanier locomotives, but between 1939 and 1942, these were 2-8-0 locomotives for the Ministry of Supply. No less than 208 of these Stanier Class 8F designs were built, in four orders, many of which, with modifications, were for 'war service' in such locations as the Sudan, the Middle East, and Turkey.

The LMS 8F 2-8-0 was adopted by the War Department as the standard locomotive, and NBL's first order, received in December 1939 (L932), is noted in the drawing office register as built to 'LMSR drawings'. In all, some 849 of these engines were built, many by NBL's competitors, as well as the railway workshops of the GWR, LNER and Southern railways. Examples of the design could be found fitted with oil burning equipment, both for service overseas and later, for experiments on the home railways after the war, when good quality coal was in short supply.

The LMS had introduced the type in 1935, along with other new LMS 'standard' designs, and although the 2-8-0 was common on other railways, the Stanier design was the most modern, and least complicated. Having said that, it possessed, along with other Stanier types, a distinct GWR 'feel', with its taper boiler, and flat topped Belpaire firebox – not so surprising in view of Stanier's training and background at Swindon. LMS locomotives at this time could be said to be a development of GWR locomotive practice, and with the 2-8-0, the LMS men in the drawing offices contributed in no small way to the modification processes. In 1934, when the first 2-8-0 appeared, there was too much GWR influence, and the locomotive was described as heavy at the back end. To compensate for this, the drawing offices modified the design by raising the pitch of the boiler, which resulted in clearance for the rear coupled wheels, and getting the weight further forward. By the time NBL were charged with building these 2-8-0s, the design was well proven, and a large number had been built. The principal dimensions were as follows:

Order No.	L932, L936, L937, L938
Works Nos	24600-24659 (L932)
	24688-24732 (L936)
	24733-24765 (L937)
	24766-24815 (L938)
Class	8F
Running Nos.	–
Wheel arrangement	2-8-0
Wheel dia. (coupled)	4ft 8.5in
Wheel dia. (bogie)	3ft 3.5in
Heating surface	
tubes	1,479.00 sq ft
firebox	171.00 sq ft
superheater	230.00 sq ft
total	1,880.00 sq ft
Grate area	28.65 sq ft
Boiler pressure	225 lb/sq in
Cylinders(3)	18.5 x 28in
Tractive effort	32,438 lb
Weights	
engine	72tons 2cwt
tender	53tons 13cwt
total	125tons 15cwt

Almost a year after the first order for 60 (L932), NBL received a second order (L936), for 62 engines initially, but which was increased to 65, to provide replacements for three locomotives that had been destroyed. This second order carried WD running numbers 360–399, and 500–524, whilst the third order (L937), carried numbers 540–571, and 623. The final order for Stanier's LMS Class 8F 2-8-0s was placed in the late summer of 1941, as NBL order L938, for 50 engines, and which were allocated LMS running numbers 8176 to 8225.

Events that took place in the LMS motive power and mechanical engineers' departments in the early years of the war period, were to prove important for North British. The reorganisation and staff changes moved R. A. Riddles to the Ministry of Supply, where he began work on a new design of 2-8-0, similar in size to the Stanier 8F, but which could be constructed simply and quickly. The LMS Derby Locomotive Drawing Office saw some of its staff move to Glasgow, where they worked at NBL on the 2-8-0, and a follow up 2-10-0 design. In the summer of 1942, to order L943, no fewer than 545 of the Riddles 'Austerity' 2-8-0s were ordered from NBL, and built at the Hyde Park and Queen's Park works. The following summer, 1943, order L945 was placed, for a batch of 100 of the 2-10-0 'Austerity' design.

NBL had by this time, a long history, and respected reputation for being able to design and build large numbers of steam engines quickly, although its commercial fortunes were, to say the least, mixed, during the 1920s and 1930s. In January 1943, exactly 40 years after its formation, NBL delivered the first of the Riddles and NBL designed 2-8-0 'Austerity' engines. This was a very simple design, with much of the construction consisting of fabricated components, and two-cylinder propulsion, with outside, easily maintained valve gear. Had such dramatic changes in steam locomotive design been proposed at any other time, it is doubtful if such large numbers would have been ordered straight off the drawing board. NBL had been in a similar position before, with the LMSR 'Royal Scot' class, but there were only 50 on that order, and the design drew quite heavily on existing practices, particularly from the Southern Railway. The 'Austerities', both 2-8-0 and 2-10-0 versions, were a great success, and large numbers of them continued in service after World War II with British Railways. The principal dimensions of these two designs were as follows:

2-8-0 'Austerity'

Order No.	L943	
Works Nos.	25321-25435	24971-25020
	25021-25320	24891-24970

Class	WD
Wheel arrangement	2-8-0
Wheel dia.	
(coupled)	4ft 8.5in
(bogie)	3ft 2in
Heating surface	
tubes	1,412.00 sq ft
firebox	168.00 sq ft
superheater	311.00 sq ft
total	1,991.00 sq ft
Grate area	28.60 sq ft
Boiler pressure	225 lb/sq in
Cylinders (3)	19 x 28in
Tractive effort	34,215 lb
Weights	
engine	70tons 5cwt
tender	55tons 10cwt
total	125tons 15cwt

2-10-0 'Austerity'

Order Nos	L945 L948
Works No.	25436-25535, 25596-25645
Class	WD
Wheel arrangement	2-10-0
Wheel dia.	
(coupled)	4ft 8.5in
(bogie)	3ft 2in
Heating surface	
tubes	1,759.00 sq ft
firebox	192.00 sq ft
superheater	423.00 sq ft
total	2,374.00 sq ft
Grate area	40.00 sq ft
Boiler pressure	225 lb/sq in
Cylinders (3)	19 x 28in
Tractive effort	34,215 lb
Weights	
engine	78tons 6cwt
tender	55tons 10cwt
total:	133tons 16cwt

A typical duty for a NBL-built 2-8-0, No. 90086 in British Railways service. Compare this view with the official view of the 2-10-0, and note that the only observable difference is the wheel arrangement – and the grimy condition!

Lens of Sutton

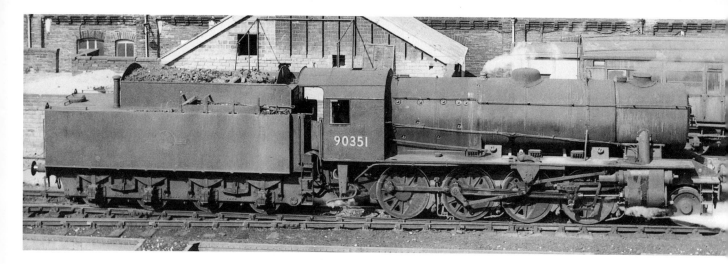

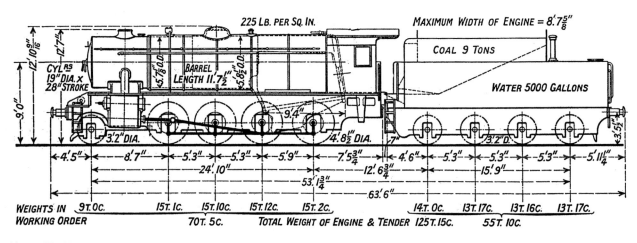

225 LB. PER SQ. IN.

MAXIMUM WIDTH OF ENGINE = 8'.7⅝"

COAL 9 TONS

WATER 5000 GALLONS

CYL⁀ᴿˢ 19" DIA. X 28" STROKE

BARREL LENGTH 11.7½"

WEIGHTS IN WORKING ORDER

Above: The WD 'Austerity' 2-8-0s were built in huge numbers by NBL during the Second World War.

Railway Gazette

Below: All of the 150 'Austerity' 2-10-0s were built by NBL in two orders; L945 and L948.

Railway Gazette

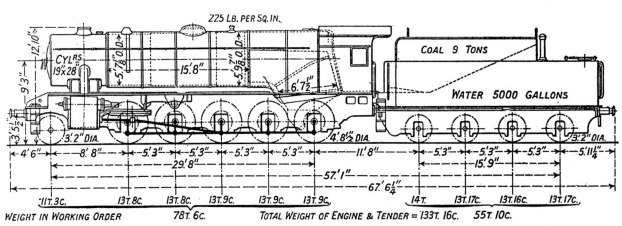

225 LB. PER SQ. IN.

COAL 9 TONS

WATER 5000 GALLONS

CYL⁀ᴿˢ 19 x 28

WEIGHT IN WORKING ORDER

7

Export Orders 1929–1953

From a commercial viewpoint, the years from 1929 to 1953 saw the company struggling desperately to survive, in the face of a dramatic and prolonged recession. On top of this, the company failed to convert from one of the world's leading steam locomotive builders, to a similar position with diesel and electric traction. The innovation that had been a characteristic of the company in its formative years seemed to be elusive later, and the company was firmly committed to steam traction until after the Second World War. The non-steam traction orders built by North British are related in Chapter 8, and those reviewed here are steam orders for the traditional marketplaces of NBL products. Between 1929 and 1953, NBL's works were the recipients of 162 orders for steam locomotives, 135 of which were for overseas. At the time of NBL's silver jubilee in 1928, the order books had reached number L859, but the order rate had already declined dramatically, and continued at its very low level for many years.

In 1929, three orders for overseas were received, for South Africa, Malaya and Brazil, and although the intervening years saw some very famous types built, at the time of the company's golden jubilee, only South African customers, and for industrial locomotives at that, were placing orders. True, in 1950, the famous R class for Victorian Railways in Australia, and more JAs for New Zealand were ordered, and a year later, India placed an order for 100 of the famous YP class Pacifics.

Africa produced by far the largest numbers of both orders and locomotives for NBL during its second 25 years, with South Africa far and away the most frequent customer. The Far East was less important than previously, but the most noticeable tailing off in orders was from South America, which had previously come to Springburn frequently, for many locomotives. The core markets for NBL during this period were Africa, India, Australia and New Zealand. North America had never ordered many locomotives from Glasgow, excepting the Newfoundland Railway in Canada. In the 1930s, curiously perhaps, once again, the Newfoundland Railway placed a number of orders on NBL, but this time, not the 4-6-0s of earlier years, but 2-8-2s, to its own design. Having said that, the five orders that were placed from Canada, only resulted in the building of eight engines, which was not good business, and these orders were spread over a five year period between 1935 and 1940!

Orders Out of Africa

Between order L859, placed in 1929, and order L55 (L999 had already been passed, and order numbers were allocated starting at L1 again), placed in 1953, a total of 92 orders were received for 1,085 steam locomotives. Although South Africa ordered most locomotives from NBL, Egypt and Rhodesia/East African Railways came to Springburn for 251 steam engines. On the industrial front, no less than 57 orders were received by NBL, for what were, frequently, small wheeled tank engines. The industrials brought in construction work on only 113 locomotives in this 25 year period, and averaged two engines on each order. Overall though, out of the total orders for steam locomotives placed in the second quarter century, more than 56% came from Africa.

The first new order received by NBL was L859, on 4th March 1929, for another 13 of the highly successful 12A class 4-8-2 goods locomotives. NBL had built the first of these superb locomotives back in 1919, and with order L859, they were building the last too. There were 67

On 17th February 1947, SAR ordered no less than 100 of the Class 24 2-8-4s. This new design was built under order L976 at Hyde Park Works, and was one of the most successful of the company's orders for the 3ft 6in gauge. An unusual feature of the construction was the use of a one-piece steel casting for the locomotive frames. They were put to work in 1949, in South West Africa, and were only displaced by diesels on the branch line services for which they were largely used in later years, No. 3607 is depicted.
Mitchell Library Collection

engines in all in this long-lived class; orders were shared between NBL and their German competitors, Henschel & Sohn, although Springburn constructed most of the class, 48 in all.

Order No	L859
Works Nos	23891-23903
Class	12A
Running Nos	2126-2138
Wheel arrangement	4-8-2
Wheel dia. (coupled)	4ft 3in
Heating surface	
tubes	2,301.00 sq ft
firebox	209.10 sq ft
superheater	466.00 sq ft
total	2,976.10 sq ft
Boiler pressure	190 lb/sq in
Cylinders(2)	24 x 26in
Tractive effort	41,840 lb

The 12As were designed as a supplement to the Class 12 locomotives, hard at work on the Witbank to Germiston coal trains in the Transvaal. The early 12As were first put to work on those services, but they were so successful that re-allocation to other routes and workings took place. At the time, D. A. Hendrie was Locomotive Superintendent, and the new locomotives, with their large combustion chamber fireboxes and free steaming boilers were considered his most notable achievement. In later years, beginning during World War II, the 12As were reboilered, when Dr M. M. Loubser became CME of South African Railways, and they became Class 12AR. Not all of the class received the massive new boilers, leaving 23 in the original condition. The reboilered engines put in a lot of work on Cape Eastern, Cape Midland and Natal, on goods and passenger workings. The 12ARs, like their predecessors, were successful and invaluable members of the SAR fleet. Interestingly, the new boiler for the 12As was adapted, in a foreshortened form, for the later S1 class 0-8-0 shunting locomotive, which included some NBL built examples ordered in 1951. That the Class 12A engines lasted until well into the 1980s, in their original form, was also testimony to the work of NBL.

The complete class of 12As appeared as follows:

Running Nos	Works Nos	Order No.	Builder	Year
1520-1539	21738-54	L685	NBL	1919
2111-2125	22751-65	L748	NBL	1921
1540-1545	21046-51	–	Henschel	1928
1546-1550	21428-32	–	Henschel	1929
2103-2110	21433-40	–	Henschel	1929
2126-2138	23891-903	L859	NBL	1929

At the opposite end of the continent, Egypt was a source of large numbers of locomotive orders for NBL, although during the recession, the company were tendering at less than cost in some cases, and even then losing out to other builders. Of the seven orders coming from Egypt, all except two were placed before the Second World War, for 120 locomotives. The remaining two orders were placed in 1947 and 1949, for 38 new 4-6-0 locomotives.

The first order – L865, in 1929, was for 20 passenger tank engines, whilst the largest Egyptian order was placed in 1935, for 50 engines, as a new design of 2-6-0. This order (L892) included 30 engines fitted with conventional Walschaerts valve gear, and 20 fitted with Caprotti poppet valve gear. They were quite advanced designs, incorporating such features as steel fireboxes, and rocking grates, and were constructed at Hyde Park Works. The principal dimensions were as follows:

Order No.	L892
Works Nos	24246-24295
Running Nos	625-674
Wheel arrangement	2-6-0
Wheel dia.	
(coupled)	5ft 6.75in
(bogie)	3ft 8.75in
Wheelbase (engine)	23ft 11.5in
(engine & tender)	47ft 8in
Heating surface	
tubes	1,257.00 sq ft
firebox	149.00 sq ft
superheater	250.00 sq ft
total	1,656.00 sq ft
Grate area	25.00 sq ft
Boiler pressure	225 lb/sq in
Cylinders(2)	17.75 x 28in
Tractive effort	25,270 lb

The locomotives' boilers were steel throughout, with steel tubes, and although, paired with their Belpaire pattern fireboxes, looked parallel, the rear boiler ring was slightly coned. The Superheater Company had been providing their design of superheaters for many of the locomotive types built by NBL, and in this design, the multiple valve header type, with 24 elements was fitted. Frame construction was traditional steel plate, with cast steel stretchers, underhung leaf springs, and the leading truck was fabricated from steel plate, with a swing bolster, and overhung springs.

There were a variety of fixtures and fittings installed on these locomotives, and included five engines fitted with ACFI feed water heaters, five with the Heinl design, five with Kylchap blastpipes, and a further ten with the Clyde soot blowers. Modifications to lubrication arrangements were seen on different members of the class, but in almost all of these modifications, the aim was to reduce the costs and demands of maintenance on Egypt's rail network. By and large they were not exceptional types, although two years later, in 1937, a very curious locomotive was built,

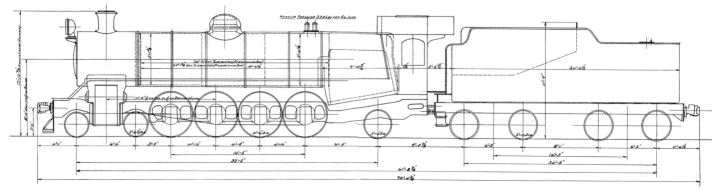

The last order for these Class 12A 4-8-2s for South African Railways, were built by NBL in 1929, to order L859.

Mitchell Library Collection

The official photograph of No. 279, one of the unique NBL-Sentinel locomotives, built in 1937 to order L908, shows them to have been just as odd looking outside, as the internal design provided some peculiar construction arrangements. Only four locomotives were built, for Egyptian State Railways.

Mitchell Library Collection

well, with NBL as sub-contractors to Sentinel Wagon actually. Under order L908, four geared locomotives were built, dispensing with the traditional valve motion in favour of a geared drive.

These unique engines were ordered from Sentinel, with the primary objective of reducing the operating problems caused by the environment. Their appearance, of a relatively conventional steam locomotive above the footplate, but with the radical departure in mechanical design was hinted at only by the fact that the axleboxes and springs were clearly visible outside the frames. They looked – albeit without coupling rods – more like an old style outside frame locomotive. The basic dimensions of these unusual locomotives were as follows:

Order No.	L908
Works Nos	24413-24416
Running Nos	276-279
Wheel arrangement	2-4-2
Wheel dia.	
(coupled)	3ft 8.75in
(bogie)	3ft 0.75in
Wheelbase	
(engine)	23ft 6in
(engine & tender)	46ft 0.25in
Heating surface	
tubes	1,072.00 sq ft
firebox	118.00 sq ft
superheater	290.00 sq ft
total	1,480.00 sq ft
Grate area	21.00 sq ft
Boiler pressure	200 lb/sq in
Cylinders (4)	11 x 12in
Tractive effort	15,290 lb @ 75% B.P.

NBL were subcontracted by Sentinel to construct the locomotives and tenders, excluding the steam engines and geared drive. Two of the locomotives were oil-fired, and

The unique Sentinel/NBL 2-4-2 locomotives for Egypt were built by NBL in 1937, to order L908.   *Mitchell Library Collection*

two coal-fired. A conventional locomotive boiler (to the same design as the new 4-4-0s ordered at the same time) and tender were provided, and the locomotive, with an all up weight of 56 tons 13 cwt for the coal fired, and 56 tons 9 cwt for the oil fired version, gave an axle weight of only 17 tons. More interestingly though, the Sentinel engine units completely eliminated wheel hammer blow.

Each locomotive was fitted with a pair of self-contained engine units, consisting of twin 11 in by 12 in cylinders, driving a gearbox mounted directly onto each axle. Steam to the cylinders of both the front and hind engine units was taken from the superheater by way of the steam pipes, visible above the footplate in the accompanying photograph. To absorb any effects from undulation in the track, each of the steam and exhaust pipes to the engine units were fitted with three ball and socket joints. The steam engine units themselves were mounted on cross beams, and provided with rubber pads in a three point suspension, to absorb any shocks to the cylinder casings. Each engine and drive unit was a totally enclosed assembly, with the final drive gears supplied to the same specification as those used on London Underground. The gears themselves were immersed in an oil bath with roller bearings fitted not only to the short crankshafts, but to the driving wheel axleboxes. Intended not for long haul services, but short suburban type workings, they were quick starting and rapid braking. These locomotives were something of an experiment, and NBL never received any further contracts for this design.

In the same year, 1937, Egyptian State placed two more orders, directly with North British, for 26 new 4-4-0 passenger locomotives and 20 new 2-6-0s. As orders L907 and L915 respectively, these were the final orders before the war, at a time when the company was already building light tanks, and other material for the war effort. The new 4-4-0s were all fitted with Caprotti poppet valve gear, which had found greater popularity during the depression years, and like their earlier, 2-6-0 counterparts, were all built at Hyde Park. The class was intended for working lightly loaded passenger trains in northern Egypt, where the route profiles were relatively flat. The overall design was produced by the Egyptian State Railways, and resulted in a quite attractive, if typically British design.

Of the 26 ordered at the beginning of 1937, all had been completed by the end of September, with 18 locomotives

fitted for coal burning, and the remaining eight for oil-burning. The main dimensions were as follows:

Order No.	L907
Works Nos	24387-24412
Running Nos	237-254 (coal burners)
	255-262 (oil burners)
Wheel arrangement	4-4-0
Wheel dia.	
(coupled)	5ft 6.75in
(bogie)	3ft 0.75in
Wheelbase	
engine	23ft 9in
engine & tender	46ft 6in
Heating surface	
tubes	1,072.00 sq ft
firebox	118.00 sq ft
superheater	290.00 sq ft
total	1,480.00 sq ft
Grate area	21.00 sq ft
Boiler pressure	180 lb/sq in
Cylinders (2)	17 x 26in
Tractive effort	17,220 lb @ 85% B.P.

The boiler and firebox for the 4-4-0s were also used in the four Sentinel engines, as was the tender, although the working pressure was increased to 200 lb for the geared locomotives. As with other designs for Egypt, steel fireboxes were almost standard practice, and the variety of fittings within the class continued. Of the coal burning 4-4-0s, three were also fitted with Nicholson thermic syphons within the firebox, and all featured the rocking grate which appeared on the 1929 order for 2-6-0s. The oil burners, as with previous classes were an NBL design, with the nozzles fitted to the front of the firebox. Unlike earlier NBL built 2-6-0s, these new locomotives were not fitted with feed water heaters, although injectors, of the Friedmann type, supplied the boiler through top feed.

The weight in working order of the 4-4-0s was just 54 tons 11 cwt, two tons less than the Sentinels then being built, and with the tender weighing 43 tons 10 cwt when full, the locomotive tipped the scales at 98 tons 1 cwt. The tenders, common with the Sentinels, carried 6 tons of coal, or 1,000 gallons of heavy fuel oil, and 3,700 gallons of water.

African Railway Orders 1929–1953

Railway	Year	Order No.	Works Nos	Qty	Works	Type
South African	1929	L859	23891-903	13	?	4-8-2 Class 12A
Egyptian State Rly.	1929	L865	23952-71	20	Atlas	2-6-4T similar L824
Rhodesia Rly.	1929	L866	23972-77	6	Atlas	4-8-2 similar to L755
Benguela Rly.	1929	L867	23978-95	18	Queens Park	4-8-0 similar to L780
Rhodesia Rly.	1929	L868	23996-24007	12	Atlas	4-8-2 similar to L817
South African	1929	L869	24008-25	18	Atlas	4-8-2 similar to L849
Tharsis Sulphur Co.	1930	L871	24034-37	4	Queens Park	2-8-0T
Central Africa Rly. Co.	1930	L873	24063-68	6	Hyde Park	4-8-0 to designs of Hawthorn, Leslie
Various mines	1930	L874	24069	1	Queens Park	4-8-2 similar to L857
Kenya–Uganda Rly.	1930	L875	24070-79	10	Atlas	4-8-2+2-8-4 'Garratt'
Tweefontein Colliery	1930	L877	24086	1	Queens Park	4-8-2T similar L874
Gold Coast Rly.	1931	L880	24094-98	5	Queens Park	4-6-0 to Robt. Stephenson & Co. drawings
Northern Lime Co.	1933	L884	24114	1	Hyde Park	4-8-2T similar L874
South African	1934	L887	24168-217	50	Queens Park	4-8-2 new Class 19C
ICI South Africa	1934	L888	24218	1	Hyde Park	2-6-2T new NBL design
Crown Mines	1935	L891	24245	1	Atlas	4-8-2T similar L874
Egyptian State Rly.	1935	L892	24246-95	50	Hyde Park	2-6-0 new design
Randfontein Estates	1935	L893	24296	1	Hyde Park	4-8-2T new NBL design
Randfontein Estates	1936	L897	24374	1	Queens Park	4-8-2T same as L893
South African Rlys.	1936	L899	24379	1	Atlas	2-10-4 new Class 21 experimental design
City Deep Mining	1936	L900	24380	1	Atlas	4-8-4T new NBL design
Tweefontein Collieries	1936	L902	24382	1	Atlas	4-8-2T similar L874
Crown Mines	1936	L903	24383	1	Hyde Park	4-8-2T similar L891
Witbank Colliery	1936	L904	24384	1	Hyde Park	4-8-2T similar L856

Nourse Mines	1936	L905	24385	1	Atlas	4-8-2T similar L903
Witbank Colliery	1936	L906	24386	1	Atlas	4-8-2T similar L904
Egyptian State Rly.	1937	L907	24387-412	26	Hyde Park	4-4-0 new design
Egyptian State Rly.	1937	L908	24413-16	4	Hyde Park	2-4-2 new design of geared loco. to Sentinel designs
East Rand Pty.	1937	L909	24417	1	Hyde Park	4-8-4 new design
Egyptian State Rly.	1937	L915	24439-58	20	Hyde Park	2-6-0 new design
South African Rly.	1937	L917	24463-506	44	Hyde Park	4-8-2 Class 15F
Randfontein Estates	1937	L918	24507	1	Hyde Park	4-8-2T similar L893
Crown Mines	1938	L921	24520	1	Hyde Park	4-8-2T similar L903
City Deep Mining	1939	L927	24581	1	Hyde Park	4-8-4T similar L900
Coronation Colliery	1939	L929	24597	1	Hyde Park	4-8-2T similar L857
Simmer & Jack Mines	1939	L930	24598	1	Hyde Park	4-8-2T similar L874
Witbank Colliery	1939	L931	24599	1	Hyde Park	4-8-2T similar L906
Brakpan Mines	1940	L933	24660	1	Hyde Park	4-8-2T similar L893
Various mining Cos	1942	L941	25896-900	5	Hyde Park	4-8-2T similar L921
Various mining Cos	1942	L942	25901-902	2	Hyde Park	4-8-2T similar L909
Various collieries	1942	L944	25903-906	4	Hyde Park	4-8-2T similar L859
South African Rly.	1944	L947	25536-595	60	Hyde Park	4-8-2 Class 15F
Leopoldina Rly.	1944	L952	25913-15	3	Hyde Park	0-6-0T same as L855
Coronation Colliery	1945	L953	25916	1	Hyde Park	4-8-2T similar L874
Vryheid Colliery	1945	L954	25917	1	Hyde Park	4-8-4T similar L909
Vogels G. M. & Co.	1945	L955	25918	1	Hyde Park	4-8-4T similar L900
St Helena Gold Mine	1945	L956	25919	1	Hyde Park	4-8-4T similar L933
Enyate Colliery	1945	L960	25940	1	Hyde Park	4-8-4T similar L954
South African Rly.	1945	L961	25941-26040	100	Hyde Park	4-8-2 Class 15F similar to L947
South African Rly.	1945	L962	26041-90	50	Hyde Park	4-8-2 Class 19D
Springs Mines	1946	L964	26241	1	Hyde Park	4-8-2T similar L958
Simmer & Jack	1946	L965	26242	1	Hyde Park	2-6-2T similar L888
African Explosives	1946	L966	26243	1	Hyde Park	4-8-2T similar L874
Tweefontein Collieries	1946	L967	26244	1	Hyde Park	4-8-2T similar L902
South Witbank Colliery	1946	L968	26245	1	Hyde Park	4-8-4T similar L954
Anglo Alpha Cement Co.	1946	L969	26246	1	Hyde Park	4-8-4T similar L955
Vereeniging Brick Co.	1946	L970	26247	1	Hyde Park	4-8-2T similar L953
Van Dyksdrift Colliery	1947	L971	26248	1	Hyde Park	4-8-2T similar L956
Nigerian Rlys.	1947	L973	26250-91 & 26726	43	Hyde Park	2-8-2 to Vulcan Foundry drawings
Egyptian State Rlys.	1947	L974	26292-311	20	Hyde Park	4-6-0 new design
Rand Collieries	1947	L975	26312	1	Hyde Park	4-8-4T similar L954
South African Rlys.	1947	L976	26313-412	100	Hyde Park	2-8-4 24 Class new design
Nyasaland Rlys.	1948	L979	26540-44	5	Hyde Park	2-8-2 similar to L973
Tanganyika Rlys.	1947	L983	26675-80	6	Hyde Park	2-8-2 – cancelled
West Reefs Exploration	1948	L984	26681	1	Hyde Park	4-8-2T similar L941
Tharsis Sulphur & C. Co.	1948	L989	26702-05	4	Hyde Park	0-8-0T new 'F' class
Transvaal Collieries	1948	L991	26727	1	Hyde Park	4-8-2T similar L941
Transvaal Collieries	1948	L995	26759	1	Hyde Park	4-8-2 same as L944
Rand/Northern Lime	1948	L999	26899	1	Hyde Park	4-8-4T similar L942
Sudan Government	1949	L1	26900-04, 26949-58, 27080-03	19	Hyde Park	2-8-2
East African Rlys.	1950	L2	26905-20	16	Hyde Park	2-8-2 metre gauge
Egyptian State Rlys.	1949	L3	26931-48	18	Hyde Park	4-6-0
Benguela Rly. Co.	1949	L4	26959-64	6	Hyde Park	4-8-2
East African Rlys.	1950	L6	27060-77	18	Hyde Park	4-8-2T metre gauge
East African Rlys.	1950	L10	27085-88	4	Hyde Park	2-8-2 similar to L2
Cape Explosives	1950	L11	27089	1	Hyde Park	4-8-2T similar L874
Anglo American Corp.	1950	L13	27090-93	9	Hyde Park	4-8-2T similar L874
Vryheid Collieries	1950	L18	27099	1	Hyde Park	4-8-4T same as L942
Sudan Government	1951	L23	27225-34, 27251-58, 27561-80, 27478-79, 27640-41	42	Hyde Park	4-8-2 oil burners
Nigerian Railways	1951	L26	27239-45	7	Hyde Park	2-8-2 similar to L973
South African Rlys.	1951	L28	27261-85	25	Hyde Park	0-8-0 new design
Nyasaland Railways	1951	L29	27249-50	2	Hyde Park	2-8-2 same as L26 built at same time
Tharsis Sulphur & C. Co.	1951	L30	27259-60	2	Hyde Park	0-8-0T similar L989
South African Rlys.	1951	L31	27287-96, 27311	25	Hyde Park	4-8-4 non-condensing
Various mines	1951	L32	27286, 27404-05	3	Hyde Park	4-8-2T similar L13
Nigerian Railways	1951	L34	27299-310	12	Hyde Park	2-8-2 same as L26
South African Rlys.	1951	L35	27312-27400	89	Hyde Park	4-8-4 condensing
Witbank Colliery	1951	L39	27406	1	Hyde Park	4-8-2 similar to SAR class 12A
New Largo Colliery	1952	L41	27469	1	Hyde Park	4-8-4T
East African Rlys.	1952	L45	27436-46	11	Hyde Park	2-8-2 class 29
East African Rlys.	1952	L46	27447-68, 27474-77	26	Hyde Park	2-8-4 class 30
Tharsis Sulphur & C.Co.	1952	L49	27480-81	2	Hyde Park	0-8-0T class 'F' same as L30
Various mines	1953	L55	27535-36, 27587	3	Hyde Park	4-8-2T same as L13

Country	No. of orders	No. of engines	Avg. engines/order
South Africa	13	581	44.7
Egypt	7	158	22.6
Rhodesia/EAR	7	93	13.3
Nigeria	3	62	20.7
Nyasaland	2	7	3.5
Kenya/Uganda/Tang.	1	10	10
Sudan	2	61	30.5
Mines & others	57	113	2
Total	92	1085	11.8

Last of the orders before WWII was a new design of 2-6-0 for mixed traffic working, and once again, fitted with Caprotti valve gear. The similarity with previous designs continued, whilst the boiler assembly was an enlargement of previous type, with a working presure of 225 lb, and a heating surface of no less than 1,696 sq ft. The superheater was identical to the earlier design of 2-6-0, with 24 elements, and all were equipped with ACFI feed water heaters. Most of the fittings, like the Friedmann live steam injectors, and Stone's lighting equipment, were common with both the 4-4-0s and 2-6-0s. Perhaps the only significant design change was the all-welded tender construction, which additionally, was fitted with roller bearings.

NBL was producing some sophisticated designs for exported locomotives, with a wide range of features, typical of specialist companies. With this in mind, it is perhaps not surprising that the company felt it was better able to design locomotives for the home railway companies, and not the railways themselves. The home market did, as we have seen, come to NBL for its expertise as well as its workshop facilities, on many occasions.

After the war, Egypt came back to Springburn for a new design of 4-6-0, 38 of which were built in two orders, placed in 1947 and 1949. The work was shared between two works, with L974 (20 locomotives) built at Queen's Park and L3 (18 locomotives) allocated to Hyde Park. They were oil burners, with double bogie tenders, and the last were scheduled for delivery in 1950.

Also after the war, the Sudan Government came back to Springburn for more locomotives, in two orders, L1 and L23. The Sudan, as with Egypt, was a former British colony, but the previous order placed from that country was back in 1926, for the 220 class Pacifics, and a further 23 years elapsed before another order (L1), was placed. The initial order was for five 180 class 2-8-2 freight engines, but under order L1, in 1949, additional contracts increased the number of engines to be built, to 19. Unlike Egypt though, Sudan Railways was built to the almost universal African gauge of 3ft 6in, and the first of the new 2-8-2s appeared in service in 1952. The main dimensions of these locomotives were as follows:

Order No.	L1
Works Nos	26900-26904
	26949-26958 & 27080-27083
Class	180
Running Nos.	310-328
Wheel arrangement	2-8-2
Wheel dia.	
(coupled)	4ft 3in
(leading)	2ft 7in
Wheel dia. (trailing)	2ft 9in
Wheelbase	
engine	28ft 1in
engine & tender	53ft 2.5in
Heating surface	
tubes	983.00 sq ft
firebox	142.00 sq ft
superheater	260.00 sq ft
total	1,385.00 sq ft
Grate area	26.00 sq ft
Boiler pressure	180 lb/sq in
Cylinders (2)	19 x 24in
Weight in w.o.	
engine	61 tons 7 cwt
engine & tender	113 tons 17 cwt
Fuel capacity	
coal	8 tons
water:	4,130 gallons
Tractive effort:	25,992 lb @ 85% B.P.

In March 1949, Egyptian State Railways came to NBL for 18 of these standard gauge 4-6-0s, for mixed traffic duties. Under order L3, they carried works numbers 26931–26948. Optimistically, given the steel shortage in post-war Britain, the NBL Order Book states that delivery was to begin in January 1950, and be completed by the end of February 1950.

Mitchell Library Collection

These Mikados were not the last orders for Sudan, this distinction befalling the 42 locomotives ordered under NBL order L23. In fact, the original order, placed on 13th March 1951, was for ten new oil-burning locomotives, to be known as the 500 class, and intended for working on routes where the axle load was very restricted. In fact, at 15 tons, the axle load of these 4-8-2s was less than the recently completed 4-6-0s for Egypt, under NBL order L3. Between March 1951, no fewer than five separate contracts from Sudan increased the total locomotives of this class on order to 42, with the final change of order placed in January 1954, and adding two more engines to this class. Like all of the recently delivered locomotives to the Middle East and North Africa, they included some of the most modern features, with all-steel fireboxes, thermic syphons and manganese steel liners to the coupled axleboxes, along with more extensive use of roller bearings. The Class 500 4-8-2s were shipped from Stobcross Quay fully assembled, and entered service from 1955. They had the following dimensions:

Order No.	L23
Works Nos	27225-27234, 27251-27258, 27478-27479, 27561-27580, & 27640-27641
Class	500
Wheel arrangement	4-8-2
Wheel dia.	
coupled	4ft 6in
bogie	2ft 4.5in
trailing	2ft 9.5in
Wheelbase	
engine	33ft 10in
engine & tender	61ft 10in
Heating surface	
tubes	2,027.00 sq ft
firebox	203.00 sq ft
superheater	542.00 sq ft
total	2,772.00 sq ft
Grate area	40.00 sq ft
Boiler pressure	190 lb/sq in
Cylinders(2)	21.5 x 26in
Weight in w.o.	
engine	88 tons 0 cwt
engine & tender	148 tons 0 cwt
Fuel capacity	
oil	8 tons
water	5,500 gallons
Tractive effort	35,940 lb @ 85% B.P.

The other major orders received by NBL from Africa were the seven placed by Rhodesia and East African Railways, for a total of 93 locomotives. Only two of these orders, L866 and L868, for 18 4-8-2s, were placed before the war, in 1929 in fact, with a gap of 21 years before the next order was received from East African Railways in 1950. Order L866, for six of the 4-8-2s, was based on order L755 as 10th class and in turn the design could be traced back to 1912 and order L508, when the first superheater fitted 10th class 4-8-2s appeared from Springburn. The second order, L868, was for another twelve 4-8-2s and was placed only four months later, in December 1929, but was designated the 12th class, all of which were built by NBL. North British constructed all of Rhodesia's 10th class engines too, with the fourth and final batch represented by order L866 and having the following main dimensions:

Order No.	L866
Works Nos	223972-23977
Class	10th
Running Nos	241-246
Wheel arrangement	4-8-2
Wheel dia.	
coupled	4ft 6in
bogie	2ft 4.5in
trailing	2ft 9in
Wheelbase	
engine	31ft 8in
engine & tender	60ft 9.25in
Heating surface	
tubes	1,374.00 sq ft
firebox	173.00 sq ft
superheater	488.00 sq ft
total	2,035.00 sq ft
Grate area	32.00 sq ft
Boiler pressure	180 lb/sq in
Cylinders (2)	20 x 26in
Weight in w.o.	
engine	76 tons 12 cwt
engine & tender	130 tons 3 cwt
Fuel capacity	
coal	9.5 tons
water	4,500 gallons
Tractive effort	29,466 lb @ 85% B.P.

Rhodesia's new 10th class cost £8,655 each, although by the end of the Second World War some inroads had been made into the numerical strength and in 1949, only five of the final order remained in service. Very little had changed

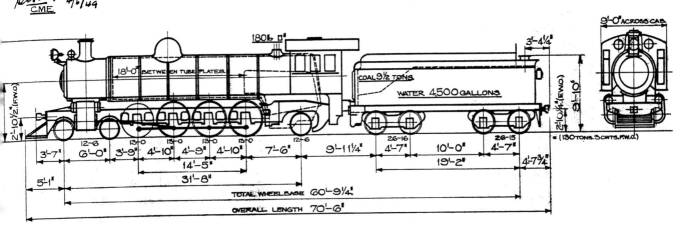

Rhodesia Railways 10th Class 4-8-2, built by NBL in 1929/30, to order L866.

Mitchell Library Collection

about these locomotives in the 18 years that they were in production and the weight diagram only shows the increased size of the tender as the major change. At 18ft 0in long and 5ft 0in in diameter the boiler was certainly large, with a combustion chamber firebox and was common, with some changes in piston valve diameter and axlebox dimensions. The almost uniform axle loading of 13 tons gave the locomotives a wide range of operation.

The second of the 1929 orders was for the 12th class, another 4-8-2, although earlier examples had been built by NBL since 1926. The main dimensions of the 1930 batch IV, were as follows:

Order No.	L868
Works Nos	23996-24007
Class	12th
Running Nos	247-258
Wheel arrangement	4-8-2
Wheel dia.	
coupled	4ft 3in
bogie	2ft 4.5in
trailing	2ft 9in
Wheelbase	
engine	32ft 3in
engine & tender	57ft 7.25in
Heating surface	
tubes	1,890.00 sq ft* inc. water tubes
firebox	130.00 sq ft
superheater	362.00 sq ft
total	2,379.00 sq ft
Grate area	32.50 sq ft
Boiler pressure	190 lb/sq in
Cylinders (2)	20 x 26in
Weight in w.o.	
engine	78.12 tons
engine & tender	131.47 tons
Fuel capacity	
coal	10 tons
water	4,250 gallons
Tractive effort	32,940 lb @ 85% B.P.

The East African Railways system however, was set to metre gauge and the two orders placed with NBL in 1950 were for a total of 20 2-8-2 types. Orders L2 and L10, the metre gauge 2-8-2s, were built together, and the orders were merged, and constructed at Queen's Park Works, for delivery towards the end of 1951. The design was based on the Crown Agents 2-8-2 prototype for general service, and which had already been built for the 3ft 6in gauge lines of Nigeria, by both NBL and Vulcan Foundry.

Just before order L10 was placed, the Crown Agents for the Colonies had placed an order for East African Railways with NBL, in January 1950, for 18 4-8-2 tank engines. These oil-fired locomotives were originally scheduled to be built at Hyde Park, but in February 1951, were re-allocated to Queen's Park, to allow Hyde Park to build the 100 YP class locomotives for India, which had been ordered in January 1951. East African Railways & Harbours had the distinction of placing the final orders for steam from Africa, with the exception of South Africa's GMA/M class Garratts. Orders L45 and L46, for Class 29 2-8-2s and Class 30 2-8-4s were received in April 1952, with construction at Queen's Park Works.

There was some change to the order for these locomotives, with the Class 29 having originally been allocated order L46, and Class 30 to order L45. The order numbers were swapped in May 1952, and eleven locomotives were scheduled for delivery starting between November 1953 and January 1954, carrying works numbers 27436-27446. The 2-8-2s were fitted with 18in by 26in cylinders, 4ft 0in coupled wheels, and carried 2,375 gallons of oil and 4,000 gallons of water on the double bogie tenders. British locomotive engineers on the home front had not adopted the widespread use of roller bearings, although their use on valve gear had been progressed by Nigel Gresley in the 1930s. The order book notes that the special features of the EAR 2-8-2s, were to be the roller bearings applied to driving crank pins only. Perhaps further evidence of British influence on colonial railway engineering.

The Class 30 locomotives were similar in most respects to the Class 29, with the most obvious departure being the use of six-wheeled, as compared with four-wheeled bogies on the tender. Delivery of these 2-8-4s was to follow the 2-8-2s and be completed by the end of 1954. The order was reduced from 38 to 26, under modifications to the contract, although two contracts actually covered the locomotives, one for 22 engines, the other for four. Interestingly, when the original order was entered in the company order books it was for 22 locomotives.

Before East African Railways came into being, the metre gauge lines were organised as the Kenya, Uganda & Tanganyika Railway, and under that administration, order L875 was placed back in 1930. This order resulted in the appearance of ten Garratt type locomotives, with a 4-8-2+ 2-8-4 wheel arrangement. This was an interesting design,

Another twelve of the Rhodesian Railways 12th Class were ordered in 1929 (L868), and were again built at Queen's Park. Running numbers 247–258, and works numbers 23996–24007, were carried by this new order. The 1929 order included some detail changes, but was largely the same as the earlier batch. This view shows the left-hand side of No. 247.

Mitchell Library Collection

In January 1951, Festival of Britain year, no less than 100 of these YP class 4-6-2s were ordered from NBL under order number L21. For metre gauge locomotives they were truly massive engines, as evidenced by the man standing alongside the first of the order, outside the Hyde Park shops. Some interesting design changes were made before delivery, such as the substitution of cast iron, instead of the original cast steel cylinders, and the use of aluminium alloy for the cab and the platforms and running boards. Forty years later, a number of these engines were still to be seen at work. (See illustrations in Chapter 9.)

Mitchell Library Collection

In appearance, these were very attractive locomotives, and perhaps represented a really good mix of the best of British and American locomotive practice on Indian railways. Free steaming and running locomotives, they were amongst the few Indian designs to be equipped with smoke deflectors, and at 57 tons, their appearance belied their relatively small size perhaps. As built by North British, the Class YP Pacifics were fitted with aluminium cabs and running boards, an unusual, if not entirely new feature on NBL built locomotives. Although officially noted as an order for the Indian Government Railways, the contract, like its predecessor for the WG class engines, was with the India Store Dept. Curiously, the order has a comment that the contract for the Class YP engines did not cover 'as mades', or photographs!

India and Ceylon Railway Orders 1929–1953

Railway	Year	Order No.	Works Nos	Qty	Works	Type
Nizam State Rly.	1929	L861	23912-05	4	Hyde Park	4-6-2, "Class XB", to Vulcan Foundry drawings
Nizam State Rly.	1929	L862	23916-20	5	Queens Park	2-8-2, "Class XD", to Vulcan Foundry drawings
BB & CI Rly.	1931	L878	2408790	4	Queens Park	2-8-2 similar to L862
South Indian	1931	L879	24091-03	3	Queens Park	2-8-2 similar to L862
Nizam's State Rly.	1932	L881	24099-103	5	Hyde Park	2-8-2 similar to L879
Nizam's State Rly.	1932	L882	24104-05	2	Hyde Park	2-8-2 similar to L881
Nizam's State Rly.	1934	L886	24165-67	3	Queens Park	2-8-2 similar to L881
East Indian Rly.	1939	L928	24592-96	15	Hyde Park	2-8-2, "Class XE", cancelled
Indian Store Dept.	1944	L949	25646-705	60	Queens Park	2-8-2 similar to L886
Indian Store Dept.	1944	L950	25706-55	50	Hyde Park	2-8-2 similar to L886
Indian Store Dept.	1948	L978	26415-514	100	Queens Park	2-8-2 Class 'WG' new design
Indian Govt. Rlys.	1951	L21	27120-219	100	Hyde Park	4-6-2 Class 'YP' new design

Country	No. of orders	No. of engines	Avg. engines/order
India	12	351	29.3
Ceylon	0	0	0
Total	12	351	29.3

Australia and New Zealand

No orders came from either Australia or New Zealand between 1924 and 1937, although NBL had built some of the most famous Class Ab Pacifics for New Zealand, and during the period from 1929 to 1953, were to build the equally famous Class Ja 4-8-2s. From the end of the First World War to 1928, New Zealand was the source of most orders for NBL, but in the period under review, Australia came to Springburn more frequently than its neighbour.

Having said that, the first locomotives from Australasia was an industrial type – to be precise, a single 4-8-4 tank engine for the Mount Lyell Mining & Railway Co., under order L910 in 1937.

The following year, 1938, witnessed the placing of an order for 40 Class J locomotives for New Zealand, at the end of the most economically depressed period for the locomotive business. The principal dimensions of these new 4-8-2s for New Zealand were as follows:

Order No.	L923
Works Nos	24523-24562
Running Nos	1200-1239
Class	J
Wheel arrangement	4-8-2
Wheel dia.	
coupled	4ft 6in
Wheelbase	
engine	33ft 1.5in
total	58ft 0in
Overall length	66ft 11.5in
Overall height	11ft 7in
Overall width	8ft 6in
Heating surface	
tubes & firebox	1,469.00 sq ft
superheater	283.00 sq ft
total	1,752.00 sq ft
Grate area	39.00 sq ft
Boiler pressure	200 lb/sq in
Cylinders (2)	18 x 26in
Tractive effort	24,960 lb @ 85% B.P.
Weight in w.o.	
engine	68 tons 11 cwt
tender	40 tons 7 cwt
total	108 tons 18 cwt

New Zealand Railways Class J, No. 1227, in original condition, with air-smoothed casing. This locomotive was built in 1939, at the time of the outbreak of World War II, under order L923. All of the class were safely delivered by early 1940.

New Zealand Rly. & Loco. Society (Inc.) Archives Collection

These 40 locomotives were, and indeed will remain, some of the most attractive designs produced for the 3ft 6in gauge. Carrying running numbers 1200 to 1239 the first of the class entered service in September 1939. There were to have been another ten of the class, built by NBL, and another twelve in New Zealand, for delivery in 1941, but shortages of materials, not to mention the outbreak of war, meant that they were never built. More of the 4-8-2s were ordered from NBL, but not until well after the Second World War.

The design of the Class J was prepared by New Zealand Railways, and the specifications dispatched to the High Commissioner in London, in 1938. NBL won the contract,

Class Js, Nos. 1202 and 1203 on board the SS *Northumberland*. Built under order L923, they carried works numbers 24554 and 24555 respectively. Both were delivered to New Zealand Railways in 1939.

New Zealand Rly. & Loco. Society (Inc.) Archives Collection

The post-war order from New Zealand Railways for the oil-fired Class Ja locomotives, were built to order L19. Here, carrying works number 27107, is No. 1278, at Paekakariki Depot on the 6th November 1960 – early summer in New Zealand, with No. 1234 alongside.

New Zealand Rly. & Loco. Society (Inc.) Archives Collection

and the finer details of the design and the locomotive building was completed at Springburn, with NZR's Design Engineer R. J. Gard, on site. All 40 locomotives were delivered between September 1939 and 21st March 1940, with, despite the hostilities, none of the locomotives being lost through enemy action.

All of the original NBL built Class Js were built up on rolled steel bar frames, with the cylinders cast in steel, and integral with the smokebox saddle. The cylinders were fitted with cast iron liners, and the piston valves operated by Baker valve gear. Up to that time, New Zealand had used Walschaerts valve gear, but the Class Js marked the end of its use on new locomotives. New technology was employed on these engines too, with all axles fitted with roller bearings, and manganese/molybdenum alloy steel coupling and connecting rods, to reduce weight. Perhaps the most notable feature of the Js, was the streamlined casing carried when new along the top of the boiler, with additional casings for the Westinghouse pumps carried on the front footplates. The streamlining was removed from the NBL built Class Js between 1948 and 1953. All of these locomotives were equipped with electric lighting, with generators from Pyle National, though this was changed to Stones equipment in the later 4-8-2s ordered from NBL.

With an axle load of no more than 11.5 tons, these locomotives were suitable for the lightweight tracks on both North and South Island, and were a very successful design. Three of the NBL built engines have been preserved – numbers 1211, 1234 and 1236. At the same time as the streamlining was removed, twelve locomotives from the original

40 were converted to oil burners, and reclassified 'Jb', but retained the original running numbers.

Another 16 locomotives were ordered from NBL twelve years later, in 1950, but without the streamlining, and fitted for oil firing, amongst other modifications. The first of the Class Ja 4-8-2s was built by New Zealand Railways at its Hillside Works, and entered service in March 1947. The new class displaced a number of South Island Class Js, ten of which were sent to the North Island during 1949 and 1950, and remained there until dieselisation overtook them in the early 1960s, when they returned to the South Island.

The order from New Zealand in 1950 was allocated order No. L19, and covered works numbers 27104 to 27119, with the main dimensions as for the 1938 order. The locomotives carried running numbers 1275 to 1290 and were originally scheduled for delivery between December 1951 and August 1952.

The same Vanderbilt tender was provided, but this time holding 1,400 gallons of fuel oil instead of 6 tons of coal, along with 4,000 gallons of water. Departures in construction for the Class Ja included wider use of welding on the tenders, and the provision of roller bearings for all axles. Roller bearings were fitted to the Baker valve gear too, but at Springburn, only on the big ends and centre couplings, though some of the New Zealand engines had roller bearings on coupling rods too. The trailing truck fitted to both the 1938 Class J and 1951 Class Ja was known as the Hodges design, and was in fact first introduced on locomotives built for New Zealand by Baldwin in 1915 – the Class Aa Pacifics.

Like their precursors, the Class Ja 4-8-2s were a highly successful design, and turned in noteworthy performances, whether on freight or passenger duties. Fortunately, one of the NBL built examples from 1952, running number 1275, is preserved. Officially, the 40 Class Js were withdrawn from traffic between 1964 and 1971, including the twelve converted to oil burners as Class Jb. The Class Jas were all withdrawn between 1964 and 1968.

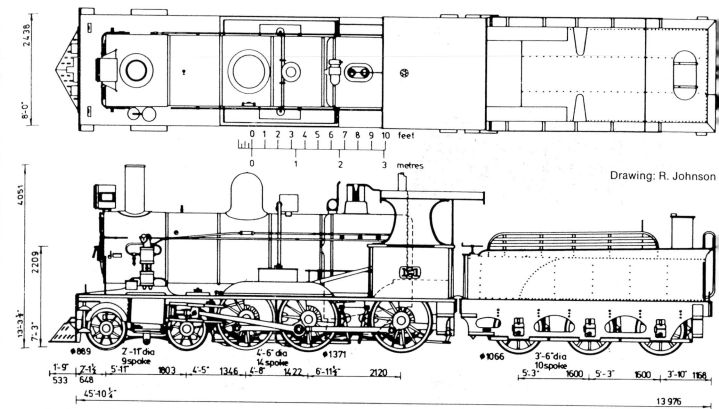

Drawing: R. Johnson

South Australia's Rx Class 4-6-0 was replaced by the 750 Class 2-8-2s, under 'Operation Phoenix', and the Rx Class 4-6-0s had been supplied by NBL in 1912, to order L526.

Australia too placed three orders with NBL after World War II, as L980, for Western Australia, L996 and L7 for Victoria, with the last order being for the famous Class R 4-6-0s. The Class PM Pacifics ordered for Western Australia were similar to the ten Class P's built at Queen's Park in 1924, under order L793, also for the 3ft 6in gauge. The order was placed in June 1947, by the Government of Western Australia, but for only 25 locomotives, and originally scheduled for delivery from the second quarter of 1949 onwards. However, in January 1949 the order was increased by ten locomotives, bringing the total to 35, with delivery at the rate of three engines per week, and the whole order to be completed by February 1950.

Victoria's railways were built to the 5ft 3in gauge, and were the third different gauge for Australia's main line railways. The first post-war order was for 50 of the new Class N 2-8-2s, for freight service, to NBL order L996, but this design took account of plans to standardise rail gauges in Australia, and were constructed so that they could be easily converted from 5ft 3in gauge to the standard, 4ft 8½in gauge. They were ordered in September 1948, with delivery required at the rate of six locomotives a month, beginning in the second quarter of 1950. Constructed at Hyde Park, like the locomotives for Western Australia, the production followed on from the previous order, and the NBL shops were certainly showing signs of the effects of a post-war boom in manufacturing at this time. The principal dimensions of the Class N 2-8-2s, were as follows:

Order No.	L996
Works Nos	26760-26809
Running Nos	450-499
Class	N
Wheel arrangement	2-8-2
Wheel dia. coupled	4ft 7.1875in
Wheelbase	
engine	30ft 9in
total	57ft 11.625in
Overall length	67ft 7.625in
Overall height	13ft 11.66in

Heating surface	
tubes	1,250.00 sq ft
firebox	203.00 sq ft
superheater	324.00 sq ft
total	1,777.00 sq ft
Grate area	31.00 sq ft
Boiler pressure	175 lb/sq in
Cylinders (2)	20 x 26in
Tractive effort	284,650 lb @ 85% B.P.
Weight in w.o.	
engine	76 tons 0 cwt
tender	48 tons 13 cwt
total	124 tons 13 cwt

The state of Victoria was in the process of 'rehabilitating' its railway system after the Second World War, under the slogan 'Operation Phoenix', and both the Class N and Class R orders were a part of that process. This activity included no fewer than 210 steam locomotives, on order from Britain, but there was also the prospect of the first diesel-electric types, and the electrification of the Gippsland line. As a result of these developments, Victoria Railways considered it might actually have more steam locomotives than it actually needed, and agreed to sell ten of the new N class to South Australia, which was also desperately short of motive power after the war.

It has been said that the N class 2-8-2s were an unremarkable design, being largely based on the similar Class N locomotives built in 1925. However, the modifications that were incorporated by NBL in the post-war construction included an all-welded steel firebox with thermic syphons and combustion chamber. Other details included provision of a two-section rocking grate, and ashpan doors operated by compressed air, with a self-cleaning spark arrester fitted into the smokebox. Changes in the design of Australian locomotives resulted in appearance which was much less oriented towards the typically British style, with clean simple lines, and a simple black livery, with only details picked out in red.

In South Australia, the new 2-8-2s were known as the 750 class, and replaced the Rx class 4-6-0s, which had been

The 50 Mikado type 2-8-2s for Victorian Railways were ordered in September 1949 (L996), and carried works numbers 26760–26809. This view shows the first of the class, No. N455, in as-built condition, before dispatch to Australia. A comparison with the illustration of one of the engines sold to South Australia shows the side buffers as they were originally provided on this order.

Mitchell Library Collection

in service with South Australia's railways for many years. The light axle loading of the new 2-8-2s meant that they had almost universal route availability. They were put to work between Mile End, Port Adelaide and Dry Creek, and were very widely used on goods trains, including some of the Murrayland lines, which could take only light axle loads. The Rx class that they replaced were pensioned off to finish their working lives on suburban services. The Class 750

2-8-2s had a very short working life, for the most part, of barely ten years, and were superseded in their turn by the diesel revolution. No modifications were made to the original Victoria Railways N class, as sold to South Australia, but they were eventually renumbered, and one member of the class, No. 752, is preserved at South Australia's Port Dock Railway Museum. Details of the numbering and renumbering of the 750 class are given below:

Designated the 750 class on South Australia's railways, this locomotive was built under order L996 for Victoria in 1951. As one of the ten purchased by South Australia, this locomotive became N Class No. 753. Seen here on shed at Mile End, South Australia, the buffers have been removed, but it still carries its original Victorian Railways number N465.

State Transport Authority (S. Australia)

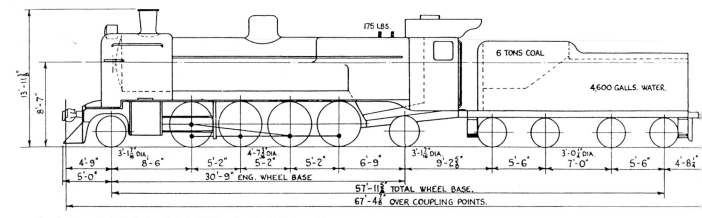

South Australia's 750 class 2-8-2, NBL order No. L996, and later reclassified as N class.

Mitchell Library Collection

SAR No.	VR No.	Works No.	In service on VR	In service on SAR	Condemned
750	474	26784	9/2/51	21/2/51	9/7/61
751	471	26781	24/1/51	5/2/51	6/7/61
752	477	26787	16/2/51	2/3/51	21/8/69
753	465	26775	11/12/50	5/1/51	9/7/62
754	461	26771	15/09/50	8/1/51	9/7/62
755	485	26795	28/2/51	12/3/51	7/9/67
756	491	26801	7/3/51	5/4/51	9/7/62
757	490	26800	11/4/51	30/4/51	9/7/62
758	494	26804	13/4/51	30/4/51	9/7/62
759	495	26805	13/4/51	8/5/51	16/7/63

The Class R 4-6-4s though, were the most memorable design of this period, and preserved examples featured in Australia's bicentenary celebrations. Like the N class 2-8-2s, these locomotives too were a part of 'Operation Phoenix', and were something of a departure from previous practice, where small engines were employed to run the trains across the state, with its numerous branch lines serving the agricultural flat lands of the region. The North British order also owed something of its design to a Victoria Railways 4-8-4 type, with a solitary example nicknamed 'Heavy Harry', which proved too heavy at 260 tons, for the lightly laid tracks and bridges. In the main though, the increasing weight of passenger trains, and the fact that the Class A2 4-6-0s were nearing the end of their working life, demanded a new passenger design. Initially, a Pacific type was proposed, but this was later altered to the 4-6-4, or Hudson arrangement – an arrangement not seen on any other Australian locomotive type.

Australia and New Zealand Orders 1929–1953

Railway	Year	Order No.	Works Nos	Qty	Works	Type
Mount Lyell Mining & Railway Co	1937	L910	24418	1	Hyde Park	4-8-4T new design
New Zealand Rlys	1938	L923	24523-62	40	Hyde Park	4-8-2 new 'J' class
West Aust. Govt	1947	L980	26545-69 & 26921-30	35	Hyde Park	4-6-2 similar to L793
Victorian Rlys	1948	L996	26760-809	50	Hyde Park	2-8-2, new 'N' class
Victorian Rlys	1950	L7	26990-27039 & 27040-59	70	Hyde Park	4-6-4 new 'R' class
New Zealand Rlys	1950	L19	27104-119	16	Hyde Park	4-8-2 JA class oil-fired

Country	No. of orders	No. of engines	Avg. engines/order
Australia	4	156	39
New Zealand	2	56	28
Total	6	212	35.3

Against the background of a backlog of repairs from the Second World War, Victoria Railways had no capacity to build new locomotives, and NBL won the contract in 1949, with order L7, for 50 locomotives. This was amended in January 1950, by the addition of a further 20 locomotives on the same contract, with delivery to be completed in 1951. The main dimensions of these prestigious locomotives were:

Order No.	L7
Works Nos	26990-27039 & 27040-59
Running Nos	700-769
Class	R
Wheel arrangement	4-6-4
Wheel dia. coupled	6ft 0.94in
Wheelbase	
coupled	12ft 10in
total	67ft 0in
Overall length	77ft 3.25in

Heating surface	
tubes	1,958.00 sq ft
firebox	285.00 sq ft
superheater	462.00 sq ft
total	2,705.00 sq ft
Grate area	42.00 sq ft
Boiler pressure	210 lb/sq in
Cylinders (2)	21.5 x 28in
Tractive effort	32,080 lb @ 85% B.P.
Weight in w.o. engine	107 tons 12 cwt
tender	79 tons 16 cwt
total	187 tons 8 cwt

The new locomotives were bar framed, from rolled slabs, having a thickness of no less than 5in, with a cast steel dragbox as a single assembly, attached to the rear of the main frames. At the leading end, a single steel casting incorporated the headstocks, to which the cylinder castings were attached. The boiler was a large parallel type, with an all-

Eight of these metre gauge Pacifics were built under order L860 for the Federated Malay States in 1929, and were a second batch to this new design, first built by NBL in 1927. The second order ,like the first, was constructed at Hyde Park, and carried works numbers 23904-23911.

Mitchell Library Collection

welded steel firebox, combustion chamber, and thermic syphons. The planned heavy workload of the class, which eventually was to cover Inter State expresses to New South Wales, required mechanical stokers to deliver the 6 tons of coal from the tender to the firegrate. Whilst North British had designed its own mechanical stoker, these new locomotives were equipped with type MB-1, designed by the Standard Stoker Co. Between 1954 and 1957, to make use of the low grade brown coal, engine number 707 was fitted with equipment from Stug, to cope with pulverised fuel. All axles, on both engine and tender, were equipped with self-aligning roller bearings, and the class was put to work on the high speed passenger services of Victoria.

Designs for the new locomotive were prepared by Victoria Railways, and one of the first Class R 4-6-4s (running number 704), was specially finished by NBL for display in Glasgow during the 1951 Festival of Britain. Like the Class N 2-8-2s, all of the Class Rs were transported to Melbourne as deck cargo. The R class attracted an enthusiastic following, and no less than six were set aside for preservation (Nos 700, 707, 711, 753, 761 and 766), and for use on steam specials. They were a most successful and attractive steam locomotive, and were the fitting final order for main line steam locomotives in Australia.

Orders from the Far East and China
Between 1929 and 1953, 7.4% of all locomotives built for export were dispatched to either China or Malaya, in four,

and eight orders, respectively. The majority of these in turn – both orders and locomotives – were sent to Malaya, initially as the Federated Malay States, and later as Malayan Railways. The first order was placed by Malaya in 1929 for another eight of the Class S three-cylinder Pacifics, first ordered in 1927. The 1929 order was L860, and all were built at Queen's Park Works, and was the last order to be received at Springburn from that country until 1937, when another new Pacific design for the metre gauge was built in Glasgow. The orders placed by Malaya in the period under review included two Pacific types, and a 4-6-4T design.

Although there were two Pacific classes built, the second of the two designs was perhaps the most notable, and included poppet valve gear in a series of modifications from the more or less conventional 4-6-2s supplied previously. In 1937, order L911 was placed with NBL, for eleven new locomotives, of the 0.1 class', which carried running numbers 60 to 70. The basic dimensions of the new locomotives were:

Order No.	L911
Works Nos	24419-29
Running Nos	60-70
Class	0.1
Wheel arrangement	4-6-2
Wheel dia. coupled	4ft 6in
Heating surface	
tubes	960.00 sq ft
firebox	149.00 sq ft
superheater	218.00 sq ft
total	1,327.00 sq ft
Grate area	27.00 sq ft
Boiler pressure	250 lb/sq in
Cylinders (3)	12.5 x 24in
Tractive effort	22,130 lb @ 85%

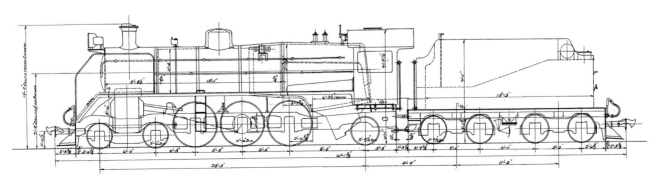

The 0.1 class Pacifics were built for Federated Malay States Railways in 1937/38, under NBL order L911.   *Mitchell Library Collection*

The locomotives were built to the metre gauge, and were put to work on passenger trains between Singapore, Kuala Lumpur and Prai. The locomotives had to be built to a very tight axle load limit of 12.75 tons, with NBL adopting every weight saving measure possible, including the use of bar frames and nickel steel boiler shells and were a very successful design, with their work being taken over long after the Second World War, by diesel-electric types. A further two orders for these Pacifics were placed on NBL, as orders L919 and L926, for another 17 locomotives, with the last order before WWII appearing on 8th March 1939. In the period under review, the final order from Malaya was placed in 1945, for Malayan Railways, for the reclassified 564 class Pacifics. These were essentially the same design as before, but in July 1945, order L957 was received at Springburn for no fewer than 40 of these very successful locomotives, marking perhaps the beginning of the post-war boom in locomotive building.

Another interesting design for Malaya, was the 4-6-4T design, for which NBL received three orders, in 1938, 1939, and 1940. The first order for this new design, L920, was taken in March 1938, for six locomotives, to be classified C2, and numbered 23 to 28. They were delivered during 1939, with the designs prepared by the Federated Malay States and NBL, and like all colonial orders, the Crown Agents for the Colonies took some part in the process. The main dimensions of the first order were as follows:

Order No.	L920
Works Nos	24514-24519
Running Nos	23-28
Class	C2
Wheel arrangement	4-6-4T
Wheel dia. coupled	4ft 6in

Heating surface	
tubes	853.50 sq ft
firebox	136.50 sq ft
superheater	180.00 sq ft
total	1,033.50 sq ft
Grate area	28.00 sq ft
Boiler pressure	250 lb/sq in
Cylinders (2)	14.5 x 24in
Tractive effort	18,200 lb @ 85% B.P.

The main characteristics of these locomotives were the same as the Pacific locomotives, then recently built by NBL for Malaya. These tank engines were also a new design for the metre gauge lines, with the same weight limitations of 12.75 tons axle load. Again, they included bar frames and poppet valve gear, and were as successful in service as the larger Pacific type. The network of Malaya's metre gauge lines covered a total track mileage of 1,000 miles at the time these engines went into service. They were intended for suburban traffic, particularly around Kuala Lumpur, where all imported locomotives were assembled, and heavy repairs undertaken. The second order for the new C2 tank engines was placed on the same day in March 1939, as the third order for the 0.1 class, whilst the final order was placed during the Second World War, in June 1940, for six 4-6-4Ts. No further orders for tank engines were to come from either the colony, or later, Malayan Railways, for this type of locomotive. The final order for steam locomotives for Malaya, was L957, for the 40 Pacifics from the 0.1 class, placed in 1945. NBL did construct another order for Malaya, but this was a diesel-hydraulic 0-6-0, ordered in 1952, under order L50, and was itself the final order for locomotives for the Far East.

China and Far East Orders 1929–1953

Railway	Year	Order No.	Works Nos	Qty	Works	Type
Fed. Malay States	1929	L860	23904-11	8	Queens Park	4-6-2 similar to L840
Nanking–Shanghai Rly.	1930	L870	24026-33	8	Hyde Park	4-6-2 new design
Peiping–Liaoning Rly.	1930	L876	24080-5	6	Queens Park	2-8-2 to railway co.'s designs
Tientsin–Pukow Rly.	1932	L883	24106-13	8	Hyde Park	4-6-2 to railway co.'s designs
Fed. Malay States	1937	L911	24419-29	11	Hyde Park	4-6-2 new design
King Kan Rly.	1937	L912	24430-35	6	Hyde Park	0-8-0 new design
Fed. Malay States	1938	L919	24508-13	6	Hyde Park	4-6-2 same as L911
Fed. Malay States	1938	L920	24514-19	6	Hyde Park	4-6-4T new design
Fed. Malay States	1939	L925	24565-9	5	Hyde Park	4-6-4T similar to L920
Fed. Malay States	1939	L926	24570-80	11	Hyde Park	4-6-2 similar to L919
Fed. Malay States	1940	L934	24661-66	6	Hyde Park	4-6-4T similar to L925
Malayan Rlys.	1945	L957	25758-95	40	Hyde Park	4-6-2 similar to L926

Country	No. of orders	No. of engines	Avg. engines/order
China	4	28	7
Malaya	8	93	11.6
Total	12	121	10.1

The British presence in China was a major factor in the locomotive builders in Britain securing orders for locomotives, including North British. A number of locomotives had been delivered from Glasgow to various Chinese railways, but like all other work, during the depression years, there was a dramatic fall in this work. Only four orders were received from China, between 1929 and 1953, for no more than 28 locomotives, and these orders were placed in 1930 (2), 1932 (1), and the final order in 1937. The locomotive types included a Pacific, a 2-8-2 Mikado, and an 0-8-0 shunting locomotive. The orders for the Far East were under severe pressure from American builders in particular, and

the two Pacific designs, one for Nanking–Shanghai (L870), and the other for Tientsin–Pukow (L883), were for standard gauge lines.

The second of these orders, placed in 1932, was for eight locomotives, and they presented a distinctly 'American' appearance. In fact, most of the features of this design were North American, which reinforced the severe competition for locomotive orders during the depression years. Amongst the features were: the Franklin firedoor, American designed multiple throttle, Westinghouse brake gear and heating equipment, Alco power reverse, and American Railroad Association 'D' couplers. All eight locomotives were trans-

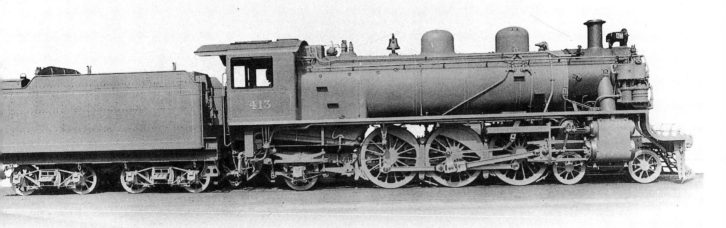

The largest of only three orders placed with NBL in 1932, and even then, for only eight engines, for the Tientsin–Pukow Railway in China. These 4-6-2s were all built at Hyde Park in 1933, and carried works numbers 24106–24113 (running numbers 413–420).
Mitchell Library Collection

ported from Hyde Park, to Stobcross Quay, where they were loaded on board the MV *Beldis,* and sailed from Glasgow on 8th July 1933. Like many locomotives before them, they had a difficult road journey from Springburn, compounded by the height of the locomotives – the Chinese loading gauge being generous for standard gauge locomotives. The main dimensions were as follows:

Order No.	L883
Works Nos	24106-24113
Running Nos	413-420
Wheel arrangement	4-6-2
Wheel dia.	
coupled	5ft 9in
bogie	3ft 0in
trailing	3ft 6in
Wheelbase	
engine	32ft 1in
engine & tender	60ft 4in
Heating surface	
tubes	1,745.00 sq ft
firebox	202.00 sq ft
superheater	443.00 sq ft
total	2,390.00 sq ft
Grate area	43.50 sq ft
Boiler pressure	200 lb/sq in
Cylinders (2)	20 x 28in

Weight in w.o.	
engine	90 tons 10 cwt
engine & tender	147 tons 18 cwt
Fuel capacity	
coal	9.84 tons
water	5,289 gallons
Tractive effort	27,600 lb @ 85% B.P.

The American theme in Chinese locomotives was continued in the final North British order for that country, when in 1937, order L912 was placed, for six new 0-8-0 shunting engines for the King Kan Railway. Although this was noted as a new design, its appearance was remarkably similar to steam engines of this type used in the USA for shunting purposes, even down to the wedge shape of the tender superstructure. Although numerous orders had been built for Chinese railways prior to the First World War, the orders were never regained, and the competition was not just from America, as the massive freight engines from Vulcan Foundry, placed during the 1930s, bear testimony.

The Americas
Not surprisingly perhaps, orders from North America were always few and far between, although occasionally, railroads in Canada came to Springburn for locomotives. Newfoundland had placed orders on NBL between 1903 and 1928, and again came to NBL in 1935 for a pair of 2-8-2s. Between 1935 and 1940, NBL received four orders from the Newfoundland Railway, and a 2-8-2 of the same basic design was ordered by Associated Newspapers of Newfoundland in 1937. No orders were taken from Central America for main line service during this period, although NBL had supplied a number of 'Modified Fairlie' types to Mexico on previous occasions.

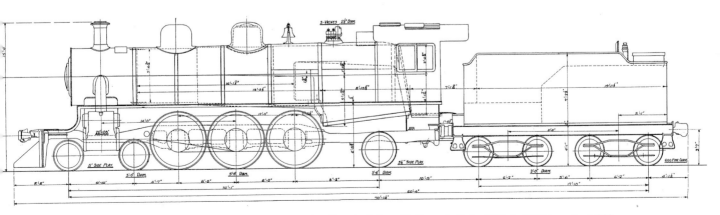

The penultimate order for China, were these Pacifics for the Tientsin-Pukow Railway, built by NBL in 1933 to order L883.
Mitchell Library Collection

The locomotives for Newfoundland were actually built to the 3ft 6in gauge, and were primarily for freight service, hauling timber and paper pulp across the province. The railways of Newfoundland totalled 740 route miles, with some very severe gradients, especially on the 546 mile run from St Johns to Port-aux-Basques. They were typically North American in appearance, with bar frames, two outside, 18 by 24 in cylinders, operated by Walschaerts valve gear. All of the locomotives were built at Hyde Park, and carried running numbers 1002 to 1008, with order L922 for Associated Newspapers carrying running numbers 14 and 15. Although these last two engines were in fact bought by the Botwood

Railway in 1937, and lasted 20 years before being withdrawn. The railway itself was sold to the Grand Falls Central Railway Co. in 1957, as part of the Anglo-Newfoundland Development Corporation. The design was actually produced by the Newfoundland Railway's engineers, with the final locomotive, number 1008, being built in 1940, under order L935.

The 2-8-2s ordered by the Newfoundland Railway were also the only known North British built locomotives to run under Canadian National Railways ownership, with the six engines transferring to CNR in 1949. All six locomotives survived to 1957, when they were finally withdrawn.

North and Central American Orders 1929–1953

Railway	Year	Order No.	Works Nos	Qty	Works	Type
Newfoundland Rly.	1935	L894	24297-8	2	Hyde Park	2-8-2 to railway co.'s designs
Newfoundland Rly.	1937	L913	24436	1	Hyde Park	2-8-2 similar to L894
Assoc. Newspapers of Newfoundland	1937	L914	24437-8	2	Hyde Park	2-8-2 similar to L913
Newfoundland Rly.	1938	L922	24521-2	2	Hyde Park	2-8-2 similar to L913
Newfoundland Rly.	1940	L935	24667	1	Hyde Park	2-8-2 similar to L922

Country	No. of orders	No. of engines	Avg. engines/order
Canada	5	8	1.6
Others	0	0	0
Total	5	8	1.6

NBL Ord. No.	Works No.	Newfound-land No.	CNR No.	Built	W/dn
L894	24297	1002	302	1935	5/57
L894	24298	1003	303	1935	9/57
L913	24436	1004	304	1937	3/57
L922	24521	1005	305	1938	11/57
L922	24522	1006	306	1938	3/57
L935	24667	1008	307	1941	5/57

The prolific ordering from South America that had been seen in previous years, especially from Argentina and Brazil, was obviously affected by the depression years. But, in the quarter century from 1929 to 1953, only eight orders were received by NBL, five from Brazil, two from Argentina, and a single order from Venezuela, which was subsequently cancelled. The order from Venezuela may be seen as unusual, if only from the fact that it was placed at

all – that country is not noted for its extensive rail network. Another of the South American orders that was cancelled was from Argentina, which would have resulted in the building of 20 Pacifics at Hyde Park in 1948/49. In view of the question of payment for orders from Argentina, referred to in Chapter 8, and negotiations between that country and Britain and the economic climate of the post-war period, perhaps that cancellation is not so surprising. In total then,

There were a number of orders for this design of passenger tank locomotive for the 5ft 3in gauge Sao Paulo Railway in Brazil. This order was placed in November 1944, for another six of these Class J tank engines of which this is No. 81. In fact, the earliest order in 1911, was for the first locomotives for the railway, to be fitted with the Schmidt type superheater.

Mitchell Library Collection

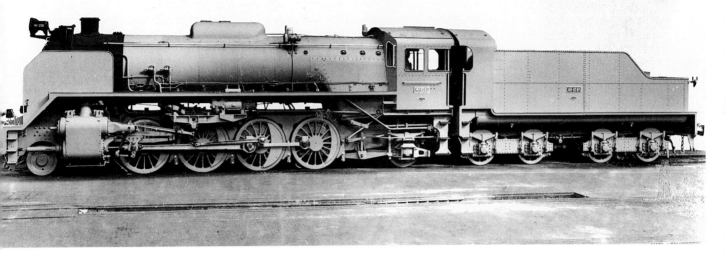

The arrival of an order from Spanish National Railways in August 1949 (L5), for 25 of these Mikado 2-8-2s, ended a drought of European orders of many years. NBL had built quite a number of orders for Europe, before the First World War, including some for the privately owned Spanish railways.

Mitchell Library Collection

only six of the recorded orders resulted in 42 engines being built, 22 for the Sao Paulo Railway in Brazil, and 20 for the Central Argentine Railway.

The order in 1929 (L864) was the first of three, for a total of 16 Class J 2-8-4 tank engines, which was a superheated type. The design dated back to 1911/12, when the first orders for this suburban 2-8-4T were placed, and a mixture of both saturated and superheated engines were delivered. Interestingly enough, the first order was equipped with a Schmidt superheater, back in 1912, when this step change in steam technology was beginning to be implemented. The 1929 order was built at Queen's Park, but all subsequent orders for the Class J passenger tank were built at Hyde Park, for the 5ft 3in gauge Sao Paulo lines.

Six years after the new Class J tank engines appeared, in 1935, NBL produced a design for a massively proportioned 4-6-4 tank engine for Sao Paulo. In total, only six of these fine engines were built, to orders L895 and L898, placed in 1935 and 1936 respectively. The first order was for two engines, which carried running numbers 171 and 172, and works numbers 24299 and 24300, whilst the second order

was for four engines; running numbers 173 to 176 and works numbers 24375 to 24378. Their appearance of great size was exaggerated by the short, but large diameter boiler, topped, in the first order, by the ACFI feed water heating equipment. The coupled wheels, at 5ft 6in diameter were driven by Walschaerts valve gear, and two 21.5 by 26in stroke cylinders were fitted. The large (11in diameter) piston valves have been noted as providing a very free steaming engine, and with the boiler pressed to 200 lb/sq in, a nominal tractive effort of no less than 26,000 lb was achieved in these coal fired locomotives.

Neighbouring Argentina had placed numerous orders with NBL, particularly before the First World War, but only one order, L959, for 20 CS6 class 4-8-0 locomotives resulted in engines being built in 1948. The order was actually placed in August 1945, with works numbers 25920 to 25939, and they were built at Hyde Park. In design, they were a development of the 40 locomotives ordered back in 1914, which in turn were a combination of the tenders fitted to the same railway's Pacific engines, and a 2-8-0 freight engine for the Buenos Aires & Rosario Railway.

By 1948, the Class CS6 heavy freight locomotives were fitted with 19in diameter, by 26in stroke cylinders, compared with the 21in diameter cylinders fitted to order L625, but retained the original 4ft 7.5in diameter coupled wheels. The original boiler design, fitted with the Robinson superheater, provided a heating surface of more than 1,700 sq ft. Later NBL built locomotives included mostly 'Melesco', or

South American Orders 1929–1953

Railway	Year	Order No.	Works Nos	Qty	Works	Type
Sao Paulo Rly.	1929	L864	23946-51	6	Queens Park	2-8-4T, "Class J", same as L823, but s/heated
Sao Paulo Rly.	1935	L895	24299-300	2	Hyde Park	4-6-4T new NBL design
Sao Paulo Rly.	1936	L898	24375-78	4	Hyde Park	4-6-4T similar to L895
Sao Paulo Rly.	1937	L916	24459-62	4	Hyde Park	2-8-4T, "Class J", same as L864
Sao Paulo Rly.	1944	L951	25907-12	6	Hyde Park	2-8-4T same as L916
Central Argentine	1945	L959	25920-39	20	Hyde Park	4-8-0 similar to L625
Argentine Rly.	1948	L992	26728-47	20	Hyde Park	4-6-2, "Class PS11", cancelled
Venezuela Rly.	1948	L993	26753-55	3	Queens Park	4-8-2T cancelled

Country	No. of orders	No. of engines	Avg. engines/order
Brazil	5	22	4.4
Argentina	2	40	20
Venezuela	1	3	3
Total	8	65	7.3

Superheater Co.'s superheaters. The Belpaire pattern firebox included a grate area of some 32.5 sq ft. The 1948 locomotives were almost identical in appearance with the original design, with the obvious external difference being the fitting of top feed apparatus to the front boiler ring. These locomotives were the last to be built by North British for Argentina, and continued the typically British designs prevalent on British owned railways in Argentina.

Overseas orders showed some signs of recovery towards the end of, and just following the Second World War, and continued into the 1950s. The sources of orders were not so wide ranging as before, in part due to the rapid expansion of diesel and electric traction, and in addition, the demise of colonial rule, as more, former British territories gained independence. The last few orders for steam locomotives in the early 1950s came, not surprisingly perhaps, from India and South Africa in the main, with the latter obtaining the last steam locomotive built by North British. So far as the locomotive building business was concerned, NBL's dominance had been challenged, even for steam orders by Vulcan Foundry, Robert Stephenson & Co., and Beyer-Peacock, and the growth of non-steam traction was to prove even less successful in the post-war years. Most of the final orders for steam from overseas, were from industrial and colliery railways, and as seen in the comparison between the number of orders and number of locomotives built, industry placed a large number of orders, but these were frequently only for one or two engines. However, during the 1950s, as NBL attempted to convert its locomotive building business from purely steam, to every kind of motive power, some of its most famous steam locomotives were built at Hyde Park and Queen's Park.

8

Diesel & Electric Traction Orders

The first essay that involved NBL in constructing loco-motives for anything other than conventional steam traction, was its own steam turbo-electric locomotive of 1909. This prototype was never developed, but was re-cycled after the First World War into the Reid-Ramsay con-densing geared turbine. Neither of these imaginative attempts at improving the efficiency of the steam locomo-tive were at all successful, and the company itself did not believe in the long term future of non-steam traction before the Second World War. Ironically, it was as sub-contractor to the English Electric Co. that NBL was set to work on its first electric locomotive. There were two orders from Japan, in 1922, and English Electric went to Springburn for the mechanical portions, under NBL orders E2 and E3, all 34 of which were built at Hyde Park.

The first major non-steam locomotive produced by NBL did not materialise until 1946, by which time the company had concentrated its entire effort on steam locomotive building. The growth of electrification in countries where coal was not an indigenous fuel was not seen by the com-pany as a particular commercial threat, nor was the gradual improvement of diesel traction. During the 1920s and 1930s, even in Britain – a coal economy – the LMSR were putting diesel shunters to work, from suppliers like English Electric and Hunslet. Even the LNER, GWR, and Southern Railway toyed with the new traction in these years, though as a rival to steam in the UK, it did not really take off until the 1950s.

Diesel Traction

In 1946, the locomotive policy of North British showed a marked change of direction, as a project to design and build a diesel locomotive took shape. It has been said that it was a characteristic of NBL's approach to locomotive building, that this was not a standard gauge, surface unit, but a low-powered locomotive for mine working. Many of NBL's cus-tomers were mines, and other extractive industries, and so the choice of a mining locomotive was perhaps not so illog-ical as it might at first seem. Under order L972, two 100hp 0-4-0 diesel-mechanical prototypes were built at Queen's Park, for 2ft 6in gauge, and carrying works numbers 26248 and 26249. This first order was officially recorded as being placed in 1947, and after a couple of years of design and testing, the NBL 'Miner' series was successfully launched. Later developments saw the use of hydraulic, rather than mechanical transmissions, for the specialised, and volatile environment of mine working.

Late in 1947, one of the most important early orders for diesel locomotives was placed with NBL, by the LMSR, in

Built for East African Railways, under order L52 (1952) and look-ing quite massive in appearance, these 0-8-0 diesel-hydraulics developed only 300hp. Fourteen of these metre gauge locomotives were ordered, as Class 83, fitted with a Paxman diesel engine, and of course, a Voith-NBL transmission. This 1954 view shows No. 8303 outside Queen's Park Works, before being shipped to East Africa.

Mitchell Library Collection

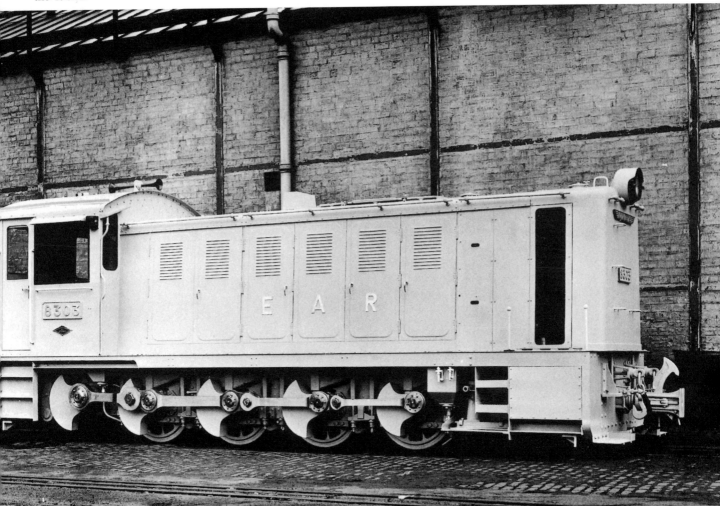

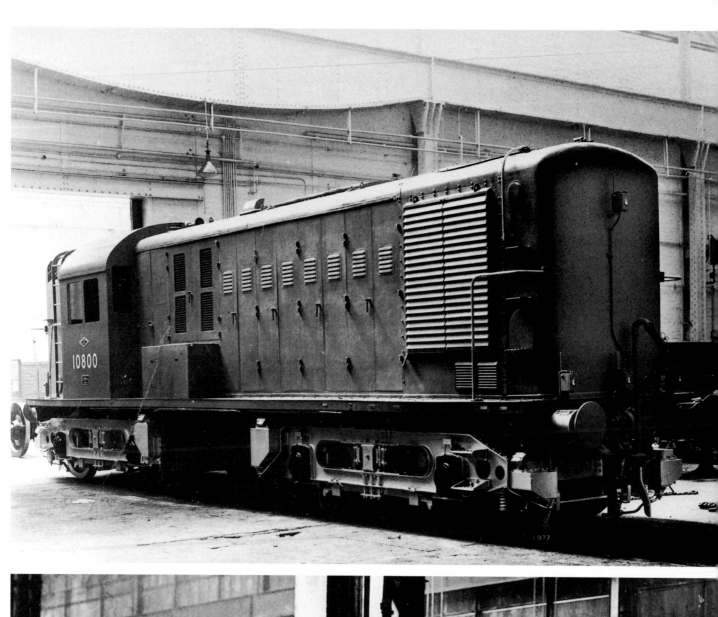

Above: North British built the very first of what was classed as mixed traffic diesel locomotives in 1950. Ironically, in view of NBL's later commitment to hydraulic transmission, No. 10800 was a diesel-electric type. This is a rare view of the solitary locomotive in revenue earning service at Birmingham New Street, in April 1955. The locomotive had arrived on the 6.35am ex-Yarmouth. It was later sold to Brush Traction, and provided a test bed for advanced electric traction and control systems, developed by the company in the 1960s.

Roger Shenton

Opposite Top: Order L977 was placed by the LMSR in 1947, and was intended as a mixed traffic diesel-electric for secondary duties. NBL's order included design work, and the supply of mechanical parts, with the Paxman diesel engine and GEC electrical equipment supplied to the Queens Park Works, where No. 10800 was built. This view shows the locomotive inside the works after completion but before delivery.

Mitchell Library Collection

Opposite Below: The very first of the North British mines locomotives were ordered in 1948, to order L972, although at first mechanical transmission was employed in the 0-4-0 100hp locomotives. The original order was for only one, but two were built as a prototype for NBL stock. The engine was a six-cylinder design from Paxman, and paired with a fully flameproofed gearbox, and jackshaft final drive. This was builder's No. 26249.

Mitchell Library Collection

its final weeks of life, before Nationalisation. Under order L977, Queen's Park Works were allocated the job of constructing an 800hp diesel-electric Bo-Bo, carrying works number 26413, and later, the BR running number 10800. In its way, this locomotive was a model for almost all future diesel freight locomotives for BR, until the 1980s.

The principal dimensions of the NBL diesel-electric were as follows:

Order No.	L977
Works Nos	26413
Running Nos	10800
Wheel arrangement	Bo-Bo
Wheel dia. (bogie)	3ft 6in
Diesel engine	Davey Paxman, 16 cyl., 827bhp
Electrical eqpt	British Thomson Houston
Tractive effort	34,500 lb

The LMSR locomotive was intended for branch line and secondary workings, with a maximum designed speed of 70 mph. The diesel engine's crankshaft was directly coupled to the main generator, with an auxiliary generator positioned above, and chain driven. The control systems followed similar arrangements provided by BTH for other diesel and electric traction equipment, with electro-pneumatic contactors. This was the preferred system for other AEI group companies, such as Metropolitan-Vickers, compared with English Electric's electro-magnetic systems. The NBL-Paxman diesel remained a one-off example, and was not joined by any other similar types, until 1957, when English Electric-Vulcan Foundry launched British Railways' most successful Type 1 diesel locomotive.

The following year, 1948, the Ceylon Government Railways ordered eight 625hp Bo-Bo diesel-electrics for its 5ft 6in gauge lines. This was not a new venture for Ceylon, since it already had multiple units and railcars in service, but for North British, it was the first major order from overseas for the mechanical parts of more than one diesel locomotive. The general appearance and layout was similar to the LMSR order of 1947, with a single full-width cab at one end, and a long bonnet or hood covering the engine and generator compartments. The four-wheeled bogies, with

Another 5ft 6in gauge diesel-electric, was this 625hp Bo-Bo type for Ceylon, No. 553 of Class G2, and built at Springburn, under order L990. Only eight were built, with Paxman diesel engines, and GEC electrical equipment.

Mitchell Library Collection

their outside frames and overhung leaf springs were very much steam age technology, a perspective enhanced perhaps by the jacks carried on the front footplate. These eight locomotives carried works numbers 26706–26713 and were Ceylon Railways Class G2. The next major order from overseas for a 'main line' locomotive was not placed until 1953, when the India Store Dept. came to Springburn for 20 metre gauge locomotives. These had the same wheel arrangement, and the Paxman 12-cylinder power unit, but were fitted with Voith hydraulic transmission.

On the whole, 1948 was a reasonably successful year for the company, securing six orders for diesel and electric types, although two of these orders were the new 100hp underground locomotives, which were initially built for stock. Ten were built under order L987 for 2ft 6in gauge, with mechanical transmission using either SLM (Swiss Locomotive & Machines) 2-speed, or Self Changing Gears 3-speed final drive. The six 3ft 0in gauge locomotives – both types were 0-4-0 – were all fitted with the SLM 3-speed final drive. The last order taken in 1948 was L994, for a pair of diesel-mechanical shunters for Coalvilles Ltd, in the Transvaal, South Africa.

Only one order was placed in 1949 – again for stock, and this was for a prototype diesel-hydraulic shunter for industrial use. This was also the first occasion that Voith transmissions were installed in a locomotive built by NBL. By 1949, NBL's order numbers had got beyond L999, and the decision was taken to go back to allocating order numbers from L1 again, and the latest contact was allocated NBL order number L8. These locomotives were 0-4-0 wheel arrangement for standard gauge and carried works numbers 27078 and 27079. Both remained on NBL's books for some time before being sold – 27078 in September 1951 to Stewart & Lloyds steelworks, and 27079 in June 1955 to

Esso. As these were prototypes, two different power units were used, to gain experience; a 200hp National diesel engine was fitted into 27078, and a 200hp Paxman RPHL/1 into 27079. Both locomotives were fitted with Voith's type L33y hydraulic transmission.

In 1950, ten diesel-hydraulic locomotives were built, mostly at Queen's Park, all of which were for industrial/mine operations. Atlas Works was again building locomotives, after a gap of more than 20 years, which included the only diesel-mechanical locomotives ordered in 1950. These latter were a pair of 2ft 6in gauge 'Miners' for Logue Industrial Equipment Ltd, an agency representing the Dominion Coal & Steel Corporation, in South Africa. The 'Miner' was a successful experiment for NBL, and its attributes, extolled by the company, were the fact that it was compact, and powerful, and not much bigger than a mine tub. A number of the 'Miner' type 100hp units were ordered by various companies over the next decade, with the last being ten locomotives built for stock in 1956, but later sold for use in Canada.

The power units installed in the 'Miner' locomotives were either Crossley Type BWL5, five-cylinder engines, or Paxman 6RQE, six-cylinder types. Electrical equipment was fully flameproofed, and supplied by either CAV or GEC. The final drive for the solitary diesel-mechanical order was provided through a 3-speed SLM transmission. By 1950, NBL were building hydraulic transmissions under licence from Voith in Germany, although these were still small in number. The 'Miners' with hydraulic transmission were equipped with the Voith-NBL type L22, whilst higher powered diesels at that time were fitted with the type L37.

An interesting, and solitary order in 1950 from Australia, well Tasmania to be precise, was allocated number L9, and was for a single 500hp 0-8-0. The order was originally placed by agents Knox, Schlapp (Pty) Ltd, for operation on the Emu Bay Railway, which had previously been a customer for NBL steam types. The power unit was once again a Paxman engine, with NBL supplying the gearing for the final drive, and the hydraulic transmission the Voith type L37.

Most of the diesel traction orders placed with NBL at this time were being built at Queen's Park, which was being gradually modernised to cater for the new technology. In 1951, six orders were allocated to Queen's Park, and three to Hyde Park. All were for either 0-4-0 or 0-6-0 industrial, mining or shunting locomotives. In November 1951, John Summers & Sons placed an order with NBL for a single 400hp 0-6-0, with the Paxman engine and Voith transmission. The order was added to in the same month by Stewart & Lloyds, whilst NBL decided to build three for stock in January 1952, which were later sold to the National Coal Board, and John Summers. These were not the most powerful shunters built by NBL, but continued a trend towards building some locomotives for stock on the back of other orders. Later in the 1950s, many more orders were built for stock, most of which were subsequently sold.

This locomotive No. 3001, was one of 20 metre gauge locomotives ordered in 1953 (order L54), and delivered two years later. These B-B diesel-hydraulics were fitted with 12-cylinder Paxman diesel engines, originally rated at 605hp but engine design changes increased this to 625hp in June 1954.

Mitchell Library Collection

A solitary export order for NBL was the single Bo-Bo electric locomotive for the Estoril Railway in Portugal, built in 1948/49, to order L986 (works number 26683). NBL had begun to establish a partnership with GEC, who supplied the electrical equipment, which was in evidence in later orders for electric locomotives for British Railways. NBL supplied the mechanical parts for this locomotive for the 5ft 6in gauge line, which was supplied with power at 1,500V dc. In total the locomotive weighed 50 metric tons, and developed a tractive effort of 40,000 lbs.

Mitchell Library Collection

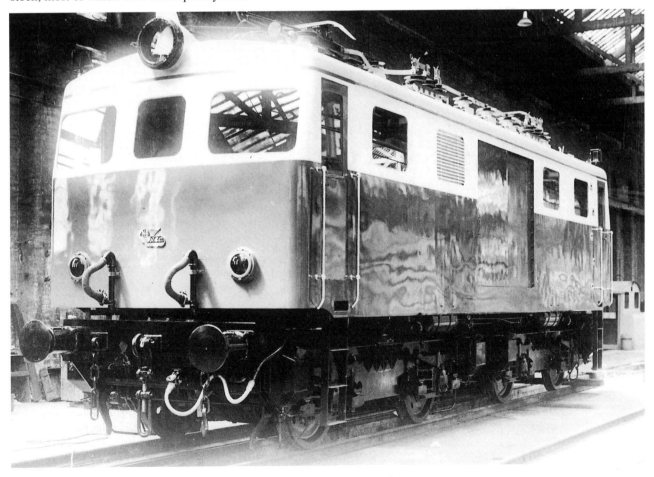

In collaboration with GEC, NBL built the 40 Class 4E 1Co-Co1 locomotives for South African Railways. These locomotives were ordered under L998, and were the second and last electric locomotives built by NBL for export. The order was originally allocated to Hyde Park, but transferred to Atlas, due to the large number of steam types under construction at Hyde Park

Mitchell Library Collection

Electric Locomotives

Apart from another prototype locomotive for the standard gauge, NBL's next non-steam locomotive order actually came from overseas, from the Estoril Railway in Portugal. In 1948, order L986 was recorded, for a single locomotive, fitted with power equipment from GEC in Birmingham, this mixed traffic design being delivered just under two years later in 1950. The association with GEC, for electrical equipment, was to continue for over ten years, and the company's financial support was very important for NBL in the late 1950s.

The second, and last of NBL's orders for electric locomotives for overseas, in partnership with GEC, came on 30th September 1948, in the shape of the mechanical parts for 40 1Co-Co1 locomotives for South Africa. These became Class 4E, and were numbered E219 to E258 on South African Railways, and although the order was placed in 1948, delivery was not scheduled until March 1951, but they did not enter service until 1952 in any numbers. The South African market for electric traction was not an easy place to break into, even for the likes of GEC, since Metropolitan-Vickers, and the AEI group had been supplying large orders for some 30 years to SAR. The Class 4Es were a heavy locomotive, and developing 3,030hp, they remained South African Railways' most powerful locomotives until 1970, when the Class 6E Bo-Bo's arrived.

They were not particularly successful in service however, and modifications at NBL's cost – referred to in Chapter 9 – were not good news for the company. The difficulties experienced in operating this 1Co-Co1 wheel arrangement on the 3ft 6in gauge forced an alteration to the Co-Co arrangement in the mid 1950s. The principal dimensions of this class were as follows:

Order No.	L998
Works Nos	26859-26898
Running Nos	E219 – E258
Wheel arrangement	1Co-Co1
Overall	
length	71ft 8in
width	9ft 6in
height	13ft 7in
Wheel dia.	
(powered)	4ft 3in
(carrying)	2ft 6in
Bogie wheelbase	15ft 2in
Bogie pivot centres	35ft 5in
Power equipment	4 GEC, nose suspended axle hung traction motors. 505hp @ 1 hr rating.
Weight in w.o.	155 tons
Maximum speed	60 mph
Tractive effort	72,000 lb

Intriguingly, there are some comments in the NBL order book which suggest that the locomotive was estimated to weigh 132 tons, and develop a tractive effort of 63,500 lb. Clearly, the latter would be influenced by whether the continuous, or one hour rating of the traction motors was measured. The locomotives were to have been delivered at the

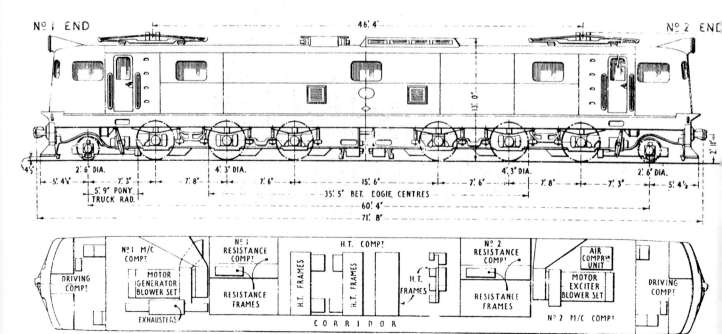

The Class 4E electric locomotives for South Africa were built by NBL in 1949, to order L998.

The bodies and complex bogies for the SAR 3,000hp locomotives, were transported to Finnieston Quay separately. Here, one of the bogies is seen leaving the works on a Pickfords low loader, starting its journey through Glasgow, from Springburn to the Clyde.
Mitchell Library Collection

rate of three per month to start with, but increasing to four per month until completion of the contract.

South African Railways had completed the latest stage of their 3,000V dc electrification programme in 1953, covering the Cape Western main line, the suburban section of which had been converted from 1,500V dc. The NBL built Class 4Es were intended to haul both passenger and freight trains over the 149 miles route from Cape Town to Touws River. The line, which was newly electrified from beyond Bellville, included a section of line at a ruling gradient of 1 in 66. Thirty of the class were to operate over this route,

whilst the remaining ten were delivered to Natal, where SAR had been running over the electrified lines through the Drakensberg Mountains since the 1920s.

The general layout of the locomotives included a fabricated main frame/underframe, built up in three separate sections, welded together to form a single unit. On top of this, a full width body with a driving cab at each end, housed the main transformers, power and control equipments. The

From the largest to the smallest. This view, taken at Atlas Works, probably in 1950, shows a 3,000hp electric locomotive of Class 4E for South Africa, dwarfing one of the diminutive 100hp 'Miner' locosmotive, for underground service (possibly order L12, part of which was constructed at the Atlas Works). The transition from steam to non-steam traction building was very difficult for NBL, and proved to be a major factor in the eventual demise of the company.
Mitchell Library Collection

three-axle bogies and pony truck units were fitted with side bearers opposite the bogie pivot, and at each end of the bogie frame, with the pivot itself carrying no weight. Overhung leaf springs were the main suspension, with the two bogies connected together in an early form of intercoupling, with the buffing and drawgear carried on the headstocks of each bogie frame.

The six traction motors were four-pole, series wound force-ventilated machines, supplied by GEC, with all the remaining power equipment and electro-pneumatic control system. Interestingly perhaps, NBL sub-contracted out the manufacture of the final drive gears to Alfred Wiseman Ltd, but in later locomotive construction, manufactured the gearing themselves at Queen's Park. As was becoming standard practice for dc electric locomotives, the power was collected from roof-mounted pantographs, and fed through isolating switches to the main high tension compartment in the centre of the locomotive. The electro-pneumatic control system provided the driver with the ability to switch in and out various combinations of resistances, through contactors, to control the power supplied to the traction motors. In appearance, the NBL locomotives set some new standards for South African Railways, and some family likenesses can be seen with later generations of electric traction in South

NBL's only 25kV ac locomotive, for British Railways was the Class AL4, ten of which were built at Hyde Park to order L91. The locomotives were originally numbered E3036–E3045, but later renumbered 84001 to 84010. This view shows the then last remaining locomotive in service, No. 84010 (works number 27802) passing Lancaster Castle in August 1979.

Author's Collection

Africa. In fact, in 1954, Metropolitan–Vickers supplied a batch of Co-Co locomotives which were very similar in appearance, but without the additional pony trucks. This may have been, sadly perhaps, NBL's only export contract of any note in association with GEC, but it was not the last order for electric locomotives. That dubious honour befell the company on 18th February 1957, when GEC placed order L91, for ten sets of mechanical parts for 25kV ac electric locomotives for British Railways.

The British Transport Commission's Modernisation Plan for British Railways envisaged large scale electrification, including the King's Cross to York, and Euston to Liverpool/Manchester main lines. As it turned out, this ambitious plan – scheduled to be completed in 1960 – was curtailed, and restricted to the London to Liverpool and Manchester lines, itself not completed until the late 1960s. British Railways placed orders with various electrical companies, AEI, English Electric, and of course GEC, for various designs of electric locomotive. The solitary order GEC received, was for ten type A locomotives, later known as Class AL4, and later still as Class 84, and the partnership with NBL resulted in the appearance of NBL order L91. The leading dimensions of this final order for electric traction from NBL, as sub-contractors, were as below:

Order No.	L91
Works Nos	27793-27802
Running Nos	E3036-E3045 (later 84001-84010)
Class	AL4 (later 84)
Wheel arrangement	Bo-Bo
Overall	
length	53ft 6in
width	8ft 8.25in
height	12ft 4.44in
Wheel dia. bogie	4ft 0in
Bogie wheelbase	10ft 0in
Bogie pivot centres	29ft 6in
Power equipment	4 GEC, nose suspended axle hung traction motors, type WT501
Weight in w.o.	76.5 tons
Maximum speed	100 mph
Tractive effort	48,000 lb

The Class AL4 electric locomotives were built at Hyde Park Works, with the locomotive body constructed from mild steel, and as an integral structure, without the heavier style of construction used on earlier locomotives. In fact, the body itself was constructed from mild steel sheet, overlaid on a framework of a type known as Vierendeel truss. It was extremely light, but strong, and was also adopted by Brush/Birmingham Railway Carriage & Wagon, for the *Falcon* diesel prototype. In BR's electric locomotive fleet, this style of construction was unique, and dispensed with the need to use fibreglass, or glass reinforced plastic, for mouldings, such as the cab area, to reduce the locomotive's weight. All fabrication in the locomotive body was welded, in order to minimise stress concentration. The NBL/GEC locomotives were the fourth of BR's 25kV ac electric locomotives, which were to form the backbone of the electric traction fleet. All were similar in outward appearance, but with differences in construction techniques, while bogie design and traction motor mountings were generally similar too. Electrical equipment was also largely the same, although its installation and configuration varied according to the supplier.

The NBL built bogies were fabricated, and unlike other locomotives, carried frame-mounted traction motors, driving the wheels through a Brown Boveri–SLM spring drive. The only other locomotives to be so fitted were the Class AL3, English Electric–Vulcan Foundry locomotives. The traction motors and other electrical equipment was cooled by fans, driven by motor-generator sets, an arrangement which differed from the other electric locomotives for BR at this time.

Other electrical equipment carried by the NBL-built locomotives included the mercury arc rectifiers, and on-load (high tension) tap changing for the main transformer. Only the Metropolitan–Vickers–Beyer Peacock locomotives featured on-load tap changing, an arrangement which was adopted as standard in later designs, until the advent of high power thyristors.

In service, the class proved troublesome, and in the early days, the bogie gave a poor ride, and some modifications were made. Other mechanical problems to afflict the class, and which was a contributory factor in its withdrawal, was the excessive wear on components of the BB-SLM final drive. The cause of the excessive wear was noted as a misalignment of the axle vertically, in relation to the traction motor, and the meshing of the final drive gear. Modifications to the motor mounting and axle and gear alignment were made during repairs, although this in turn is reported to have caused lubrication problems.

Electrical equipment came in for some attention too, and the mercury-arc rectifiers originally fitted proved a troublesome feature, and were later replaced by semiconductor rectifiers. Transformer windings were being damaged in the late 1960s on these locomotives, until it was revealed, following test runs, that the speed of operation of the tap changer mechanism was the root cause of flashovers. Similar problems affected the GEC six-pole traction motors, and the mechanical strength of the motor windings caused insulation breakdown, leading to flashovers. Some modifications were made here also, but the motors continued to prove less than reliable in service, and in the mid-1970s, they were rewound, but it was decided only four years later, to withdraw this small class of locomotives. They had to all intents and purposes been withdrawn some years earlier, in 1963, following the numerous problems with electrical equipment, although the major reason for their eventual demise was the final drive failures.

Construction of the class at Hyde Park was slow, and BR had required on site acceptance tests for all of its ac locomotive fleet. The initial allocation of the locomotives was of course to Longsight, for the Manchester to Crewe (Styal) line workings. Their survival into the late 1970s was in the main due to BR's need to keep costs down, after completion of the West Coast Main Line electrification. Fittingly perhaps, the class finished its days in regular service working into Scotland, but mainly on freight and freightliner trains.

The British Transport Commission Diesel Orders

In 1948, when the four main line railway companies were nationalised as British Railways, they were included as part of the British Transport Commission umbrella. BTC were also responsible for road transport, waterways, some coastal shipping, and other services, like hotels and catering. British Railways though, was the largest segment of the BTC empire, and began life with a large collection of diverse steam locomotives inherited from its predecessors. Some diesel and electric traction services were already provided, but these were limited, except for the Southern Region's extensive electrified system, and a few other electrified lines away from southern and eastern England. Diesel locomotives were, with two notable exceptions, restricted almost entirely to either 0-4-0s or 0-6-0s for shunting purposes.

The early to middle 1950s were a period of experimentation, most of it planned, where British Railways would introduce prototype diesel, electric and gas turbine motive power for trials. Steam was still supreme, and the introduction of a new 'Standard' range of designs suggested it would continue for many years to come.

By 1955, the gentle march of progress was accelerated, and the BTC instigated a radical programme of modernisation, to introduce large numbers of diesel and electric locomotives, and extensive electrification schemes. The railway industry, including NBL, were required to produce examples of various types of diesel and electric locomotive, for pilot scheme trials and evaluation.

North British already had agreements with diesel engine builders, hydraulic and electric transmission suppliers, and had built BR's first mixed traffic diesel locomotive, with electric transmission. NBL's main platform for the BTC modernisation programme, was for diesel-hydraulic locomotives, with a single class of diesel-electric, and as sub-contractor for the mechnical portions of GEC electric locomotives.

The initial BTC plan was to cover a pilot of both diesel-electric and diesel-hydraulic locomotives, to assess their suitability for British Railways. This small number of locomotives and the pilot scheme itself was overturned barely a year after its announcement, as a direct result of the explosive growth in the competition to railway transport. The burgeoning deficits of British Railways demanded action, and the decision was taken to order and build large numbers of diesel-electric locomotives, some designs almost straight off the drawing board. This was very bad news for NBL, who had nailed its own colours to the diesel-hydraulic mast. However, the orders that were placed by the BTC included at least one class of the most famous diesel locomotives to run in Britain – the Western Region's 'Warship' class. There were in fact two varieties of this class, and NBL also supplied more mixed traffic locomotives, similar to that ordered originally by the LMS. In addition, shunting locomotives were built, and two classes of passenger locomotive, one with hydraulic, and one with electric transmission, in the same power range.

The first orders from BTC came in 1955, with order L76, for a batch of five 2,000hp diesel-hydraulic locomotives, to a North British/BTC design. This order was one of four placed by the BTC, with NBL, on the same day, 16th November 1955, and delivery was scheduled to begin 15 months later, in February 1957. In the event, the first locomotive, carrying BR Western Region running number D600, was placed in service in January 1958, and was eventually named *Active*. The two engines in the D600 series locomotives were NBL/MAN L12V 18/21S, and built at Atlas Works, like many other NBL/MAN diesel engines, and were high speed engines, developing 1,000hp at 1,445 rpm. The final drive was of course hydraulic, through a Voith L306r transmission, connected to each of the outer axles on each bogie, through cardan shafts. In common with other diesel locomotive designs of this era, they were 'heavyweights', and adopted construction practices similar to steam locomotives – these first 'Warships' even had main frames! The principal dimensions of these important locomotives were as follows:

Order No.	L76
Works Nos	27660-27664
Running Nos	D600-D604
Wheel arrangement	A1A-A1A
Wheel dia. bogie	3ft 7in
Bogie wheelbase	15ft 0in
Diesel engine	NBL/MAN L12V 18/21S
	12 cyl., 1,000bhp
Transmission	Voith L306r
Tractive effort	50,000 lb

The first of the British Transport Commission orders, and the first 2,000hp diesel locomotive for British Railways were the five 'Warship' class. The orders from the BTC appeared to give North British a rosy future, but troubles with the diesel-hydraulic designs and the much larger numbers of diesel-electrics, spelled disappointment for the company. Here though, soon after delivery in June 1958, No. D600 *Active* is heading up Dainton Bank on a West of England express.

Lens of Sutton

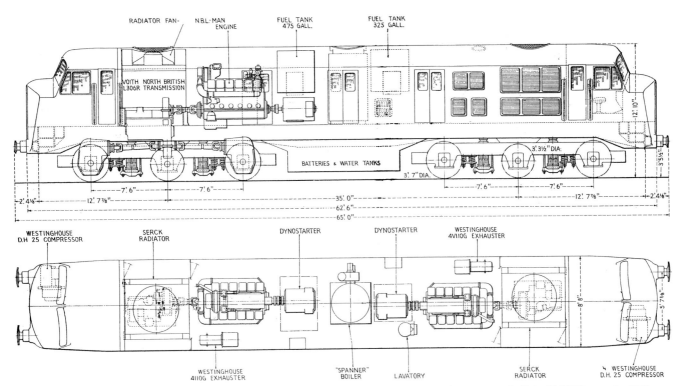

The D600 series of 'Warship' class diesel-hydraulics for the Western Region of British Railways, were built in 1957/58, to order L76.

The heavy weight of these first locomotives, at 117.5 tons, stands out in comparison with the later series of 'Warships', which were based on the German State Railways V200 series. The later locomotives developed the same horsepower, for a weight of only 78 tons, pushing the power to weight ratio up from 17.1 hp/ton, to more than 25.6 hp/ton. NBL had entered into arrangement with MAN, to build its designs of diesel engine in Glasgow. The NBL/MAN engines installed in these, and other main line diesel-hydraulics, featured crankcases and engine blocks built up from steel plate, with the former carrying cast steel bulkheads to support the main bearings. The crankshafts were hardened, with ground alloy steel forgings.

The transmissions, built by NBL at Queen's Park to Voith designs for these locomotives included three torque converters, transforming the power applied from the engine to the input shaft, to ouput to the cardan shafts, to drive the wheels. The smaller diesel-hydraulic locomotives built by North British included transmissions with only a single torque converter, and fluid couplings, and a gear train to transform the power generated by the diesel engine. The heart of the transmission in all cases was, and indeed is, the torque converter, whose essential function is to multiply the engine torque, for application at the wheels, in a similar manner to a gearbox. The transmissions operated in both cases by the filling and emptying of the oil circuits associated with each converter.

Overall design of the locomotives was the responsibility of North British, although the heavy steel structure resulted from the British Transport Commission's insistence on using thicker plate than was necessary. The range of diesel types ordered under the Pilot Scheme all differed in appearance, unlike the standard steam types then in production for British Railways in the various railway workshops. The NBL 'Warships' were a distinctive design, but sported much of the paraphernalia of steam traction, such as steam heating, and the headcode discs for train identification. Multiple locomotive working was also seen as a commonplace event, just as with steam locomotives, and the provision of flexible bellows connections in the nose of each locomotive, allowed the crew to cross from one locomotive to another. In practice these were not normally used, and later diesel locomotive types discarded their use altogether.

On entering service, the NBL 'Warships' were assigned immediately to top link duties, and were regular performers on the principal expresses, such as the 'Cornish Riviera Express'. A demonstration run with a nine-coach train from London to Bristol and back was made on 17th February 1958, and on the return journey, one of the diesel engines was switched off, and the rest of the run completed on a single engine. Trials were held in the summer of 1958, between D601, the second locomotive, and various steam engines, over the South Devon lines, between Newton Abbot and Plymouth. The reason behind the trials was to find out how the diesels would perform when double headed with a steam engine, and the most appropriate loadings for the heavy trains during the summer months. It was also thought that there would not be enough diesels available to cope with the traffic, and that steam engines would be used as additional power.

The NBL D600 series 'Warships' were:

Works No.	Running No.	Name	Introduced	Withdrawn
27660	D600	Active	1/58	12/67
27661	D601	Ark Royal	3/58	12/67
27662	D602	Bulldog	11/58	12/67
27663	D603	Conquest	11/58	12/67
27664	D604	Cossack	1/59	12/67

Soon after the arrival of the NBL 'Warships', the Swindon built versions of the German V200 were putting in apperances in ever increasing numbers, and were outperforming the NBL versions. The NBL 'Warships' suffered from poor engine performance and this, coupled with the lower level of confidence of maintenance staff, edged the original 'Warships' from Glasgow out of the front line duties. The NBL 'Warships' lasted less than ten years, and their demise was foreshadowed when British Railways implemented the National Traction Plan in 1967. In this plan, classes of locomotive were 'phased out' under the following headings; (i) Elimination of types which had given trouble, (ii) those having excessive maintenance costs, and (iii) classes of low numerical strength. The original NBL 'Warships' fitted all three categories, and after having spent most of their working lives based in Plymouth, were all withdrawn in December 1967.

Even less successful than the 48 1,100hp diesel-electrics, were the 1,000hp diesel-hydraulics for the Western Region. 58 of these locomotives were built to orders L77 (6) and order L97 (52). No. D6344 is seen here at Exeter St Davids in the early 1960s.

G. W. Sharpe Collection

Under the same contract, but allocated NBL order number L77, six 1,000hp diesel-hydraulics were ordered, with a B-B wheel arrangement. The power equipment installed in these locomotives consisted of a single NBL/MAN L12V diesel engine, and Voith L306r transmission – the same as used in the 2,000hp 'Warships'. These were classified as Type 2 diesel locomotives, compared with Type 4 of the 'Warships', and for comparison, the BTC ordered 10 diesel-electric Bo-Bo locomotives, fitted with the same NBL/MAN 1,000hp diesel engine. These latter were covered by NBL order L79, and were built at Queen's Park, along with the diesel-hydraulics. There appears to have been some confusion in allocating the work on order L77 originally though, since they were first going to be built at Queen's Park, later transferred to Hyde Park, but finally were completed at Queen's Park. The principal dimensions of both these orders are given below:

Diesel-Hydraulic Type 2

Order Nos	L77 & L97
Works Nos	27665-27670 [L77]
	27879-27930 [L97]
Running Nos	D6300-D6357
Wheel arrangement	B-B
Overall	
length	46ft 8.5in
width	8ft 8in
height	12ft 10in
Wheel dia. bogie	3ft 7in
Bogie wheelbase	8ft 6in
Bogie pivot centres	23ft 0in
Diesel engine: (L77)	NBL/MAN L12V 18/21A
(D6300-6305)	12 cyl., 1,000bhp

Diesel engine (L77 & L97)	NBL/MAN L12V 18/21B
	12 cyl., 1,100bhp
Transmission	Voith L306r
Weight in w.o.	65 tons
Maximum speed	75 mph
Tractive effort	40,000 lb

Diesel-Electric Type 2

Order No.	L79 & L94
Works Nos	27681-27690 [L79]
	27840-27867 [L94]
	27942-27961 [L94]
Running Nos	D6100-D6157
Wheel arrangement	Bo-Bo
Overall	
length	42ft 6in
width	8ft 8.5in
height	12ft 6in
Wheel dia. bogie	3ft 7in
Bogie wheelbase	8ft 6in
Bogie pivot centres	28ft 6in
Diesel engine	NBL/MAN L12V 18/21B
	12 cyl., 1,100bhp
Transmission	4 GEC, nose suspended
	axle hung traction motors
Weight in w.o.	72.5 tons
Maximum speed	75 mph
Tractive effort	45,000 lb

The original order for six diesel-hydraulics was planned for delivery in or about May 1957, but it was not until January 1959 that the first was put into service. This was an almost unacceptable delay, but NBL were struggling to keep their business viable at this time, and the problems with designs, and the new technology were taking their toll. The second order for 1,000hp diesel-hydraulics was placed in November 1957, and delivery was rather better on this order, with the first appearing only seven months late, compared with over a year and a half for the earlier order.

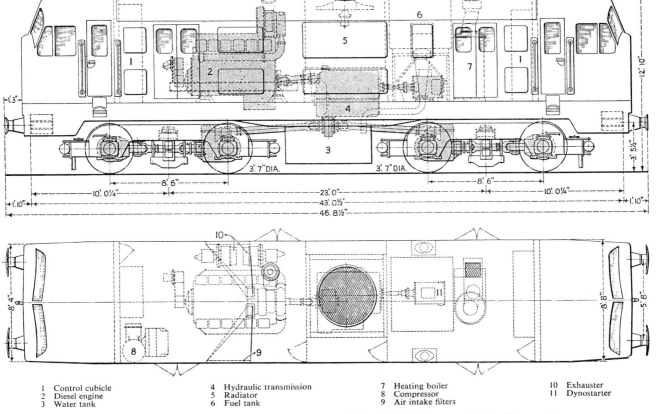

1	Control cubicle	4	Hydraulic transmission	7	Heating boiler	10	Exhauster
2	Diesel engine	5	Radiator	8	Compressor	11	Dynostarter
3	Water tank	6	Fuel tank	9	Air intake filters		

Layout of equipment and principal dimensions of the 52 1,100-h.p. production locomotives

British Railways (WR) Type 2 diesel-hydraulic locomotives carried running numbers D6300-D6357, and were built by NBL to orders L77 and L97.

Interestingly, the second order was placed with NBL more than a year before delivery from the first order, and various modifications agreed with BTC had increased the price, and spares were also included in the contract.

The modifications included an uprated engine, delivering 1,100bhp, in line with the engine installed in the diesel-electric version, and alterations to the transmission design

Another of the ill-fated D6300 series, number D6313 is seen here with Southern Region steam locomotives for company. All of these Type 2 diesel-hydraulics were allocated to Plymouth Laira depot.

G. W. Sharpe Collection

included a lighter, more compact Voith LT306r. The Western Region were implementing standardisation on two engines and two transmission makes, covering the Maybach/Mekydro, and NBL/MAN-Voith. The power systems were supposed to be interchangeable across the locomotive fleet, including the larger Type 4 locomotives. The first locomotives (order L77) had engines positioned slightly off-centre, and with all the Voith transmission units made in Glasgow. Whereas the later series (order L97) had the engines located centrally, with different mountings, and the new transmissions were supplied from Glasgow, and Voith's home plant in Heidenheim, Germany.

These Type 2 locomotives were intended to handle all the

800 B.H.P. DIESEL-ELECTRIC
LOCOMOTIVES
FOR BRITISH RAILWAYS

NORTH BRITISH
LOCOMOTIVE
CO., LTD.

N B
L O C O

G.E.C.

THE GENERAL ELECTRIC CO. LTD.
OF ENGLAND

Reprinted from " Diesel Railway Traction," November, 1958

North British Locomotive Company Limited, Glasgow

Publication No. 1055

Western Region's freight and secondary passenger duties in the Devon and Cornwall area initially, and working in tandem with their larger Type 4 cousins, the 'Warships'. Locomotive control systems were electro-pneumatic on order L77, but all-electric on the later order. The locomotives with electro-pneumatic control were able to work in multiple with the NBL built 'Warships', Nos D600–D604, whilst the later Type 2 B-Bs, Nos D6306–D6357 were fitted with the same control system as the D800 series 'Warships'. The first locomotives were confined to the far West Country throughout their life, whilst the locomotives from order L97 were to be found almost anywhere on the Western Region. Withdrawals of both orders began at the end of 1967, whilst the last to go were Nos D6338 and D6339, officially recorded as being withdrawn in January 1972.

The Type 2 diesel-electrics, ordered at the same time, were almost identical in appearance externally, although the bogies were naturally different in design and construction. The fuel and water – for the steam heating boiler – was another difference in appearance that could identify the D6100 series locomotives. As in the previous designs, the 1,100hp diesel-electrics had a fabricated steel underframe, with the superstructure built up of aluminium sheet and sections in order to keep the total weight down. With GEC as principal sub-contractor, it is interesting also to note in the list of other contractors, the Carntyne Steel Castings Co., already a member of the NBL organisation. As in other locomotives built by NBL, they supplied some of the principal castings, including, with the diesel types, the wheel centres.

The ten locomotives built under order L79 had their engines set to run at 1,500 rpm, and develop 1,000hp initially, but the GEC supplied generators were designed to

No. D6128 was based, like all of the other members of this class of 1,100hp diesel-electrics, on the Scottish Region. The first order was placed in 1955, for ten locomotives, with a second order in 1957 for 28, increased in 1958 to 48. No. D6128 was from the second order L94, and based at Glasgow Eastfield depot. The original MAN engines were later replaced with engines from Davey-Paxman, and this example is seen in original condition, although looking in a sorry state after an engine room fire.

G. W. Sharpe Collection

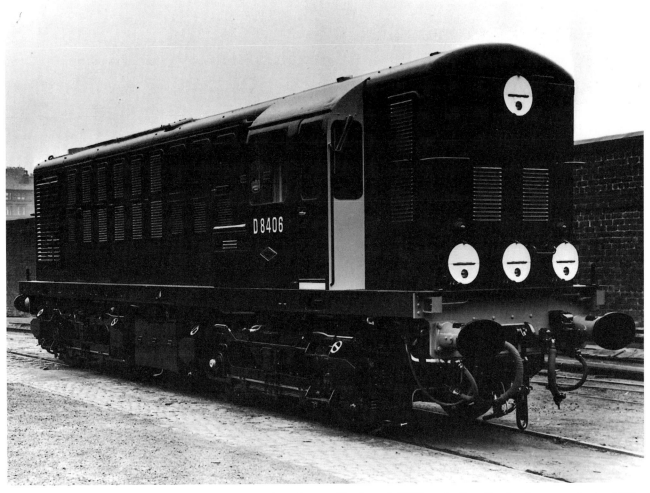

take power from the engines without changes, when they were uprated to 1,100hp. The electrical equipment was similar to that supplied by GEC for the ten Bo-Bo Type 1s, ordered under L78. The main generator was a type WT880, and was a six-pole, self-ventilated machine, delivering 1,700 Amps continuously, at 1,500 rpm. The auxiliary generator was flange-mounted to the main machine on an extension of the armature shaft. Traction motors, all series wound, force ventilated machines, were designated type WT440, and rated at 189hp, running at 375 rpm.

The initial idea was to introduce these Type 2s on the Eastern Region, as with the Brush Type 2s, although the same delays beset the diesel-electrics, and it was not until February 1959 that the locomotives entered service. The first order (L79), were all scheduled for delivery to the Eastern Region, whilst the second order, (L94), originally for 28 locomotives, was extended in July 1958 to include a further 20, but for service on the Scottish Region from the outset. However, the allocations to the Eastern Region were relatively shortlived, and they were quickly reallocated to the Scottish Region, where they were allocated to Glasgow Eastfield, and in North East Scotland, to Kittybrewster. Here they spent their working lives, before again, as with the diesel-hydraulic types, being withdrawn under the criteria of the 1967 National Traction Plan.

Order L78 – the third of the group of four placed by BTC on 16th November 1955 – was for the ten Bo-Bo Type 1 freight locomotives mentioned above. The agreed delivery schedule was 21 months from the date of settlement of technical details, not the placement of the order, making the first locomotives due in August 1957. In fact, the NBL Type 1s did not appear until the late summer of 1958, a year behind schedule. The general appearance of the locomotive, for freight working primarily, was similar to the solitary 827hp

The last of NBL's main line diesel orders were the ten 800hp Bo-Bos for secondary and goods workings. The locomotives were built at Queen's Park works to order L78. The order was placed in November 1955, but the locomotives did not appear until 1958. They were fitted with a 16-cylinder Paxman engine, and electrical equipment from GEC. The locomotive shown, No. D8406 carried works number 27677, but sadly, like other diesels for British Railways, they were not a success, and there were no further orders.

locomotive, ordered by the LMS in 1947, and delivered to BR in 1950.

Generally, fabricated main frames running the full length of the locomotive supported the Paxman 16-cylinder 16YHXL engine, and was carried on a pair of four-wheeled bogies, with a single driving cab. The engine itself was Paxman's preferred vee form, and at 1,250 rpm, it developed 800bhp, driving the GEC main and auxiliary generators. The same arrangement was adopted for these latter, as in the D6100 series, although the six-pole, self-ventilated main generator was now running at 1,250 rpm, and developing 550kW, 1,700 amps, designated type WT881. The traction motors were identical with the D6100 series, but were downrated to 152hp, running at 420 rpm, with the electro-pneumatic control system, as in the D6100 series. In service with British Railways Eastern Region, they carried running numbers D8400–D8409, but were not equipped with train heating boilers. They spent all of their working life at Stratford depot, in East London, and once again, like their NBL built contemporaries, suffered an early withdrawal under the criteria of the National Traction Plan.

The principal dimensions of these locomotives were as follows:

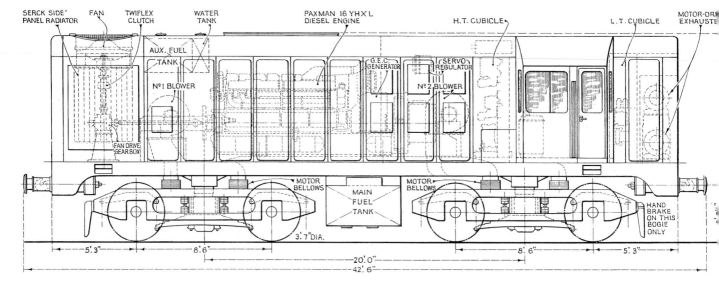

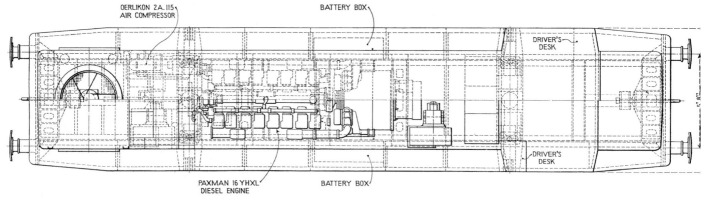

General arrangement of the 800 bhp North British Bo-Bo diesel-electric locomotives, British Railway Nos D8400-8409.

Order No.	L78
Works Nos	27671-27680
Running Nos	D8400-D8409
Overall length	42ft 6in
width	8ft 8.5in
height	12ft 6in
Wheel arrangement	Bo-Bo
Wheel dia. bogie	3ft 7in
Bogie wheelbase	8ft 6in
Bogie pivot centres	20ft 0in
Diesel engine	Paxman 16YHXL
	16 cyl., 800bhp
Generator, Main	GEC Type WT881
Auxiliary	GEC Type WT761
Transmission	4 GEC, WT441
	nose suspended
	axle hung traction motors
Weight in w.o.	68 tons
Tractive effort	60,000 lb

The final orders from the British Transport Commission were placed in 1958, even before most of the previous orders had been delivered. Between July and December 1958 NBL received orders L100 to L102, the first of which was for MAN engined 'Swindon Warships', whilst the last two were for diesel-hydraulic shunters. By the time L102 was placed by the BTC in December 1958, NBL had received 82 orders for diesel and electric types, and order L102 was the last for British Railways.

Diesel-hydraulic transmissions for main line diesel locomotives had not progressed beyond the Western Region, and British Railways were, in the late 1950s, ordering large numbers of diesel-electrics for other regions. The diesel-hydraulics of the NBL 'Warship' design were supplemented in 1958 by a similar powered design, but based on German Railways V200 class. Here was an example of locomotive

procurement that the British locomotive industry was worried about, and NBL in particular. The prospect of buying locomotives from outside the UK, and from the likes of General Electric and General Motors in the USA for diesel-electric types, had already been considered by the BTC. In the diesel-hydraulic category, only Western Germany had exploited the arrangement with success, for high powered locomotives. The BTC and British Railways Board had introduced more 'flexible management' of the BR regions in the middle 1950s, which the Western Region authorities used to pursue their diesel-hydraulic traction policy. This was perhaps a ghost of the individuality developed by the old Great Western Railway, since the broad gauge days, and I. K. Brunel.

It was hoped in the initial stages, that simply transcribing the German design, with minor variations to suit BR operations would work, but it did not. With the assistance of reams of technical information from German Federal Railways, which even went to the extent of an English translation of the German painting instructions, Swindon Locomotive Drawing Office designed its locomotive. In principle it followed the V200 design, except that it was smaller, and having adopted this unconventional design, Swindon went still further, and dispensed with the then fashionable underframe/chassis as found on other diesel locomotive types. The entire locomotive was designed and built around two 6.5in diameter tubes, running the full length of the locomotive.

At the time the order was placed with NBL, there were three of these new 'Warships' in service, the first of which had emerged from Swindon Works in August 1958. The engines in these were Bristol Siddeley Maybach MD650, and rated at 1,100hp – two of which were installed in every locomotive. This bears direct comparison with the NBL/MAN L12VB engine, which had been uprated to 1,100hp, for installation in the D6300 series B-B Type 2 locomotives. The order book states that L100 was scheduled for delivery 18 to 21 months after the order was placed, giving a planned introduction in either February or May 1960. Delays on this order were limited, and NBL delivered its first of this new class of 'Warship', in June 1960, only a month late. The entry to traffic date is officially recorded by BR Western Region as July 1960, and the order for all 33 locomotives was completed by May/June 1962. Ironically, the final Swindon design of 'Warships' were supplied a few weeks after the company had gone into liquidation, in April 1962. The main dimensions of order L100 were as follows:

Order No.	L100
Works Nos	27962-27994
Running Nos	D833-D865
Wheel arrangement	B-B
Overall length	60ft 0in
width	8ft 10in
height	13ft 0.75in
Wheel dia. bogie	3ft 3.5in
Bogie wheelbase	10ft 6in
Bogie pivot centres	37ft 9in
Diesel engine (2)	NBL/MAN L12V 18/21B
	12 cyl., 1,100bhp
Transmission	Voith LT306r
Weight in w.o,	79 tons 8 cwt
Maximum speed	90 mph
Tractive effort	52,400 lb

Having said that there was a lesser delay in delivering these locomotives, the order book states that the date of the order was actually a letter of intent, so the delays were perhaps rather more attributable to British Railways than NBL. True, the company was going through a particularly difficult time, commercially in the mid to later 1950s, but the inconsistency in British Railways' ordering, and indeed decision making process at this time, did not help NBL. On the technical front, the hydraulic transmissions were the modified L306r, which had been installed in earlier NBL locomotives, but the modifications from Voith, with a lighter, more compact design, were included in the new 'Warships' from the first. The Swindon Works-built locomotives, with their Maybach engines, were paired with a Mekydro transmission, which had a single torque converter, and four-speed gearbox. This arrangement was thought to be cheaper and simpler than the Voith, although it too was new, and there was even less experience with this type of transmission. The Mekydro converter/automatic gearbox transmissions were initially supplied from Germany, but in later locomotives were built under licence by Stone & Co., in London. The NBL/Voith transmissions were all built at Queen's Park, where a large section of the works had been constructing them for a number of years, and the final few units were built by Voith Engineering (Glasgow) Ltd, following NBL's liquidation.

In service, the new 'Warships' were the mainstay of express passenger services on the Western Region, until the advent of the HST in the early 1970s, and they were supplemented in this work by the railway workshop built 'Western' series. All of the class carried names, which had also been carried, or associated with ships of the Royal Navy, a tradition carried on for many years. The first of the NBL built locomotives to go, were D848 *Sultan,* and D863 *Warrior,* in March 1969, when each was less than eight and seven years old respectively. The majority were withdrawn in 1971, once again being taken out of traffic following the criteria that had either given trouble in service, or in this case, they did not now comply with the strategy to adopt electric transmissions for main line locomotives. The

names and numbering details of the NBL D800 series 'Warships' are listed below:

Works No.	Running No.	Name	Built	W'drawn
27962	D833	Panther	7/60	10/71
27963	D834	Pathfinder	7/60	10/71
27964	D835	Pegasus	8/60	10/71
27965	D836	Powerful	9/60	5/71
27966	D837	Ramillies	11/60	5/71
27967	D838	Rapid	10/60	3/71
27968	D839	Relentless	11/60	10/71
27969	D840	Resistance	2/61	4/69
27970	D841	Roebuck	12/60	10/71
27971	D842	Royal Oak	12/60	10/71
27972	D843	Sharpshooter	1/61	5/71
27973	D844	Spartan	3/61	10/71
27974	D845	Sprightly	4/61	10/71
27975	D846	Steadfast	4/61	5/71
27976	D847	Strongbow	4/61	3/71
27977	D848	Sultan	4/61	3/69
27978	D849	Superb	5/61	5/71
27979	D850	Swift	6/61	5/71
27980	D851	Temeraire	7/61	5/71
27981	D852	Tenacious	7/61	10/71
27982	D853	Thruster	8/61	10/71
27983	D854	Tiger	9/61	10/71
27984	D855	Triumph	10/61	10/71
27985	D856	Trojan	11/61	5/71
27986	D857	Undaunted	12/61	10/71
27987	D858	Valorous	12/61	10/71
27988	D859	Vanquisher	1/62	3/71
27989	D860	Victorious	1/62	3/71
27990	D861	Vigilant	2/62	10/71
27991	D862	Viking	3/62	10/71
27992	D863	Warrior	4/62	3/69
27993	D864	Zambesi	5/62	3/71
27994	D865	Zealous	6/62	5/71

Not all of the BTC orders for diesel locomotives were for main line types and orders L101, L102, L93, L88 and L81 were for diesel shunters. However, although there were still a large number of goods yards in existence in the late 1950s, where the 0-4-0 shunters were most suitable, they were not to last for long. The smaller goods yards disappeared under the Beeching regime, and with them, the most suitable work for the 200 to 225hp 0-4-0 diesel-hydraulic shunters built by NBL. In total, the BTC ordered 88 shunters from NBL, although it had already taken delivery of six 200hp shunters, which NBL had built for stock in 1952/53.

Order L44, built at Queen's Park, included the Paxman 6RPH diesel engine, paired with Voith L33YU transmission, which in turn was based on order L8, from 1950. This prototype included engines with the Paxman engine, and a National 200hp engine, and the Paxman engined version was repeated in order L14, which NBL built for stock in 1951. In both cases, the locomotives were sold to industry, including ICI, Esso and the Singer plant in Glasgow. Order L44 was essentially the same, and were the earliest diesel-hydraulic shunters to be operated by British Railways. The later orders, from 1955, included the MAN design of engine, which NBL were then building regularly, under licence, and which developed 225bhp at 1100 rpm.

Order No.	L81
Works Nos	27703-27714
Running Nos	D2708-D2719
Wheel arrangement	0-4-0
Wheel dia.	3ft 6in

Above: Built in 1957, under order L81, with later batches from orders L93 and L102, this was another 0-4-0, diesel-hydraulic shunter, but of 225hp. In this case, number D2726 was from order L93, placed in April 1957, the locomotive was almost on home turf, seen here at Edinburgh (St Margarets) depot. All bar a few of the shunters supplied to this design were allocated to Scottish Region depots, and were based on a design built for NBL stock under order L73.

Lens of Sutton

Below: Built in 1958, under order L88, this was one of a series of diesel-hydraulic shunters built by NBL. Many of this same design were supplied to industry, such as the National Coal Board, or the electricity authorities. A second order was placed with NBL in late 1958 for three shunters of the same design, under order L101, and all were built at Queen's Park Works.

Developing 330hp, most of this class were allocated to Stratford Depot, in North London with others at Rugby, on the London Midland Region.

Lens of Sutton

Diesel engine	NBL/MAN W6V 17.5/22A
	6 cyl., 225bhp
Transmission	Voith L33Y
Weight in w.o.	30 tons 0 cwt
Tractive effort	20,800 lb

Order No.	L88
Works Nos	27751-27762
Running Nos	D2900-D2911
Wheel arrangement	0-4-0
Wheel dia.	3ft 9in
Diesel engine	NBL/MAN W6V 17.5/22AS
	6 cyl., 300bhp
Transmission	Voith L24V
Weight in w.o.	36 tons 0 cwt
Tractive effort	24,100 lb

Order No.	L93
Works Nos	27815-27839
Running Nos	D2720-D2724
Wheel arrangement	0-4-0
Wheel dia.	3ft 6in
Diesel engine	NBL/MAN W6V 17.5/22A
	6 cyl., 225bhp
Transmission	Voith L33Y & L37Y
Weight in w.o.	30 tons 0 cwt
Tractive effort	20,080 lb

Order No.	L101
Works Nos	27995-27997
Running Nos	D2912-D2914
Wheel arrangement	0-4-0
Wheel dia.	3ft 9in
Diesel engine	NBL/MAN W6V 17.5/22BS
	6 cyl., 330bhp
Transmission	Voith L24V

Weight in w.o.	36 tons 0 cwt
Tractive effort	24,100 lb

Order No.	L102
Works Nos	27998-28033
Running Nos	D2725-D2780
Wheel arrangement	0-4-0
Wheel dia.	3ft 9in
Diesel engine	NBL/MAN W6V 17.5/22B
	6 cyl., 225bhp
Transmission	Voith L33YV
Weight in w.o.	30 tons 0 cwt
Tractive effort	20,080 lb

The earliest shunters were allocated to the North Eastern Region, with some in the Scottish Region, around Edinburgh. Order L88 was originally allocated to the London Midland Region, whilst another batch of 25 of these 225hp 0-4-0s was sent to the Scottish Region from new. Industry had been buying a number of these locomotives too, and they could be found at work in sidings belonging to the Central Electricity Generating Board, Cadburys, the National Coal Board, and at numerous other locations.

In total, North British built 32 orders for diesel locomotives for stock, almost all of which were later sold, between 1947 and 1961. Only the orders the company received from industry exceeded this figure, with 38 orders in all, for a total of 111 locomotives. The late 1950s was hardly a successful time for the company, even for the burgeoning diesel and electric traction market, but it had secured a good deal of business from industry. The final orders for the company included an order for two shunters from Stewarts & Lloyds (L111), the Benguela Railways, also two locomotives (L112), and the very last order, from Richard Thomas & Baldwins, for three locomotives (L113).

Diesel and Electric Locomotive Orders

Railway	Year	Order No.	Works	Qty	Works. Nos	Type
North British Loco.	1947	L972	?	2	26249 & 26414	0-4-0 diesel-mechanical
LMSR	1947	L977	Queens Park	1	26413	Bo-Bo diesel-electric
North British Loco.	1947	L985	?	1	26682	Cancelled – 1,600hp demonstration locomotive
Estoril Rly. (Portugal)	1948	L986	Queens Park	1	26683	Bo-Bo electric
North British Loco.	1948	L987	Queens Park	10	26684-85 & 26687-94	0-4-0 diesel-mechanical
North British Loco.	1948	L988	Queens Park	6	26686 & 26695-99	0-4-0 diesel-mechanical
Colvilles Ltd.	1948	L994	Hyde Park	2	26756-57	0-4-0 diesel-mechanical
South African Rlys.	1948	L998	Hyde Park	40	26859-98	1Co-Co1, Class 4E electric
North British Loco.	1949	L8	Hyde Park	2	27078-79	0-4-0 diesel-hydraulic
Emu Bay Rly. Co.	1950	L9	Queens Park	1	27080	0-8-0 diesel-hydraulic, 500hp
Logue Industrial	1950	L12	Atlas	2	26700-701	0-4-0 diesel-mechanical
North British Loco.	1950	L14	Queens Park	6	27094-5 & 27100-03	0-4-0 diesel-hydraulic
Lithgow Valley Colliery	1950	L15	Atlas	1	27096	0-4-0 diesel-hydraulic
Shelton Iron & Steel	1950	L16	Queens Park	1	27097	0-4-0 diesel-hydraulic
Shelton Iron & Steel	1950	L17	Queens Park	1	27098	0-6-0 diesel-hydraulic
Mauritius Rlys.	1951	L22	Queens Park	2	27220-21	0-6-0 diesel-hydraulic, 625hp
Logue Industrial	1951	L24	Hyde Park	2	27235-36	0-4-0 diesel-hydraulic
Logue Industrial	1951	L25	Hyde Park	2	27237-38	0-4-0 diesel-hydraulic
English Steel Corp.	1951	L27	Queens Park	1	27246	0-4-0 diesel-hydraulic
North British Loco.	1952	L27	Queens Park	3	27413-15	0-4-0 diesel-hydraulic
Commonwealth Collieries	1951	L33	Hyde Park	1	27297	0-4-0 diesel-hydraulic

Customer	Year	Works No.	Built at	Qty	Running Nos.	Description
Ministry of Fuel & Power	1952	L36	HP & Atlas	1	27401	A1A-A1A, coal burning gas turbine
John Summers & Co.	1951	L37	Queens Park	1	27402	0-6-0 diesel-hydraulic
Stewarts & Lloyds	1951	L37	Queens Park	3	27407-09	0-6-0 diesel-hydraulic
North British Loco.	1952	L37	Queens Park	3	27410-12	0-6-0 diesel-hydraulic
Tharsis Sulphur & Copper	1951	L38	Queens Park	1	27403	0-6-0 diesel-hydraulic
Rhodesia Copper Co.	1952	L40	Hyde Park	1	27416	0-4-0 diesel-hydraulic
Coalvilles Ltd.	1952	L42	Queens Park	4	27417-20	0-4-0 diesel-hydraulic
Ministry of Supply	1952	L43	Queens Park	9	27421-29	0-4-0 diesel-hydraulic
North British Loco.	1952	L44	Queens Park	6	27430-35	0-4-0 diesel-hydraulic
Logue Industrial	1952	L47	Queens Park	3	27470-72	0-4-0 diesel-hydraulic
Logue Industrial	1952	L48	Queens Park	1	27473	0-4-0 diesel-hydraulic
Malayan Railways	1952	L50	Queens Park	6	27482-87	0-6-0 diesel-hydraulic
North British Loco.	1952	L51	Atlas	10	27488-97	0-4-0 diesel-hydraulic
East African Rlys.	1952	L52	Queens Park	14	27498-501 & 27525-34	0-8-0 diesel-hydraulic, "Class 83"
East African Rlys.	1952	L53	Queens Park	3	27502-04	0-8-0 diesel-hydraulic, "Class 84"
India Store Dept.	1953	L54	HP & Atlas	20	27505-24	B-B, 625hp diesel-hydraulic
Stewarts & Lloyds	1953	L56	Queens Park	3	27537-39	0-4-0 diesel-hydraulic
Anglo American Mines	1954	L57	Atlas	1	27543	0-4-0 diesel-hydraulic
North British Loco.	1954	L58	Queens Park	3	27544-46	0-4-0 diesel-hydraulic
Logue Industrial	1954	L59	Atlas	2	27550-51	0-4-0 diesel-hydraulic
Logue Industrial	1954	L60	Atlas	1	27552	0-4-0 diesel-hydraulic
Anglo American Mines	1954	L61	?	2	27553-54	0-8-0 diesel-hydraulic
North British Loco.	1954	L64	Queens Park	3	27547-49	0-4-0 diesel-hydraulic
North British Loco.	1954	L65	?	6	27581-86	0-4-0 diesel-hydraulic
North British Loco.	1954	L66	Queens Park	6	27588-93	0-6-0 diesel-hydraulic
Crown Agents for Colonies	1954	L68	Queens Park	10	27620-29	0-8-0 diesel-hydraulic, 888hp
North British Loco.	1955	L69	HP & Atlas	10	27630-39	0-4-0 diesel-hydraulic
Anglo American Mines	1955	L70	Queens Park	2	27642-43	0-8-0 diesel-hydraulic, 625hp
Ministry of Supply	1955	L71	Queens Park	5	27644-48	0-4-0 diesel-hydraulic
John Summers & Co.	1955	L72	Queens Park	1	27649	0-6-0 diesel-hydraulic
North British Loco.	1955	L73	Queens Park	6	27650-55	0-4-0 diesel-hydraulic
C. A. Parsons	1955	L74	Queens Park	1	27656	0-4-0 diesel-hydraulic
North British Loco.	1955	L74	Queens Park	2	27657-58	0-4-0 diesel-hydraulic
Selection Trust	1955	L75	Queens Park	1	27659	0-6-0 diesel-hydraulic
British Transport Comm.	1955	L76	Queens Park	5	27660-64	A1A-A1A diesel-hydraulic, 2000hp
British Transport Comm.	1955	L77	Queens Park	6	27665-70	B-B diesel-hydraulic, 1000hp
British Transport Comm.	1955	L78	Queens Park	10	27671-80	B-B diesel-hydraulic, 800hp
British Transport Comm.	1955	L79	Queens Park	10	27681-90	Bo-Bo diesel-electric, 1000hp
British Transport Comm.	1955	L81	Queens Park	12	27703-14	0-4-0 diesel-hydraulic
Rich. Thomas & Baldwins	1956	L82	Queens Park	2	27715-16	0-6-0 diesel-hydraulic
North British Loco.	1956	L82	Queens Park	2	27717 & 27730	0-6-0 diesel-hydraulic
North British Loco.	1956	L82	Queens Park	2	27748 & 27750	0-6-0 diesel-hydraulic
Logue Industrial	1956	L83	Hyde Park	4	27718-21	0-4-0 diesel-hydraulic
North British Loco.	1956	L83	Hyde Park	6	27722-27	0-4-0 diesel-hydraulic
North British Loco.	1956	L84	Queens Park	10	27728-29 & 27731-37 & 27813	0-4-0 diesel-hydraulic
North British Loco.	1956	L85	Hyde Park	10	27738-47	0-4-0 diesel-hydraulic
John Summers & Co.	1956	L86	Queens Park	1	27749	0-6-0 diesel-hydraulic, 500hp
British Transport Comm.	1956	L88	Queens Park	12	27751-62	0-4-0 diesel-hydraulic
North British Loco.	1956	L89	Queens Park	6	27763-68	0-6-0 diesel-hydraulic
General Electric Co.	1957	L91	Hyde Park	10	27793-802	Bo-Bo, Class AL4, electric loco.
North British Loco.	1957	L92	Queens Park	10	27803-12	0-4-0 diesel-hydraulic
British Transport Comm.	1957	L93	Queens Park	25	27815-39	0-4-0 diesel-hydraulic
British Transport Comm.	1957	L94	Hyde Park	48	27840-67 & 27942-61	Bo-Bo diesel-electric, 1100hp
North British Loco.	1957	L95	Queens Park	6	27868-73	0-6-0 diesel-hydraulic
North British Loco.	1957	L96	Queens Park	5	27874-88	0-4-0 diesel-hydraulic
British Transport Comm.	1957	L97	Queens Park	52	27879-930	B-B diesel-hydraulic, 1000hp
North British Loco.	1958	L98	Queens Park	6	27931-36	0-6-0 diesel-hydraulic
North British Loco.	1958	L99	Queens Park	5	27937-41	0-4-0 diesel-hydraulic
British Transport Comm.	1958	L100	Hyde Park	33	27962-94	B-B diesel-hydraulic, 2200hp
British Transport Comm.	1958	L101	Queens Park	3	27995-97	0-4-0 diesel-hydraulic
British Transport Comm.	1958	L102	Queens Park	36	27998-28033	0-4-0 diesel-hydraulic
John Summers & Co.	1959	L103	Queens Park	1	28034	0-6-0 diesel-hydraulic
West Minster Plant Co.	1959	L104	Queens Park	2	28035-36	0-8-0 diesel-hydraulic, 532hp
North British Loco.	1959	L105	Queens Park	5	28037-41	0-4-0 diesel-hydraulic
Benguela Railway	1960	L106	Queens Park	2	28042-43	0-6-0 diesel-hydraulic
North British Loco.	1960	L107	Queens Park	4	28044-46 & 28050	0-6-0 diesel-hydraulic
North British Loco.	1960	L108	Queens Park	1	28047	0-6-0 diesel-hydraulic – NOT BUILT
North British Loco.	1960	L110	Queens Park	1	28049	B-B 1,000hp diesel-hydraulic – NOT BUILT
Stewarts & Lloyds	1960	L111	Queens Park	2	28051-52	0-6-0 diesel-hydraulic
Benguela Railway	1961	L112	Queens Park	2	28053-54	0-6-0 diesel-hydraulic
Rich. Thomas & Baldwins	1961	L113	Queens Park	3	28055-57	0-6-0 diesel-hydraulic

Country/Company	No. of Orders	No. of engines	Avg. engines/order
British Transport Comm.	12	252	21
North British Loco.	31	164	5.29
LMSR	1	1	1
Estoril Rly. (Portugal)	1	1	1
South African Rlys.	1	40	40
Emu Bay Rly. Co.	1	1	1
Mauritius Rlys.	1	2	2
Benguela Railway	2	4	2
East African Rlys.	2	17	8.5
Malayan Railways	1	6	6
Industrials/Others	31	111	2.9
Total	84	599	7.13

Diesel & Electric Locomotive Orders
Locomotives Built for Stock

Railway	Year	Order No.	Works	Qty	Works. Nos	Type
North British Loco.	1947	L972	?	2	26249 & 26414	0-4-0 diesel-mechanical
North British Loco.	1947	L985	Queens Park	1	26682	Cancelled – 1,600hp demonstration locomotive
North British Loco.	1948	L987	Queens Park	10	26684-85 & 26687-94	0-4-0 diesel-mechanical
North British Loco.	1948	L988	Queens Park	6	26686 & 26695-99	0-4-0 diesel-mechanical
North British Loco.	1949	L8	Hyde Park	2	27078-79	0-4-0 diesel-hydraulic
North British Loco.	1950	L14	Queens Park	6	27094-5 & 27100-03	0-4-0 diesel-hydraulic
North British Loco.	1952	L27	Queens Park	3	27413-15	0-4-0 diesel-hydraulic
North British Loco.	1952	L37	Queens Park	3	27410-12	0-6-0 diesel-hydraulic
North British Loco.	1952	L44	Queens Park	6	27430-35	0-4-0 diesel-hydraulic
North British Loco.	1952	L51	Atlas	10	27488-97	0-4-0 diesel-hydraulic
North British Loco.	1954	L58	Queens Park	3	27544-46	0-4-0 diesel-hydraulic
North British Loco.	1954	L64	Queens Park	3	27547-49	0-4-0 diesel-hydraulic
North British Loco.	1954	L65	?	6	27581-86	0-4-0 diesel-hydraulic
North British Loco.	1954	L66	Queens Park	6	27588-93	0-6-0 diesel-hydraulic
North British Loco.	1955	L69	HP & Atlas	10	27630-39	0-4-0 diesel-hydraulic
North British Loco.	1955	L73	Queens Park	6	27650-55	0-4-0 diesel-hydraulic
North British Loco.	1955	L74	Queens Park	2	27657-58	0-4-0 diesel-hydraulic
North British Loco.	1956	L82	Queens Park	2	27717 & 27730	0-6-0 diesel-hydraulic
North British Loco.	1956	L82	Queens Park	2	27748 & 27750	0-6-0 diesel-hydraulic
North British Loco.	1956	L83	Hyde Park	6	27722-27	0-4-0 diesel-hydraulic
North British Loco.	1956	L84	Queens Park	10	27728-29 & 27731-37 & 27813	0-4-0 diesel-hydraulic
North British Loco.	1956	L85	Hyde Park	10	27738-47	0-4-0 diesel-hydraulic
North British Loco.	1956	L89	Queens Park	6	27763-68	0-6-0 diesel-hydraulic
North British Loco.	1957	L92	Queens Park	10	27803-12	0-4-0 diesel-hydraulic
North British Loco.	1957	L95	Queens Park	6	27868-73	0-6-0 diesel-hydraulic
North British Loco.	1957	L96	Queens Park	5	27874-88	0-4-0 diesel-hydraulic
North British Loco.	1958	L98	Queens Park	6	27931-36	0-6-0 diesel-hydraulic
North British Loco.	1958	L99	Queens Park	5	27937-41	0-4-0 diesel-hydraulic
North British Loco.	1959	L105	Queens Park	5	28037-41	0-4-0 diesel-hydraulic
North British Loco.	1960	L107	Queens Park	4	28044-46 & 28050	0-6-0 diesel-hydraulic
North British Loco.	1960	L108	Queens Park	1	28047	0-6-0 diesel-hydraulic – NOT BUILT
North British Loco.	1960	L110	Queens Park	1	28049	B-B 1,000hp diesel-hydraulic – NOT BUILT

Country/Company	No. of Orders	No. of engines	Avg. engines/order
North British Loco.	31	164	5.29
Totals	31	164	5.29

In 1960, NBL was putting in hand plans to build a 'range' of diesel-hydraulic locomotives, with the Voith transmission, known as the 'World' series. The designs, for which order numbers L108 and L110 were allocated, included a 440hp 0-6-0, and a 1,000hp B-B type, neither of which were ever built. In both cases too, the NBL/MAN engine designs were to be included, which NBL had been building in Springburn. Order No. L113 however, represents not only the last diesel locomotive to be built by NBL, but its very last locomotive. In fact, the last orders for 440hp shunters placed with NBL were actually completed by Andrew Barclay, Sons & Co. of Kilmarnock. Prior to NBL going into receivership in April 1962, Andrew Barclay completed four such orders, covering L106, L107, L112 and L113. Andrew Barclay ultimately purchased the goodwill of NBL, after that fateful day in April 1962, and continued to supply spares for all NBL built locomotives.

By the 1950s, industrial diesel locomotives were fast becoming a major product for NBL. In this example the Paxman and Voith/NBL hydraulic transmissions were paired, to produce a 500hp 0-6-0 for the Shelton Iron & Steel Co. The solitary locomotive on this order (L17), carried works number 27098.

Mitchell Library Collection

9

Changing Fortunes: 1953 to 1962

As noted in the company's commemorative brochure in 1953, NBL did not turn from steam to other motive power with any commitment until 1946, by which time, the major players in diesel and electric traction had been in business for many years. This was not going to be an easy time for the company. In the late 1940s and early 1950s the management team at Springburn were well aware of the trends in the railway industry. But, in less than a decade, the giant locomotive building works centred in the Springburn district of Glasgow had ceased to exist. The year 1953 saw North British Locomotive Co. reach its golden jubilee, but its survival was dependent on a continuing flow of orders for steam engines. In the cold light of the post-war economy, NBL was struggling to survive – shortages of steel, men and orders. As described in earlier chapters, it was not uncommon in the steam engine building business to find the major players showing great difficulty in adapting to the new forms of railway traction. The economic difficulties that had plagued the Glasgow company throughout the 1920s and 1930s, continued to a degree after the war, although a mini 'boom' in orders can be seen in the company's books.

NBL had demonstrated in the past that it had the foresight to realise the benefits of new and emerging technologies and techniques, but in the 1950s the competition from longer established companies was just too much. This statement does seem at odds with the known history of NBL and

its predecessors. What happened to the company, and the attempts it made to recover its former position – its struggle to survive – are sadly, the final phase of its development. Whilst it may be true to say that they entered the new world of diesel and electric traction too late, and were perhaps too slow to enter into partnerships with the electrical industries and diesel engine builders, there were other factors that influenced NBL's survival. Ironically perhaps, as will be discussed in the final chapter, many of the NBL built locomotives are still at work – even steam engines – on the preserved railways of Great Britain.

In the years following the end of hostilities, the economies of all European countries were in a poor state, with shortages having a marked effect on manufacturing industry in particular. Between 1948 and 1953, the company's results were quite good, although the spectre of rising costs was often referred to, and what orders that were placed, continued to be dominated by export work. Centrepiece of the 1951 Festival of Britain exhibition in George Square, Glasgow, was a YP Class engine for India,

The North British-built B1 class 4-6-0 mixed traffic locomotives were another success story, and could turn their hand to almost any duty. Here, No. 61331 is seen near Newark, passing over Muskham water troughs, with the Aberdeen to London King's Cross fish train in August 1958.

Roger Shenton

A landmark, not only on Clydeside, but also for the many thousands of steam locomotives built by NBL, was the Stobcross crane at Finnieston Quay, and, in this view, the huge crane that hoisted many steam engines on board ships bound for destinations around the world, is awaiting one of the 2-8-2s built for Spain in 1950 that is seen arriving at the quayside, prior to despatch.

Mitchell Library Collection

New Zealand Railways Class Jb, No. 1218, photographed at Thorndon in Wellington in 1949, after conversion to oil burning condition, with air-smoothed casing removed.

New Zealand Rly. & Loco. Society (Inc.) Archives Collection

Forty years on and still in normal service, Class YP No. 2625 takes water at Kanpur station in October 1992. The station's facilities are perhaps not up to full main line standards, but the character of both India's railways and the longevity of the North British built locomotives shines through.

Philip Cousins

Another surviving Class YP, No. 2463, also seen at Kanpur station in October 1992, and replenishing the tender tank. The condition of the locomotive is clearly not pristine, but still providing the motive power on many routes as the millennium approaches.

Philip Cousins

one of a few large orders for steam placed with NBL at that time. The early 1950s though provided more evidence of continually rising costs with material shortages having a detrimental effect on the company's financial position. The steel shortage, which had perhaps the most obvious repercussions, had equally adverse effects on other companies too, but in 1951, NBL's profits were down in comparison with its competitors. The following year, 1952, saw some increase, but pressure from rising costs and material shortages provided deteriorating results for NBL throughout the decade.

1953–1958

In organisation terms NBL had, by the early 1950s, established associations with other companies, such as GEC, and C. A. Parsons. The main reasons behind this was to meet the competition from, and indeed compete in the same markets for diesel and electric traction orders. In addition, NBL had already diversified its product range in association with the Baldwin–Lima–Hamilton Corporation, producing dragline excavators under the 'Lima' brand. Lima were another example of a specialist steam locomotive builder, whose diversification strategy, even in combination with the massive Baldwin organisation, was unable to meet competition from non-steam traction in the railway business.

NBL had acquired the Carntyne Steel Castings Co. and Henry Pels & Co., the machine tool maker, after World War II, as further strings to its bow. Sharp Stewart, one of NBL's predecessors had a particular reputation for designing and building machine tools, and the Henry Pels acquisition was

Almost back to its place of birth, this 'Austerity' 2-8-0, No. 90229, is resting at Motherwell, near the end of its working life in June 1963. Built in 1943, under order L943, the engine was one of 545 WD 2-8-0s built by NBL.

Roger Shenton

something of a logical step for the company. By far the most far reaching and long lasting partnership forged by North British at this time was with the German company Voith. Although NBL had taken the decision to build locomotives with hydraulic transmissions from Voith in 1949, it was not until 1953 that they were in full production at Queen's Park Works. The first shunting locomotives fitted with Voith L33y transmissions, built by NBL under licence, were to order L8 in 1950, for Esso and Richard, Thomas & Baldwins steelworks.

The company report for 1952 reflected the difficult trading conditions, but indicated that there were some grounds for optimism, and a dividend on ordinary and preference shares of 5% was declared. The order book was sound, but still with more steam than diesel or electric orders, and there was some unfavourable reporting of problems with recently completed electric locomotives for South Africa. The first Lima excavators were scheduled for completion at Queen's Park in 1953, where gearing up for large scale production of the Voith hydraulic transmissions was taking place. Queen's Park was an especially busy place to be in 1953, where the newer products of NBL were being made, and which then included the Henry Pels machine tools. Up at Springburn, attention was focused on the new Parsons-North British gas turbine locomotive – a case of *déjà vu* here without doubt. But, gas turbines, as alternative locomotive traction were fashionable, with Metropolitan–Vickers, and Brown Boveri supplying examples for trial on British Railways.

Financially, the year was not a particularly good one, although another 5% dividend was declared – NBL had to undertake corrective repairs to the South African Railways locomotives, and incurred losses of more than £100,000 on the contract. The work on the coal burning gas turbine was still in progress throughout 1953, and was expected to take until 1955 to complete. The Lima excavator however, com-

gramme for the nationalised rail system did not save it from generating huge deficits in the 1950s. The question of whether to buy home built or foreign diesel and electric locomotives aggravated the difficulties for the British locomotive industry supplying motive power to British Railways.

In general, NBL believed that they had reached a plateau in 1956, so far as locomotive building was concerned. They had established themselves as suppliers of diesel-hydraulic locomotives, and had re-equipped the works to cater for the new types of locomotive, and gained considerable experience. However, the board had also taken step to diversify the company's activities still further – the opposite approach to that taken by Walter Montgomerie Neilson in the 1800s. In 1956 they were, in addition to the work of Carntyne and Henry Pels & Co., producing pipelines for the North of Scotland Hydro-Electric Board, and pressure vessels for the oil industry. The latter was a move to utilise the boiler shops, which were already building pressure vessels – steam locomotive boilers – and maintain the skills. The primary business of NBL was locomotive building, and throughout 1956, steam and diesel locomotives were being built, for home and overseas. The British Railways 'Pilot Scheme' diesels were in hand, but the delay in placing larger orders was still a concern for the home locomotive industry. The change in policy of the British Transport Commission and British Railways, soon to be announced, turned out to be bad news for North British, as the railways nailed their colours firmly to the mast of diesel-electric traction.

As 1956 progressed into 1957 though, NBL, with its full order book, but some spare capacity in the works, was optimistic. A good indicator that all was not entirely happy at Springburn may be seen by one comment in the 1956 annual report, where, to meet the difficult circumstances, "vigorous steps to reduce overhead expenses and considerable economies have already been made". This inference is borne out by the recorded profit of a miserly £2,000 in 1957, at a time when the first effects of dieselisation and electrification were being felt on British Railways. This was indeed a bad year, and there was a loss on trading in that year, and the figures showed the company with its head just about above water, after making adjustments and transfers from various accounts. The final orders for steam locomotives were being worked on at Hyde Park during this time, but as 1957 began to run on into 1958, it became evident that the British Transport Commission was fast becoming NBL's principal customer. Worse though, the costs of re-equipping, and modifying the works to cope with the new technology was not entirely supported by operational success, especially for the British Railways orders. The hydraulic transmissions were causing problems for BR, and there were no other serious orders for diesel-hydraulic types coming from anywhere other than the Western Region of British Railways. From NBL, output was three times higher in 1957, and productivity was up by around 30%, which in the face of difficult trading conditions was no mean feat.

During the year, NBL formally established its Diesel Engine Division, and appointed Hugh Fulton as Divisional Director. Fulton was previously Managing Director of Albion Motors, and brought his experience of the automotive industry with him to NBL, which was potentially a great benefit to the company. Towards the end of the year the first 2,000hp diesel-hydraulic was completed for BR's Western Region, and became the forerunner of the first of BR's famous 'Warship' class locomotives. The final four locomotives were completed for an order from Nyasaland Railways and under order L90, placed on 15th January 1957, these were the last steam locomotives to be con-

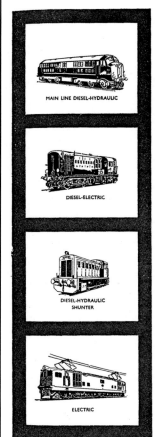
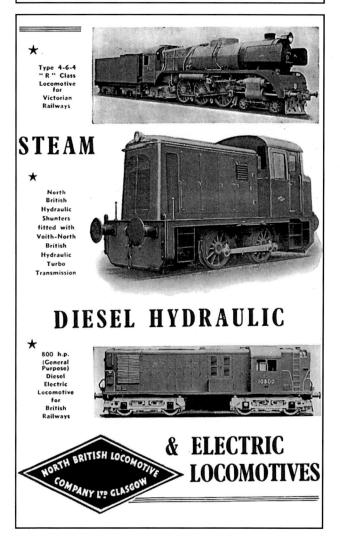

structed by North British at its Hyde Park Works. Effectively this brought to an end the company's illustrious history of steam locomotive building, and the three NBL works were then committed fully to diesel and electric traction. The company was busily supplying a significant number of its diesel-hydraulic shunting and mining locomotives for home and export. The orders on the company's books showed a healthy position, and the value was significantly higher, in no small measure due to the ordering programme of British Railways.

To cope with the increasing orders for diesels, NBL were still re-equipping, and ordering new plant, so the financial position was not so strong as might have been hoped. Although the mood of the board as 1958 approached was relatively optimistic, there were some large bills coming. The completion of the changeover from steam engine construction was still to be achieved; Hyde Park was still building, and equipped for steam. There was a concern too, that the workforce still needed increasing, and the directors paid several visits overseas to members of the traditional North British marketplace.

In 1958, the company lost its final link with the original management of 1903, when W. D. Lorimer died. The family had been associated with the company since the beginning, and before that, with Dübs & Co., at the old Glasgow Locomotive Works. The famous North British diamond it will be remembered was an impression on the bricks used in the construction of the Dübs works in Govan. Financially, 1958 was a disaster, a trading loss of over £900,000 was recorded, and the recorded profit in the balance sheet was only achieved by transferring funds from the reserve accounts. The stated reasons for the losses were two-fold. The primary cause was the lack of production, which was reportedly improved towards the end of 1958, but the reputation of the company had been affected. A second reason, and mentioned frequently in the 1950s, was the high cost of design and manufacturing of the new breed of diesel-hydraulic and diesel-electric locomotives. The new traction equipment cost NBL a lot of money to build, and the costs were not recovered quickly enough to pay the bills. On top of this, the railways were leaning increasingly towards electric transmissions, and the operational problems with hydraulic transmissions under British conditions did not help the case. The original 2,000hp 'Warship' class for the Western Region was not a huge success, and British Railways looked to the successful examples of a similar type in service in West Germany for an answer. During 1958, the 'cut down' version of the German V200 class was ordered and NBL, with their experience in hydraulic transmissions, given the opportunity to deliver a more successful locomotive. In fact they did just that, but by the time they were in service in large numbers, and had been proved operationally, diesel-electric locomotives far outnumbered diesel-hydraulic types. In 1958, the company received five orders only, and these were all from home, with no export orders at all, despite which, it was expected that the works would be fully employed for 'some time ahead'.

The NBL-Parsons Coal Burning Gas Turbine

Returning to the subject of the coal burning turbine which, still pursuing the improvement in steam locomotive efficiency, NBL were building with C. A. Parsons of Newcastle. In 1954 it was undergoing 'shop trials' in Newcastle. NBL were still very secretive about this project in their public pronouncements, referring to the gas turbine itself as being 'under construction in one of our workshops'. Having referred to this project in a somewhat jaundiced way so far, there is perhaps an element of hindsight in that view. In the light of the austerity economy of post-war

Britain, where steam traction was still supreme, and where the cost of coal was spiralling almost daily, this was a most obvious, and logical proposal. Gas turbines, using oil fuel had been ordered, and were already in service on British Railways, but the NBL-Parsons locomotive offered the prospect of using only half the coal of a steam locomotive. Coal was a major indigenous resource in Britain at the time, whereas oil had to be imported, and cheaper coal bills for BR were likely to increase the longevity of steam, and make BR's services more competitive with road transport especially.

NBL, as already discussed, had a history of innovation and experiment in steam traction, most notably in the steam-electric, and geared turbine locomotives many years earlier. The fuel costs, and efficiency factors drove the investigations into alternative locomotives during and after World War II, and after reviewing various locomotive designs, the NBL-Parsons project was born. The proposal was put to the then Ministry of Fuel and Power, and was a joint effort of NBL and C. A. Parsons. The proposal was approved by the Ministry, and order L36 was placed with North British on the 23rd December 1952 for a prototype locomotive. Typical in appearance to that of other similar designs it had a full width body, and a cab at either end. The body and power equipment were carried on a pair of six-wheeled bogies, but only the two outer axles of each bogie were driven. What was unique about the NBL-Parsons design was the way in which the power cycle, or process, was designed in order to get around the inherent problems of pulverised fuel locomotives.

The process that was to be used in the new locomotive, based on the 'exhaust heater' principle, involved admitting air to a type of boiler, where the compressed gas was heated to 1,300 deg. F, and then driving the main turbine. In turn, the turbine drove the main compressor whilst a second turbine, supplied by the 'air boiler' was used to drive the wheels directly, through gearing. In the last phase of its path through the locomotive's power train, the heated air entered a combustion chamber, where pulverised coal was blown in and burned. One of the principal reasons that the NBL-Parsons locomotive adopted this arrangement was to overcome the problems with pulverised fuel locomotives, where particles of fuel would damage the turbine blades. The choice of partners in this venture was quite appropriate, just as it had been for diesel engines, since Charles Algernon Parsons had been responsible for the development of steam turbines many years earlier. Sadly, the NBL-Parsons prototype never entered revenue earning service, and remained a final, isolated example of the ingenuity of the North British Locomotive Co. The optimism expressed by NBL in their commemorative brochure about this project, and its revolutionary qualities, were never realised.

General Engineering Activities

The diversification plans of the North British Locomotive Co. took shape with the acquisition of Henry Pels & Co. Ltd, in 1950. The following year, 1951, saw the entire shareholding of Carntyne Steel Castings Co. Ltd, come under NBL ownership. More curiously perhaps, NBL were approached by the UK and European representatives of the Baldwin–Lima–Hamilton Corp., to build, under licence, its dragline excavators. Tracked vehicles were not new to NBL experience – having built hundreds of tanks in both world wars – but, the building of a light tracked vehicle for use on marshy or boggy terrain was very different. The 'Water Buffalo' as it was named, was designed by J. A. Cuthbertson of Biggar, and with its very light (2.5 lb/sq in) track pressure, was successfully used on reclaimed land. This was not a successful venture overall, and did not result

Not all of NBL's products were enormously powerful main line steam locomotives, and the company had built hundreds of industrial type locomotives during its existence. Here, built to order L11, in July 1950, the 4-8-2 tank engine was provided for the Cape Explosive Works Ltd and named *Ryan Fry*. The design had been ordered on a number of previous occasions for South African collieries and mines.

Mitchell Library Collection

in large orders for NBL, but was a curious example of the way the company were looking at diversification in the early 1950s.

The Lima excavators were type 1201, and this was perhaps less of curious diversion, considering that there was an increasing demand for earth moving machinery. All of the examples built by NBL, again, not a great many, were of the dragline type, but convertible to shovels, clamshells and cranes. Clearly, they would have applications in opencast mining and quarrying too. There were a number of changes needed in the British built Lima excavators, with the provision of non-American proprietary fittings, generators, compressors, electric lighting, and even the engines. Curiously, NBL noted that the versions built in Glasgow had all components interchangeable with the American built units.

Carntyne Castings

This company, acquired by North British in May 1951, was formed in the Carntyne district of Glasgow in 1906, only three years after NBL. The company supplied specialised steel castings to the shipbuilding, general engineering, and locomotive industries. As the company outgrew its premises to the east of Glasgow, it was relocated to Renfrew, and the flourishing business rapidly expanded. Castings for the locomotive industry, including wheels, became a major part of the Carntyne foundries' output even before the Second World War. They became renowned suppliers of quality locomotive castings, with extensive laboratories and metallurgy departments. The company had been in the hands of North British for three years before there appeared any falling off of trade, even allowing for the postwar materials and manpower shortages.

In 1955, the Renfrew plant of Carntyne witnessed the replacement of its Bessemer converters with electric furnaces. This changeover at once improved quality and production costs were reduced, and in the same year Carntyne produced a record number of steel castings. Throughout the mid-1950s, the Renfrew plant was modernised, and the company continued to be successful and profitable, but it

was not immune to the effects of the problems affecting the parent company. The first signs of real problems came in 1959, and although there had been a slight fall in orders for 1958, in 1959, output was down by 27%, and the company recorded a loss for the first time. By 1960, the writing was clearly on the wall, and statements in the annual report like 'overproduction in the industry' were not good news for Carntyne, and another financial loss was recorded. Some improvement was recorded during 1961, but the troubles with North British Locomotive Co. were coming to a head, and the improvement was short lived.

Henry Pels & Co.

This company, taken over by NBL in 1950, produced punching and shearing machines and guillotines, and was a success throughout its association with North British, and afterwards. The provision of the right tool for the right job had been a byword in the locomotive building industry and others, and to which view NBL had subscribed since 1903. The acquisition though was not simply to provide metal forming/shaping tools for its own use, but as a useful, general engineering product range. The tools produced under the name of Henry Pels were extended, and expanded during the 1950s, and even at the time of the final reports, Henry Pels & Co. was still turning in a profit, in the face of difficult trading.

Steam Locomotives 1953–1962

In the final decade of NBL's existence, only seven orders were taken for steam locomotives, one for India, and the rest for Africa. Two of the orders (L80 and L87), were as sub-contractors to Beyer Peacock, supplying 32 of the GMA/M Garratt locomotives for South Africa. There were no orders at all from the home market in these last ten years, though British Railways were still building steam locomotives in their own workshops up until March 1960.

The first order to be placed was received in February 1953 (Order L55), and was initially for a pair of 3ft 6in gauge 4-8-2 tank locomotives. The order was increased in May 1953 to three engines. Like many overseas orders for industrial use, the order was placed through agents, in this case, Findlay, Durham and Brodie, and was similar in most respects to earlier orders. The same agents placed another two orders for colliery locomotives 18 months later, orders L62 and L63, in July and August 1954. The first of this pair were massive – by British standards anyway – 4-8-2s, and based on the SAR Class 12A goods locomotives. The two orders for these essentially shunting types, were placed by

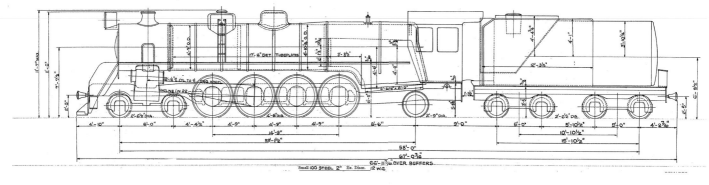

Built to order L19 in 1950, these were New Zealand Railways oil-fired Class JA 4-8-2s.

Mitchell Library Collection

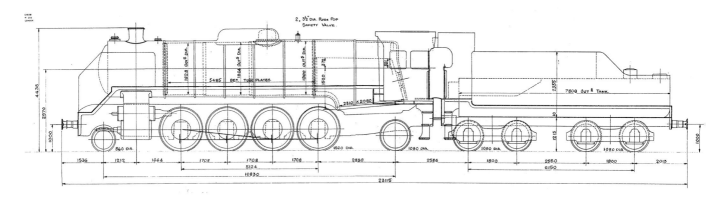

Spanish National Railways (RENFE) ordered 25 of these Mikado 2-8-2s, which were built in 1950, to NBL order L5.

Mitchell Library Collection

the Anglo American Corporation of South Africa, two (order L62) going to Blesbok Colliery, and four (order L63), to Wankie Colliery.

The second order (L63), was actually based on another NBL type for main line service on South African Railways, the 19D, but this time, with tanks and tenders similar to Rhodesian Railways Class 12A. Like the SAR Class 12A, the 19Ds were built by other makers, including Fried-Krupp, Borsig, Skoda, and Robert Stephenson & Co., but the 19Ds from NBL were easily identifiable with their cylindrical tender water tanks. Perhaps the success of the 19Ds on SAR contributed to the decision by Anglo American to buy their own!

On 8th December 1954 an order was placed (L67) through the agency of the Emergency Procurement Service, USA, for the India Store Department. This was the final order for India to be built at Hyde Park, and consisted of 25 of the 5ft 6in gauge 2-8-2s, as the 'WG class'. They were not a new design to NBL, since the company had built 100 of these engines under order L978, between June 1950 and November 1951, and described in Chapter 7. This final order carried works numbers 27594 to 27618, and in service, running numbers 9175 to 9199 were originally allocated.

The very last two orders for steam locomotives were received from Beyer Peacock in Manchester, with a sub-contract in each case, to supply 12 and 20 Garratt locomotives. Order L80 was received from the Manchester company on 29th November 1955 – South African Railways had placed a contract with Beyer Peacock ten days earlier. In fact, South African Railways had ordered 35 locomotives in 1955, with the delivery of the first required in seven months. This feat was achieved, and North British contributed its share in this major success. These were massive engines, for operation on the 3ft 6in gauge, and SAR had a number in service already, from 1954. They were costly locomotives too, at just a little under £100,000 per unit. The

main dimensions, built to Beyer Peacock designs, were as follows:

Order Nos	L80 & L87
Works Nos	27691-27702 (L80)
	27769-78 & 27783-92 (L87)
Class	GMA/M
Running Nos	4099-4110 (L80)
	4111-4120 (L87)
	4131-4140 (L87)
Wheel arrangement	4-8-2 + 2-8-4
Wheel dia. coupled	4ft 6in
Heating surface	
tubes	2,960.00 sq ft
firebox	237.00 sq ft
superheater	747.00 sq ft
total	3,844.00 sq ft
Grate area	63.20 sq ft
Boiler pressure	200 lb/sq in
Cylinders(4)	20.5 x 26in
Tractive effort	60,700 lb
Fuel	
coal	14 tons
water	2,100 gallons *

* The locomotives also had a permanently coupled tank car, which carried a further 6,800 gallons of water.

The GMA/M class was ordered in part, to ease the chronic motive power shortage on some sections of the SAR main lines. The suffix M on this class indicated its use on main lines, including the Witbank to Germiston section, which was being electrified in the mid-1950s. The final order for steam from NBL could not have resulted in a better, or more successful locomotive, and the GMA/M was a fitting tribute to NBL's locomotive building skills. The final order (L87), was placed in December 1956, through Beyer Peacock, and delivery was scheduled to take place between

March and July 1957. The very last steam locomotive built by North British carried the works number 27792, though the order was not delivered until 1958. Happily, and fittingly, one of these massive locomotives was saved from the breaker's torch, and is preserved at the Summerlee Heritage Museum in Coatbridge, Scotland.

1959–1962

The final three years of the company's independent existence were overshadowed by parlous financial results, and an almost non-existent order book. The production of shunting and mines locomotives, already produced by other UK suppliers, would not keep this engineering giant in business forever. The previous year, the board had approached HM Government, the General Electric Co., and the Clydesdale & North of Scotland Bank Ltd., for financial support. This support was indeed forthcoming, to the tune of £3.75 million, to shore up the ailing giant. The financial problems of NBL were reaching the newspapers in 1959, where the Company's shareholders gave authority to the board to borrow up to £5 million. The company though, in addition to the loans mentioned above, already had an overdraft in early 1959, of more than £3 million.

From the initially optimistic days of the early 1950s, in little more than five years NBL was, sadly heading for disaster. Only one order a year was built between 1959 and 1961, and each of these was for an average of a single 0-4-0 shunting locomotive. The export market had almost completely dried up, with only orders L106 and L122, in 1959 and 1961 respectively, for the Benguela Railway. These were powered by Paxman engines, and not the NBL-MAN design, for which so much promise was held, but which did not, in the end live up to expectations. L122 was the last overseas order secured by NBL before its demise, and during the last years the company were building shunting locomotives for stock, in the hope that railway operators could buy them 'off the shelf'. Some were indeed sold in this way, primarily for industrial service, such as Cadbury & Co., Esso, and Richard, Thomas & Baldwins steelworks.

Again, perhaps in a last ditch effort to stave off the inevitable, prototype locomotives were planned, but never completed. These are noted as orders L108 and L110 in the order books, as 'Prototype World Series' designs – a very grandiose reference. One (L108) was based around the 440hp 0-6-0 diesel-hydraulics that had been designed and built by the company, whilst the second, (L110), was a 2,000hp locomotive of broadly similar design to the NBL built 'Warships' for British Railways. The power plant in each case was the NBL-MAN engine, allied to the Voith hydraulic transmission.

The company had appointed management consultants in 1958 to review the company's organisation, and make recommendations. 1959 saw what was described as a management shake up at NBL, with T. A. Crowe retiring as Chairman and Chief Managing Director, and other organisational changes being made. But the profitability of NBL was teetering on the edge of a precipice in 1958, and by the time the 1959 results were known it had gone over the edge completely, and a loss of more than £1,200,000 was recorded. The company still had a workforce of around 5,000, and the wages and other bills still had to be paid, and the incoming Chairman, T. Coughtrie was faced with some grim prospects. T. A. Crowe was still involved with the company at board level, becoming Chief Executive, though it was a post he was hoping to give up in 1960. At the end of the annual meeting in 1960, following the review of 1959, Coughtrie sounded an optimistic note, but shareholders were still very concerned – not surprisingly, since no dividend had been paid for five years, and none was in prospect for two or three more. Although 90% of the company's activities were centred around locomotive building there were some hopeful signs, and more successful areas. The hydraulic transmissions produced at Queen's Park, under the Voith name, despite initial problems in locomotive applications, went on to become a very successful division in its own right. Carntyne Steel Castings were still relatively successful in the late 1950s, although output declined in 1958/59, and Henry Pels & Co., followed similarly successful paths. Having said that, 1959 was a loss making year for each of these subsidiaries.

There was considerable over capacity in the three works of NBL, and the reallocation of work was considered during 1959. Most of the 'newer' activities of the company were concentrated at Queen's Park Works, whilst Atlas was still struggling with the new diesel engines, and Hyde Park was still completing conversion from steam age technology. In 1960 more drastic changes were announced, and the concentration of all production at Queen's Park was settled on, with the consequent closure of the Hyde Park and Atlas works. At the same time, the elegant headquarters building

Another industrial 4-8-2 tank locomotive, in this case built to order L991 in 1950. Although obviously bearing the name 'Greenside Colliery', it was in fact ordered by the agents Findlay, Durham & Brodie for the Clydesdale Transvaal Colliery in South Africa. The agents had been responsible for acting for many of the smaller industrial and colliery lines, and appear many times in the NBL Order Books. This particular locomotive was similar to a previous order (L941), but had a steel, instead of a copper, firebox. *Mitchell Library Collection*

Just four months short of its 30th birthday, ex-LMSR 'Jubilee' class 4-6-0 No. 45571 *South Africa* was withdrawn. Here though, on an intermediate service on the West Coast Main Line, in February 1960, No. 45571 passes over Hademore Troughs. The locomotive was built by NBL under order L885, and allocated works number 24129 in 1934.

Roger Shenton

in Flemington Street was offered for sale.

The final report and accounts, at least, in their normal form, were published in the spring of 1961, and painted a very bleak picture. The locomotive marketplace had all but disappeared for North British, and, there was great disappointment at the loss of an order for diesel-electric locomotives for BR's Scottish Region. The company and its representatives made great efforts to secure orders from home and overseas railways, but the 1961 orders totalled two for home, and one for overseas. The final locomotive order was L113, placed in September 1961 by Richard, Thomas & Baldwins Ltd, of Scunthorpe, for use at their Redbourn Works.

During the year for which the final report and accounts were available, it was stated that the management changes and concentration of production at Queen's Park was complete. The manufacturing and design difficulties that NBL faced with their new diesel engines and hydraulic transmissions is given some insight from the 1960 review. It is clear that the company's reputation had suffered from the problems of the diesel-hydraulics and complaints were frequent, and repairs – both physical, and to the NBL reputation – had cost more than £250,000 in 1960. There had been differences with MAN and Voith over design faults with the products made under licence, but relations had improved with these companies by that time. Extending the general engineering activities of NBL, in the face of disappearing locomotive business, was pursued fairly aggressively. But, the new markets for which NBL was aiming could not support the large labour force of the past, and this was a problem which weighed heavily in the minds of the directors, workforce, and everyone.

By the beginning of 1961, the workforce had fallen as a result of reorganisation and the concentration of work at Queen's Park, to 1,500, from 5,000 only three years earlier. The last results of the company showed increasing deficits, and for 1960, a loss of £1,676,206 was declared.

10

Demise of a Giant

The final days of this ailing giant were the source of much anger, surprise, protest and confusion, and the eventual loss of livelihood for many skilled engineers. The immediate reaction as the news broke was for the social as well as the economic impact, although on the one hand, the reports were that the company had not seen the writing on the wall, some commentators noted that the company was seen to have been deteriorating for years. The then Lord Provost of Glasgow, Mrs Jean Roberts stated it was a 'tragic blow', and began a dialogue with the Government and Board of Trade. It is interesting that the reported comments suggest that there should have been an investigation into how the North British facilities could be used for more modern engineering. It was relatively common knowledge that the company had been in financial difficulties for a number of years, and between 1959 and 1962, the work-force reduced from over 5,000 to around 1,500. The body blow of impending liquidation broke on 4th April 1962, when it was announced the directors of the company were putting that recommendation to a meeting of stockholders and creditors on 19th April 1962. The day before the news broke, NBL's ordinary share value fell dramatically, from 3s7½d (about 18.1p) to only 7½d (about 3.1p). This may not seem a large sum by today's standards, but comparatively speaking, could represent a fall of more than 80% in the value of a major company. The £1 ordinary share value of the company had fallen away quickly from 1955, when its highest value was 28s 6d (about 142.5p), and it seemed a healthy investment, and a profitable company. The major change in the company's fortunes in the second half of the

1950s, was a rapid decline, continuous losses on trading, and no dividends paid to ordinary shareholders for more than five years. This state of affairs was even worse than the depression of the 1920s and 1930s, and NBL clearly could not continue in business.

The press was decidedly bad, and even when the company finally succumbed, its shareholders saw little or no return. The company had been supported by three major creditors in its last days – GEC, the banks, and HM Treasury – but the problems which NBL faced could not be solved without further major losses. Thomas Coughtrie, the Chairman of the company in its last days, clearly identified the cause of the failure of its financial position as the unsuccessful switch to building non-steam locomotives. Coughtrie had joined NBL in June 1959, as a condition under which the Treasury was loaning £1.75 million, to support the overdraft of £2.8 million which NBL had run up with the banks. This amount was registered in March 1959, and without the Treasury support, plus a further £500,000 from GEC, the company would not have made it to the end of 1959. The support of the creditors gave NBL just less than three more years of life, and work for its employees. Liquidation had been avoided in 1959, but only just, and the final decline had begun.

The 'Austerity' engines were as much a feature of the post-war British Railways scene, as they were a product of World War II economics. Here, classed as 8F, this 2-8-0 shows some signs of wear and tear, and carries BR running number 90127.

Lens of Sutton

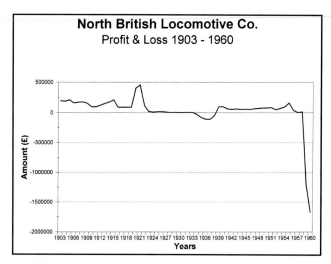

North British Locomotive Co.
Profit & Loss 1903 - 1960

NBL had in its last years, beginning in 1959, attempted to rationalise its production, and its product line, with a major concentration of work at Queen's Park Works. In 1960, a major reorganisation was begun, in the full knowledge that NBL would be able to produce in one works, the output it was then spreading across all three sites. The redundancies that were inevitable from this restructuring began in 1960, and at the same time negotiations were begun for the sale or lease, of the Flemington Street headquarters. Just one month before NBL went into formal liquidation, in March 1962 the Glasgow Education Committee announced it had bought the Flemington Street offices for £214,000. It was planned to use the NBL Headquarters for a college of engineering in the city, and as the Springburn College, its role in further education ensured the survival of this imposing building.

The company had found it difficult to obtain trained staff, especially in the high precision skills needed for diesel engine production, and the expertise that was developed, was gained at a very high cost. The concentration of production at the 23-acre Queen's Park site left a further 36 acres of works in Springburn, and another 19 acres of land in the north of the city, available for sale or lease. Interestingly, when the announcement about the liquidation was made, the Chairman's comments suggested that the shortage of skilled labour was aggravated by the concentration of work at Queen's Park, as the other sites were run down.

North British had purchased a number of properties over the years for a variety of reasons, most of these being obtained from about 1946. These properties included Hogarth Park, Elstow, and houses in Kingsborough Gardens, Marchmont Terrace, Cleveden Drive, Hamilton Drive and Cleveden Crescent. At the beginning of 1960, 22 Kingsborough Gardens had already been sold, but the remaining properties were valued at £14,895. Not a lot perhaps by today's standards. In fact, the valuation of fixed assets in 1960 provided some interesting figures, and was subsequently revalued downwards, so that the company's assets in 1960 achieved a figure not much more than the amount paid in 1903, for the three works.

Valuation of Fixed Assets 1960

Land & buildings	£1,120,000
Plant & machinery	£1,616,320
Fixtures & fittings	£ 65,937
Motor vehicles	£ 9,030
Locomotives, mobile cranes, etc	£ 52,670
Office furniture etc	£ 48,443
Patterns & drawings	£ 35,000
Total	**£2,937,100**

The effort that NBL had put into securing its future was not successful, but its liquidation in the Spring of 1962 came at a troubled time for both the engineering and railway industries. The same year that saw NBL go out of business also saw the publication of the infamous 'Beeching Plan', and the rationalisation of rail transport. The transition from steam to diesel and electric motive power can be seen with hindsight as taking too long, at least to ensure survival for some of the builders. So far as North British were concerned, the relatively poor performance of the company in securing major orders at home especially, and the limited success of its larger diesel locomotives was a serious handicap. Protracted problems with the new diesel-hydraulic locomotives for British Railways and disagreements with the Voith company were the focus of NBL's problems. In fact, the transmissions of a number of the NBL built 'Warship' class were entirely at NBL's expense, which added further delays and costs to the completion of contracts at home.

Built for the Furness Railway in 1913, under order L516 at Atlas Works, this locomotive survived until 1956, before finally being withdrawn as British Railways 0-6-0 No. 52494.

F. Dean

Previous financial arrangements on locomotive building at home included progress payments, but this was no longer available in the 1950s, and the company was unable to finance any locomotive building itself. The financing arrangements were even more difficult for export orders, and in the Chairman's statement at the time of liquidation, Mr Coughtrie noted that the credit arrangements extended to ten years and more, which made it impossible for North British to build locomotives for export.

Another interesting statement contained in the liquidation announcement, suggested that consideration had been given to not building locomotives, and concentrating on other work. Some of the efforts of NBL in diversifying its engineering activities have already been mentioned, but there is a greater irony in the idea that a specialist locomotive builder could exist without building locomotives! The *Glasgow Herald's* announcement of the closure ended with the observation that the loss of NBL meant "the virtual end of another Scottish industry". However, attempts were made to take up Tom Coughtrie's optimistic implication that opportunities were available for developers, as NBL land was freed up in the city. The most obvious of these was the continued use of the former Queen's Park Works, building hydraulic transmissions, gearing and other, general engineering products. This work, carried out under the name of Voith Engineering (Glasgow) Ltd, enabled the engineering skills and tradition of quality of North British to continue, at least for a time, in Glasgow.

To suggest pessimistically that the long tradition of locomotive building was coming to a close with the demise of NBL, did not do justice to the efforts, skills and success of Andrew Barclay of Kilmarnock. Although the name North British Locomotive Co. no longer appeared on locomotives built in Glasgow, its legacy was carried forward from the Ayrshire town, and locomotives continued to be built in Scotland.

Voith Engineering Ltd – The Queen's Park Heritage

The activities of this company, whose partnership with North British during the growing phase of dieselisation on Britain's railways, was successful and the work continued as a separate concern. Initially, a corner of NBL's Queen's Park Works, was devoted to the design and manufacture, under licence, of hydraulic transmission systems for railway locomotives. Later, this was expanded to occupy a larger area of this famous site, producing transmission systems for other industries, as well as the rail transport business.

In 1962, the separate company of Voith Engineering Ltd was set up on the Queen's Park site, and continued in business there until 1970. It was registered on 7th November 1962 as a wholly owned subsidiary of the Voith Group, then based at Heidenheim in the former West Germany. The new company took over part of the old works, the offices and 300 staff – former employees of the North British Locomotive Co. The principal activities were of course the hydraulic transmissions, with two orders being completed for British Rail in 1962/63. In addition, the supply of spares for MAN engines, installed in other British Rail diesel-hydraulics, such as the BR built and NBL 'Warship class', was assured. The new company provided continuity of manufacture for hydraulic transmissions in the UK.

The Western Region of British Railways were in the process of designing and building a more powerful diesel-hydraulic locomotive at the time of the demise of NBL. Just a few weeks before the formal announcement, the new 2,700hp 'Western' series of locomotives took to the rails, from British Rail's Swindon Workshops. The new locomotives were equipped with Voith-NBL type L630rV trans-

missions, for each of the 74 locomotives, and with Voith Engineering Ltd established in Glasgow, support was assured. Unfortunately for NBL, BR did not adopt the MAN engines which had been built by NBL under licence, but for this last and largest diesel-hydraulic type opted for the Bristol Siddeley-Maybach MD655. Although these too were a German design, from Maybach, but built under licence in the UK by Bristol Siddeley. As was the case for some of the last NBL locomotive contracts completed by Andrew Barclay, the successor company – Voith – completed delivery of the transmission order, and were responsible for spares, repairs and replacements.

The Voith company's products from Glasgow were largely known for hydraulic transmissions in the rail industry, in both main line, and industrial service, but with the new company the opportunity was taken to extend the range of products. Originally, Voith hydraulic transmissions were built under licence by the North British Locomotive Co., where the systems became widely known. As the independent Voith Engineering Ltd, the company began supplying paper making machinery and transmissions for road transport, both public and heavy industrial equipment. Under the new company's banner, former North British customers in the industrial market were supplied with transmissions built at Queen's Park. Voith also supplied transmissions to companies like Hunslet of Leeds – once former competitors of NBL for industrial locomotive orders. Ironically perhaps, the North British Locomotive Co., whether through its personnel, skills, or company goodwill, was a common link between Voith, Andrew Barclay and the Hunslet Engine Co. The latter two companies themselves, as descibed next, carried the NBL heritage forward, in more ways than one.

Sadly though, during the late 1960s, manufacturing on the Queen's Park site was stopped, and again the long saga of North British's decline cast a shadow over the area. The business of Voith Engineering Ltd became a sales and after-sales service organisation, and transferred its offices to Thornton Heath in Surrey in 1970. The impact was a further loss of jobs from former North British Locomotive employees, and the eventual cessation of engineering manufacture on the site. Voith still supply hydraulic transmissions to British Rail, but the equipment used on the latest electric locomotives, is no longer made in Glasgow.

Andrew Barclay, Sons & Co.

This long established company from Kilmarnock was a world leader in the construction of smaller steam locomotives for industrial and other uses. Unlike its larger neighbour in Glasgow, it was able to continue in the locomotive building business, with an easier transition from steam to non-steam traction. Its origins can be traced back to 1840 when, in partnership with one Thomas McCulloch, a small engineering business was set up. Andrew Barclay had served an apprenticeship as a plumber, tin and coppersmith, but his earliest foray into the engineering business was as a maker of shafting for mills and the calico printing industry. This partnership lasted until about 1842, when the two men parted company, and Andrew Barclay established an independent and rival business next door to McCulloch. The engineering business was expanding rapidly in Kilmarnock, and a further move to provide greater capacity brought the business to West Langlands Street in 1847. However, Andrew Barclay was still not in the business of building railway locomotives, and much of the work came from collieries and ironworks, in particular for winding engines. It was twelve years before the first locomotive order was received, in 1859, from the nearby Portland Iron Co., and the now established Caledonia Works continued building steam railway locomotives until the late 1950s. From this century of steam engine building, the majority of locomotives went to industry, although many were also built for main line railways.

The marketplace for industrial locomotives was less dramatically affected by the growth in road transport, and unaffected by air transport. Markets changed however, and Barclay locomotives were no longer exported around the world in the same numbers as before. The company though was able more successfully to convert from steam to non-steam construction, especially in comparison with its larger competitors. Interestingly too, the town of Kilmarnock was the birthplace of the forerunner of one of the UK's most successful builders of diesel and electric locomotives. Dick, Kerr & Co. established its manufacturing base at the Britannia Works, competing with Andrew Barclay and others for general engineering and transport orders. In later years Dick, Kerr & Co. moved to Preston in Lancashire, began building electric tramcars and railway rolling stock, and ultimately became the English Electric Co. The success of this latter company, and others, such as Metro-politan–Vickers, in delivering successful, and effective diesel and electric railway locomotives was a factor in the demise of the North British Locomotive Co.

At the time of the closure of NBL, Andrew Barclay were able to secure the important industrial contracts and market share that was held by Springburn, purchasing the company's goodwill, drawings, and other details. When NBL went into receivership, Andrew Barclay put in its offer for the goodwill, which was accepted on 30th January 1963. Andrew Barclay, Sons & Co. became the only locomotive builders in Scotland, and despite the relatively poor marketplace in the 1960s, the NBL acquisition soon proved an advantage for the company. Some of the former NBL staff went to Andrew Barclay, and the expertise of the former company has survived, in a different guise. Amongst the staff that went to Andrew Barclay were Tom McKinlay, who was appointed Contracts Manager in September 1962. Another important appointment was that of Robert Barr as Sales Manager. Robert Barr had previously been NBL's

Chief Draughtsman, and had expert engineering knowledge, especially of the former North British diesel-hydraulic locomotives.

It is true that the later industrial diesels ordered from NBL, were actually completed by Andrew Barclay, who of course were able to supply the necessary spares and other components for NBL locomotives in service with industry around the world. During 1963, Guest, Keen & Nettlefolds came to Kilmarnock with an order for a North British design of diesel-hydraulic, for two 440hp locomotives, so the acquisition paid off almost immediately. By the middle of 1963, 50% of Andrew Barclay's spares and repairs orders were from former NBL customers, and by the end of the year the commercial position was much improved. NBL markets had given Andrew Barclay £80,000 in sales, and over £100,000 in the completing of orders placed previously with North British.

Consolidation within the industrial locomotive business continued throughout the 1960s, and for Andrew Barclay, a further bonus came with the purchase of the goodwill of John Fowler & Co., of Leeds. Another famous Leeds builder – the Hunslet Engine Co. – was merged with Andrew Barclay in 1972, becoming part of the Hunslet Group. In the 1970s, personnel changes saw some of Barclay's staff move to Leeds and others retired while Robert Barr had become Technical Manager for the company. In 1982, the former Chief Draughtsman of North British Locomotive retired,

In 1963 this 0-6-0 tank was donated by the NCB to Glasgow Transport Museum for preservation. It had been built by NBL, at Hyde Park Works in 1917 for the Glasgow & South Western Railway. Although the engine ran as LMSR No. 16379, it was eventually sold to Wrexham Colliery for its last years of service. The circular plate on the smokebox side, clearly visible, shows that it was built at Hyde Park, before the familiar diamond plate was adopted as the North British trademark, and in this case the locomotive carries works number 21521. The original order from the G&SWR was L677, and was for three engines, placed in March 1916.

Roger Shenton

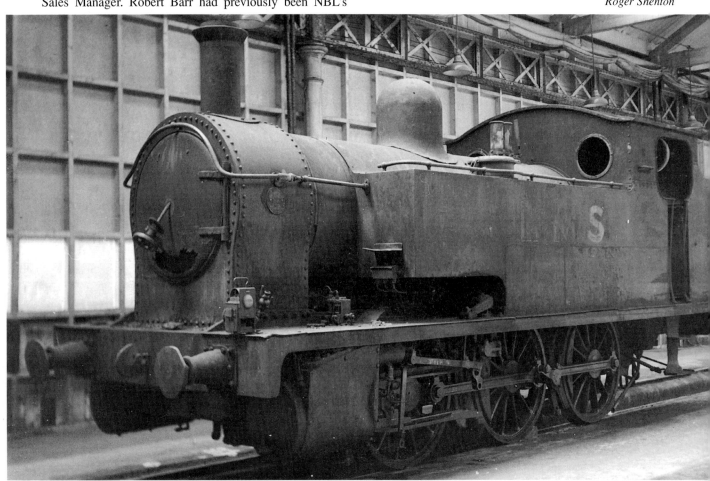

severing another link with that famous company. Four years later, in 1986, Tom McKinlay also retired, and the final, direct link with locomotive building at Springburn was ended.

Andrew Barclay, Sons & Co. was restructured during the 1980s, and the name changed in 1989, but the business of building locomotives continued. The only remaining link between the railway business of Hunslet-Barclay and the North British empire, are the NBL records and designs owned by the Kilmarnock company.

Longevity and Preservation
From the vast range of locomotives that had been built by 'The Combine', many survived almost unaltered for decades. In India especially, there remained large numbers of North British built engines in service, which in latter years gave the impression of only rudimentary servicing. There are indeed engines still in service on that continent that were built by the hands of the Springburn craftsmen. African, Australian and New Zealand orders have seen examples that survived the breakers' torches, with notable examples from South Africa being returned to the UK for preservation. Here at home, the number of NBL built engines still in traffic, hauling steam specials, and hard at work on preserved railways is testimony to the quality of the products of Hyde Park, Atlas and Queen's Park in its heyday.

British Locomotives
Although the GWR was unique amongst Britain's railways, and built almost all of its engines at Swindon, the first 50 of the 57XX series pannier tanks were built by NBL in Glasgow. Fortunately, three examples of a later NBL build (from order L872, built in 1930) survived to be preserved. The preserved pannier tanks were bought and used by both the National Coal Board and London Transport after their service on the former GWR lines came to an end. Two of the preserved panniers, Nos 7752 and 7760, went to the Birmingham Railway Museum, at Tyseley, whilst the third, No. 7754, is now on the Llangollen Railway in Clwyd.

Those locomotives built for the former LMSR and LNER have been preserved in even greater numbers, with a solitary 'King Arthur' from the Southern Railway. In fact, many of the preserved engines used to haul enthusiasts' specials, like the 'Cumbrian Mountain Express', are hauled by the products of NBL. Earlier products of the three Glasgow Works have also been preserved, including the famous Caledonian Railway single No. 123, built by Neilson, and the first 4-6-0 locomotive in Britain, David Jones' No. 103 for the Highland Railway, built by Sharp Stewart in 1894. Although only a few of the locomotives built by Dübs & Co. have survived these do include the 3ft gauge 0-6-0T *Caledonia* which has recently been restored to full working order for use on the railways of the Isle of Man. The Caledonian and Highland Railway locomotives are sadly no longer in active use, but remain as static exhibits in the Glasgow Transport Museum. Locomotives built by North British for British main line railways and the War Department, that are maintained in working condition, or are currently being restored to operational status include:

Built to order L885 in 1934 at Queen's Park Works, LMS 'Jubilee' 4-6-0 No. 45596 *Bahamas* is at Crewe Works in 1960 and shows some changes from the original build by North British. The double chimney is the most noticeable change, and the dome and top feed are separate. Compare this with the view of No. 45575 in the previous chapter. No. 45596 is now preserved.

G. W. Sharpe Collection

Railway	Locomotive	NBL Works No.	Built
GWR	0-6-0PT No. 7752	24040	1930
GWR	0-6-0PT No. 7754	24042	1930
GWR	0-6-0PT No. 7760	24048	1930
Southern	4-6-0 No. 30777 *Sir Lamiel*	23227	1925
LMSR	0-6-0T No. 47324	23403	1925
LMSR	0-6-0T No. 47327	23406	1925
LMSR	0-6-0T No. 47357	23436	1925
LMSR	4-6-0 No. 6115 *Scots Guardsman*	23610	1927
LMSR	4-6-0 No. 5593 *Kolhapur*	24151	1934
LMSR	4-6-0 No. 5596 *Bahamas*	24154	1935
WD/LMSR	2-8-0 No. 8233	24607	1940
GNR	0-6-2T No. 69523	22600	1921
LNER	4-6-0 No. 1264	26165	1947
BR(E)	4-6-0 No. 1306 *Mayflower*	26207	1948
BR(E)	2-6-0 No. 2005	26609	1949
WD/TCDD	2-8-0 No. 45160	24648	1941
WD	2-10-0 No. 600 *Gordon*	25437	1943
WD/OSE	2-10-0 No. 601 *Sturdee*	25438	1943
WD/OSE	2-10-0 No. 3672 *Dame Vera Lynn*	25458	1944

This finely preserved example of an NBL built pannier tank, was originally built in 1930, as the fourth batch of 25 of these locomotives. Built under order L872 at Queen's Park Works, GWR No. 7752 carries NBL works number 24040. The design may have been very much GWR, but the NBL diamond plate on the leading splasher is crystal clear. Now preserved at Tyseley, Birmingham, another Springburn engine is still in working order more than 60 years later.

Birmingham Railway Museum

The B1 class *Mayflower,* the K1 class 2-6-0 are not preserved in their as-built state, neither is the 'Royal Scot' class 4-6-0 No. 6115, for the LMSR. The former two locomotives were actually delivered after Nationalisation, and did not appear in the former LNER livery, and were assigned to the new British Railways Eastern Region. The 'Royal Scot', No. 6115 was dramatically rebuilt by Stanier whilst he was that railway's Chief Mechanical Engineer. It is included as a representative of a very successful design built by NBL. This engine itself survived in the original form, as built by NBL in September 1927, for 20 years, until rebuilt in its present form in 1947. As British Railways locomotive No. 46115 *Scots Guardsman* also had the distinction of being the last of the class to be withdrawn, in 1966. The same railway also ordered two batches of the famous 5XP or 'Jubilee' class 4-6-0 from NBL. Of the three running examples of this renowned Stanier and LMSR design, two were built in the Queen's Park Works in December 1934 and January 1935. The LMS came to Glasgow numerous times, as described earlier, for large numbers of locomotives, and not all of them high speed passenger types. Most of the work was carried out by NBL under pressure from the railway company, so that in turn, it could provide suitable motive power for its rapidly expanding traffic demands. That the NBL built examples of Stanier's regime at the LMS should be preserved, is a fitting tribute both to the railway company, and the North British Locomotive Co. Examples of a design attributed to Henry Fowler's days as CME for the West Coast company are also preserved. These three humble 0-6-0 tank engines, nicknamed "Jinties", were built by NBL in the mid-1920s, at a time when the LMS motive power department was under severe pressure.

The Southern Railway also entrusted NBL with larger orders for important, urgently needed locomotives, including a new batch of the 'King Arthur' class 4-6-0s in the mid-1920s. The design dated back to 1918, and the old London & South Western Railway, but No. 30777 *Sir Lamiel* was built in June 1925, and allocated to the new Western Section of the Southern Railway. *Sir Lamiel* was almost not rescued as the representative of this famous class, but No. 30453 *King Arthur* was not as suitable for the National Collection as the NBL built example.

The LNER, and its constituent companies also came to Glasgow for locomotives, often at a time of need, when their workshops, like those of the LMSR, were filled to capacity, or when they needed locomotives in a hurry. But in fact, only No. 1264 was built by North British in the last days of the LNER, during 1947 as the other B1, and K1 2-6-0 were built after the LNER ceased to exist, but remain as fine examples of the last designs of that railway. The Thompson designed B1 4-6-0s were built in large numbers, as mixed traffic engines, and by far the majority of them by North British. No. 1306 was built in April 1948, and never carried a name during its days with British Railways, with the name *Mayflower* carried by another NBL built locomotive, No. 61379. The preserved engine was given the honour of working the last steam train over the old Great Central main line into Marylebone, in August 1966, before that line was closed.

As British Railways K1 class 2-6-0 No. 62005, NBL completed this locomotive in June 1949, and it was delivered carrying the then new BR lined black livery. This K1 was another example of preserving an NBL built engine that almost did not happen. The K4 2-6-0 *The Great Marquess*, which had already been purchased privately by Viscount Garnock, was to have acquired the boiler of No. 62005. Perhaps a fitting way of providing a new boiler for the K4, since Edward Thompson had rebuilt the Gresley 3-cylinder 2-6-0 into the simpler, new K1 design. Fortunately it was decided that the older locomotive did not need the new boiler, and so 62005 was rescued for preservation in its entirety. It has also featured in the TV documentary *Diamonds Were Forever*, hauling special trains over the West Highland line between Fort William and Mallaig.

Lastly, but by no means least, only two pre-Grouping locomotive to be built by NBL are preserved, the oldest of these being former Great North of Scotland Railway Class F 4-4-0, number 49. The locomotive was built by NBL in October 1920, just over two years before the Grouping, and the railway's absorption by the LNER. In service, this engine worked all of its life in North East Scotland, particularly between Aberdeen, Keith and Elgin. No. 49 *Gordon Highlander* was the last of the class to be withdrawn, after 38 years at work, in June 1958. Like its contemporaries from the Caledonian and Highland Railway, No. 49 is now an exhibit in the Glasgow Museum of Transport.

The second of the pair is former Great Northern 0-6-2 tank engine, No. 69523 (last British Railways running number). Carrying NBL works number 22600, this was built in 1921, to order L734, when Nigel Gresley was in charge at Doncaster. In fact, the 50 Class N2 tank engines was the first order for NBL in 1920, placed on the 16th February, and all were built at Hyde Park Works. Rather like the Thompson B1 4-6-0s of later years, North British built the lion's share of these suburban tank engines. The preserved N2 was originally numbered 1744 by the Great Northern, renumbered 4744 by the LNER initially, later becoming 9523, and finally, as British Railways No. 69523.

During the build up to World War II, NBL were heavily engaged in the construction of larger numbers of locomotives for the war effort, as well as the munitions of war. In the early days of the war, the Stanier 8F 2-8-0 was selected as suitable for military service, and NBL built 2-8-0s have survived to be preserved. In 1940 No. 8233 (works No. 24607) was built for war service, under order L932, as one of a batch of 60 of these 2-8-0s. The order was actually placed with NBL on 20th December 1939, and included the other 2-8-0 on the foregoing list, carrying works number 24648, and built at the Hyde Park Works. Another three orders were placed on NBL for these Stanier 8Fs, including 50 under order L938, for the LMS, which carried running numbers 8176 to 8225. All of the 8Fs for war service were built at Hyde Park.

The WD 'Austerity' 2-8-0 and 2-10-0 types were perhaps the most well known NBL-built locomotives during the war years, and no fewer than three of the 2-10-0s have been preserved in the UK, including two repatriated from Greece.

Overseas preservation
India
The subcontinent having been the source of so many orders for NBL, should naturally preserve a number of the company's locomotives. Of course, steam has survived much longer there than anywhere else in the world too, and the collection housed in the railway museum in New Delhi contains a wide variety of locomotives, of all shapes and sizes. At the time of writing, there are still examples of North British steam in service, which will perhaps one day be rescued for posterity, either in India, or back at their place of birth, in Glasgow. The representative examples of the works of NBL, and those of its predecessors include:

Railway	Builder	Type	Gauge	Built
Nizam's State	Dübs & Co.	L class 4-6-0	5ft	1891
North Western	NBL	0-6-2T	5ft 6in	1904
GIPR	NBL	E1 class 4-4-2	5ft 6in	1907
Jodhpur Rly.	Dübs & Co.	0-4-2	Metre	1878
Sth. Mahratta	Dübs & Co.	FM class 0-6-0	Metre	1888
Darjeeling	Sharp Stewart	0-4-0ST	2ft	1889

The 4-6-0 for the Nizam's State Railway was followed by a modified series, known as Class A, with larger coupled wheels. The example that is preserved in the Rail Transport Museum has been sectioned, and was earlier used for training purposes at the Railway Staff College in Baroda, before being moved to Delhi. The 5ft 6in gauge tank engine, was originally supplied by NBL as Class ST, some of which were built under order L20, placed in 1903. These 0-6-2 tank engines were also supplied as a kit of parts, sent from Glasgow, and put together at the North Western Railway's Mughalpura Workshops.

In June 1906, NBL received order L212 from the Great Indian Peninsula Railway for a batch of 19 Atlantic type locomotives, the second of which carried works number 17780, and built by Atlas Works. This locomotive was shipped to the GIPR for working the prestigious mail trains and other express passenger services, in 1907, and was originally non-superheated, but was superheated and fitted with piston valves in 1922. In its present form it was classified EM, following modifications which included lengthening the frames, but still carrying the original running number, 922.

The two additional Dübs locomotives for the metre gauge Jodhpur and Southern Mahratta railways have also been modified from the originally delivered locomotives. Not surprisingly perhaps, considering the engines were supplied in 1878 and 1888 respectively. The diminutive 2ft gauge Darjeeling 0-4-0 saddle tanks were originally supplied by Sharp Stewart, but after 1903, NBL continued to supply another 18 similar engines. The preserved example is one of

North British Locomotive Company, Limited,
GLASGOW.

Reference No. L 525.

GAUGE OF RAILWAY, 2-ft. 0-in.

TYPE 0-4-0.   TANK ENGINE.

CYLINDERS { DIAMETER ... ... 11-in.
          { STROKE ... ... 14-in.

WHEELS ... COUPLED, DIAMETER, 2-ft. 2-in.

WHEEL-BASE ... TOTAL ... 5-ft. 6-in.

WORKING PRESSURE ... 140-lbs. per sq. in.

HEATING SURFACE { TUBES ... 276 sq. ft.
                { FIREBOX ___40___ ,,
                { TOTAL   316 ,,

FIREGRATE AREA ... ... 9 ,,

BOILER FEED ... TWO INJECTORS, No. 5.

TRACTIVE FORCE AT 75% }
    OF BOILER PRESSURE } ... 6,840-lbs.

WEIGHT IN WORKING ORDER, 15 tons 7 cwts.

TANK CAPACITY ... ... 380 gallons.
FUEL SPACE ... ... 34 cub. ft.

Above: It would be hard not to include a last look at the diminutive Darjeeling tanks, for the 2ft gauge in the jewel of the British Empire. Thankfully one of this breed is preserved at the Indian National Railway Museum in Delhi. From the largest, to the smallest of steam locomotives, North British Locomotives built them all.
Author's Collection

Opposite: NBL built a number of the 2ft 6in gauge Pacifics for the Bengal–Nagpur and North Western Railways in India, and the earliest Class C locomotives were built in 1906. Here, on shed at Bankura in 1992, is a forlorn looking No. 664, of Class CC, but still in service with the Bankura–Damodar River Railway.
Philip Cousins

the early Class B prototypes, and at the time of writing, a number of the NBL built engines are still in service. The variety of locomotives supplied to Indian railways are well represented in the national collection in Delhi, from the main lines to the hill country.

South Africa
Like India, Africa was a source of many orders for Springburn, and although steam has now ceased to play a major role on those railways, some of the largest NBL built engines have been preserved. Amongst the most famous of course are the massive GMA/M Garratt types, built in Glasgow for South African Railways. Happily, one of their number was returned to Scotland, and occupies pride of place in the Summerlee Heritage Museum at Coatbridge, just east of Glasgow. Such has been the enthusiasm for steam in South Africa that there is a campaign to return some of these giants to the UK. Types that still exist, include the following:

Railway	Locomotive	Builder	Built
Natal Govt.	Class A, 4-8-2T	Dübs & Co.	1900
Cape Govt.	Class 7A, 4-8-0	Sharp, Stewart	1896
Central S.A.	Class 11, 2-8-2	NBL	1904
SAR	Class 12A, 4-8-2	NBL	1951
SAR	Class 15F, 4-8-2	NBL	1945
SAR	Class 24, 2-8-4	NBL	1949
SAR	Class 25NC, 4-8-4	NBL	1954
SAR	Class GMA/M, 4-8-2+2-8-4	NBL	1956

From the foregoing impressive list, three are already back in the UK – a Class 7A, 25NC and of course the Garratt. In addition, some of the remainder are already set aside for either the North British Locomotive Society, or other preservation groups. Amongst the latter is well-known artist, David Shepherd, who already counts the Sharp Stewart built Class 7A 4-8-0 No. 993 amongst his collection and hopes soon to take delivery of Class 15F No. 3052. The successful repatriation of the 25NC, No. 3405, was a triumph for the NBLS, and the completion of work to preserve other NBL built engines in the UK provides further testimony to the men of Springburn.

Australia and New Zealand
The farthest corners of the British Empire saw numerous examples of the products of the North British Locomotive Co., and here again, some of the finest examples have been preserved. In New Zealand, locomotives of classes Ab, J and Ja, many of which had been supplied by NBL, were rescued for preservation, and some allowed to work along the main lines again. Others are preserved as representatives of

Above: The elegantly proportioned Class 15F, now rescued for preservation, was built by North British, in huge numbers. Out of a total of 255 of these 4-8-2s, no less than 205 were supplied by North British, with the remainder almost evenly divided between Beyer Peacock and two German builders. The NBL built 15Fs were the greatest asset of South African Railways for many years, and have been described as the equivalent of the LNER A4 Pacifics in Britain. The locomotive illustrated, No. 2929, was built to the first order, L917, at Hyde Park, in 1938.

Mitchell Library Collection

Below: No less than 205 of these elegant Class 15F 4-8-2s were built for South African Railways, and along with the Class 25NC 4-8-4s, represents perhaps the company's swan song in steam locomotives for Southern Africa.

Author's Collection

NORTH BRITISH LOCOMOTIVE CO. LTD., GLASGOW.
CLASS 15F LOCOMOTIVES FOR THE SOUTH AFRICAN RAILWAYS.

Gauge of Railway, 3ft. 6in.

TYPE 4-8-2			ENGINE.				TENDER		
Cylinders ...	Dia.	24in.		Tubes	3,179 sq. ft	Wheels, Dia.		2ft. 10in.
	Stroke	28in.	**Heating Surface**	Firebox including arch tubes ...	236 „	Wheel Base		20ft. 5in.
				Total	3415 „			
Wheels ...	Front Bogie Dia. 2ft.	6in.				Tank Capacity ...		6,050 gallons
	Coupled „ 5ft.	0in.	**Do. do.**	Superheater ...	661 „			
	Hind Truck „ 2ft.	10in.		Total	4076 „	Fuel Space (14 tons)		590 cub. ft.
Wheel Base ...	Rigid ...	15ft. 9in.	**Firegrate Area**		62·5 „	Weight, Full ...		68 tons 12 cwts
	Total ...	35ft. 8in.	**Tractive Force** at 85% of					
Working Pressure	...	210 lbs. per sq. in.	Boiler Pressure		47,980 lbs.	ENGINE & TENDER.		
Boiler Feed ...	... 2 No. 13 Injectors.		**Weight**	In Working Order -	109 tons·	Wheel Base, Total ...		65ft. 6⅜in.
				On Coupled Wheels -	72 tons.			

Boiler Plates, NICKEL STEEL.
Firebox „ STEEL.

Boiler Tubes, STEEL.

Brake on Engine. STEAM.
„ „ Tender. VACUUM & HAND.

At Taumarunui Depot, Class J No. 1239, this view showing the right side view of a locomotive in particularly clean condition. Another of the 1939 deliveries from order L923, carrying works number 24562.

New Zealand Rly. & Loco. Society (Inc.) Archives Collection

the last of both New Zealand and North British steam locomotives:

Locomotive	Built
Class Ab 4-6-0, No. 830	1925
Class J 4-8-2, No. 1211	1939
Class J 4-8-2, No. 1234	1939
Class J 4-8-2, No. 1236	1939
Class Ja 4-8-2, No. 1275	1952

In Australia, NBL built locomotives have been rescued, and one of the Victoria Railways R class Hudsons played a major role in the bicentennial celebrations. The R class, like the K1 class 2-6-0 for the LNER in Britain, also starred in the NBL documentary *Diamonds Were Forever*. Other preserved examples in Australia include:

Railway	Locomotive	Builder	Built
South Aust.	Class R 4-6-0, No. 93	Dübs & Co.	1886
South Aust.	Class Rx 4-6-0, No. 207	NBL	1913
South Aust.	750 Class 2-8-2, No. 752	NBL	1951
Victoria	Class R 4-6-4, No. 700	NBL	1951
Victoria	Class R 4-6-4, No. 704 (i)	NBL	1951
Victoria	Class R 4-6-4, No. 707 (ii)	NBL	1951
Victoria	Class R 4-6-4, No. 711	NBL	1951
Victoria	Class R 4-6-4, No. 753	NBL	1951
Victoria	Class R 4-6-4, No. 761	NBL	1951
Victoria	Class R 4-6-4, No. 766	NBL	1951

(i) On permanent display at the North Williamstown railway museum, and was displayed in Glasgow, during the Festival of Britain in 1951.

(ii) Featured in the documentary film on NBL and took part in Australia's bicentennial celebrations, and carried the name *City of Melbourne*.

The R class Hudsons for Australia, and the Class J and Ja for New Zealand, epitomise the finest work of the North British Locmotive Co. Their success in service, resulted in the preservation of a number of engines, and they continue to provide power for the world's railways.

The North British Locomotive Collection

Now resident in Glasgow's Mitchell Library is a unique photographic record of the locomotives built by the men of Springburn and Polmadie. Photographs of many hundreds of different types, though sadly not all, are held in the collection. Some unique records are also held there, of the workforce itself and the earnings of the men who built these steam locomotives, together with diagram books and details of weights and costs. More general business information and company records are kept in the Business Archives of Glasgow University.

The rise and fall of this company has been captured on film too, in the appropriately named documentary *Diamonds Were Forever*, screened on television and later available on video. Perhaps the most poignant reminder though of both the solidity and frailty of steam locomotive engineering was expertly captured by Glasgow artist George Wyley, in his famous sculpture the 'Straw Locomotive'. This sculpture was hauled through the streets of Glasgow, hung from the huge crane at Finnieston Dock, from where so many of the locomotives carrying the dia-

mond plate were shipped to all corners of the globe. Later the straw locomotive was returned to Springburn, and burnt in a spectacular finale. The only remaining evidence within the City of Glasgow of the mighty NBL are the Stobcross Crane, the Flemington Street offices – now the North Glasgow College – and the Springburn Museum. The museum is housed in a building bequeathed to the people of Springburn by the proprietors of the company that once gave them work. The skills, reputation and memory of the excellence of the steam locomotives that carried that famous diamond plate remain intact.

Above: The preserved Rx class 4-6-0 built by NBL in 1913 for South Australia Government, No. 207, is seen on a steam excursion organised by the Australian Railway. It shows a good head of steam and plenty of smoke near Millswood.

Phil Butler

Opposite top: 'Operation Phoenix' was targeted at revitalising the railways of the State of Victoria, but the neighbouring state of South Australia was short of motive power. In 1950, order L996 was placed for the N class 2-8-2 for Victoria, but several were bought by South Australia. Here, No. 755 heads an Adelaide to Tailem Bend passenger train in 1961, through the Mount Lofty ranges.

P. Bartrop

Opposite below: A parting shot, but a view that would not have been possible at the height of the success of the men of Springburn. The imposing office block that the North British Locomotive Co. built for itself in Flemington Street still provides a focus, but nowadays, as a centre of education, rather than locomotive engineering.

Author's Collection

Distribution of NBL Orders By Continent

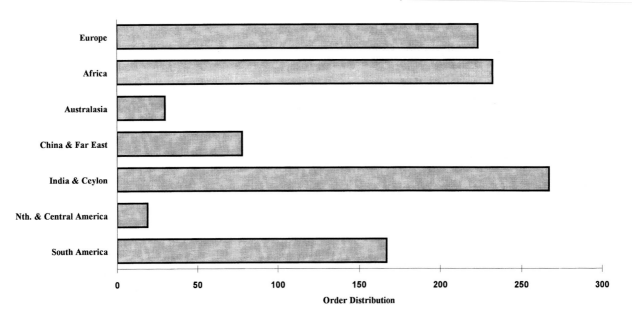

NBL Home Orders 1903 - 1953

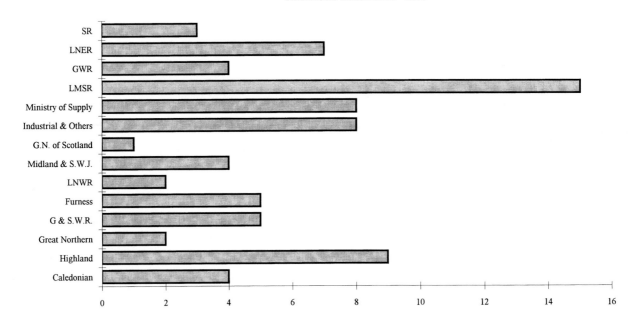

NBL Diesel & Electric Orders

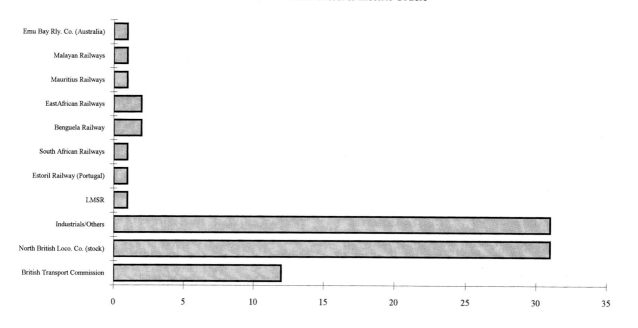

Distribution of NBL Built Locomotives By Continent

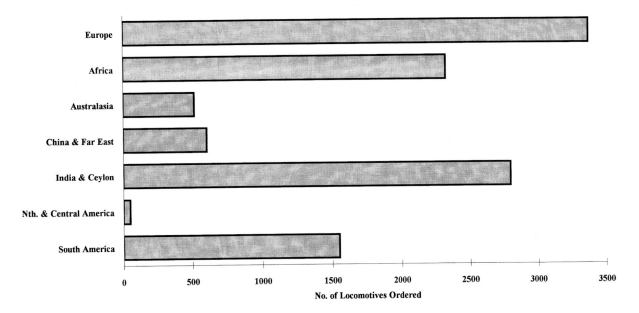

No. of Locomotives Ordered

NBL Locomotives Built for the Home Market 1903 - 1953

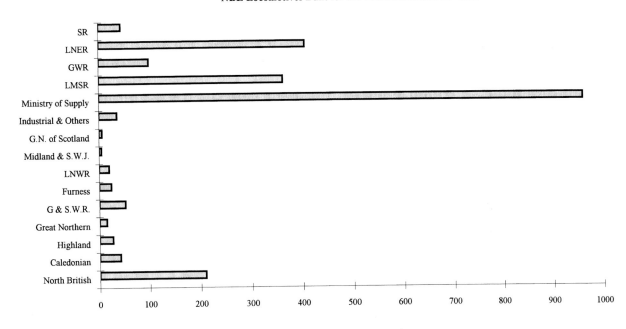

NBL Built Diesel & Electric Locomotives

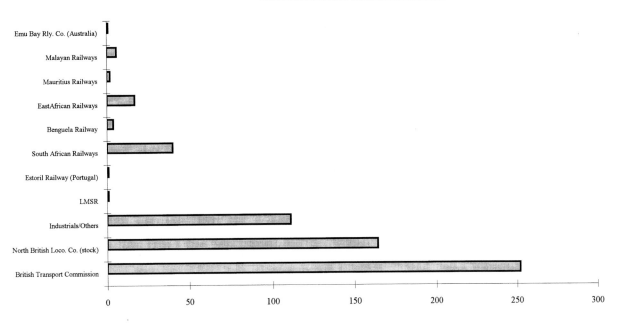

Index